Advance Praise

In *Reading the Megillot*, Mathews extends the performance-critical lens she has previously applied to prophetic texts to now examine a collection of five diverse books from among the Ketuvim ("Writings") of the Hebrew Bible. Mathews's work highlights the artistry of composition inherent in the texts of the *Megillot*, demonstrating how reading them as performances can bring certain meanings and rhetorical devices to the fore. Discussions of the texts' liturgical settings in various religious traditions as well as their resonance with the important social discourses of today reveal why these millennia-old books still demand our attention. Mathews's skill as a philologist and vibrant re-imaginings of biblical texts work together to present innovative interpretations that are both accessible to students and lay readers and illuminating for experienced scholars.

—*Dr. Rosanne Liebermann*
Aarhus University

Jeanette Mathews is well known for her creative application of insights from performance criticism when interpreting Hebrew Bible texts. This commentary on the five *Megillot* is no exception. Mathews consistently and skillfully read each of the five books from the perspective of performance criticism. She creatively translates each book as a "script" intended for aural performance. I have great appreciation for her focus on the five books' liturgical importance in the Jewish festive calendar, the commentary on each book from the perspective of performance criticism, and the author's grappling with the implications of these books (called "Connections") for postmodern societal issues like gender based violence, xenophobia, inequality, and poverty. The book illustrates that ancient biblical texts speak to us today!

—*Prof Gert T.M. Prinsloo*
Department of Ancient and Modern Languages and Cultures
University of Pretoria

By viewing the *Megillot* through the lens of performance, Mathews builds a bridge for scholars and ordinary readers, clergy and lay people, performers and audiences to meet and explore these rich texts in both old and new ways. She synthesizes the best of scholarship on the ancient situation of the Song of Songs, Ruth, Lamentations, Ecclesiastes, and Esther; leads us to see how each is used in Jewish festivals; connects each to major life events of every human; proposes fresh ways to bring them to life for modern audiences; and draws us into the struggle for justice and peace in our world. A creative and engaging book worthy of close study. I'm going to try out her proposals for performing them!

—Peter S. Perry
Associate Affiliate Professor of New Testament
Fuller Seminary

In this study of the five *Megillot*, Jeanette Mathews has reinvented the genre of biblical commentary. Her interpretation of the Song of Songs, Ruth, Lamentations, Ecclesiastes, and Esther applies multiple hermeneutical perspectives, connects the texts with Jewish festivals and other cultic practices, and offers performance-sensitive translations that invite readers to become involved in the texts. Immensely informative and based on deep knowledge of a wide range of historical, religious, and literary issues, this volume equally speaks to graduate students, biblical scholars, and a general readership.

—Werner H. Kelber
Isla Carroll and Percy E. Turner Professor Emeritus of Biblical Studies
Rice University

Working with her own translations, Jeanette Mathews engages the oral world of biblical Hebrew and the performative nature of the *Megillot*. Her work is fresh, insightful, creative—and most importantly, accessible. Cast as performances, the five scrolls come alive under Mathews's direction and readers will wonder at their own role in the story.

—Kandy Queen-Sutherland
Professor Emerita of Religious Studies
Stetson University

READING THE MEGILLOT

Smyth & Helwys Publishing, Inc.
6316 Peake Road
Macon, Georgia 31210-3960
1-800-747-3016
© 2022 by Jeanette Mathews
All rights reserved.

Library of Congress Cataloging-in-Publication Data

Names: Mathews, Jeanette, author.
Title: Reading the *Megillot* : a literary and theological commentary /
   Jeanette Mathews.
Description: Macon, GA : Smyth & Helwys, 2023. | Series: Reading the Old
   Testament | Includes bibliographical references.
Identifiers: LCCN 2022051402 | ISBN 9781641734066 (paperback)
Subjects: LCSH: Talmud. Megillah--Commentaries.
Classification: LCC BM506.M43 M355 2023 | DDC 296.1/206--dc23/eng/20221110
LC record available at https://lccn.loc.gov/2022051402

Disclaimer of Liability: With respect to statements of opinion or fact available in this work of nonfiction, Smyth & Helwys Publishing Inc. nor any of its employees, makes any warranty, express or implied, or assumes any legal liability or responsibility for the accuracy or completeness of any information disclosed, or represents that its use would not infringe privately-owned rights.

Reading the Megillot

A Literary and Theological Commentary

Jeanette Mathews

Also by Jeanette Mathews

Performing Habakkuk: Faithful Re-enactment in the Midst of Crisis
Prophets as Performers: Biblical Performance Criticism and Israel's Prophets
God by Degrees: A Practical Guide for New Theological Students

Acknowledgments

This has been a most enjoyable experience of research and writing, allowing me to discover levels of creativity that I did not know existed. I would like to acknowledge and thank those who took part in this process, whether by working on sections with me or by allowing me the space and time to write. I am grateful that my colleagues at St Mark's National Theological Centre covered my lecturing and administrative responsibilities in the School of Theology of Charles Sturt University during my period of study leave when much of this book was written. A Hebrew reading group that meets weekly at St Mark's translated and discussed with me the books of the *Megillot* over a two-year period. Among that group, my special thanks go to Jen Rose, Tjebbe Bekema, Frank Basten, and Alan Horner, some of whom also made suggestions on my final "performance" translations. John Clark, Benjamin Mathews-Hunter, Jane Foulcher, and poet John Foulcher gave valuable feedback on the Lamentations and Ecclesiastes chapters, as did Jan Smith on my "Panto Esther." Naturally, I have appreciated the encouragement and astute comments of my editor, Mark Biddle. I also want to acknowledge my first Hebrew Bible professor, Dr. Kandy Queen-Sutherland, who continues to inspire and encourage me both academically and as a friend. Her own work on Ruth and Esther has been valuable for this book.

My thanks again go to my family and friends for their love and support as I work with the ancient texts of the Hebrew Bible creatively, critically, and cooperatively. The more I study them, the more I realize they have to offer us for our own time and place.

Contents

Editor's Foreword xv

Introduction to the *Megillot* 1
    What is the *Megillot*? 1
    The Scrolls and the Festivals 3
    Reading the *Megillot* Intertextually 5
    Interpreting the Scrolls 6
        Early Jewish and Christian Interpretation—Literal, Allegorical,
            and Transformational 6
        Modern Interpretation—Historical-critical, Literary, and
            Advocacy Approaches 8
            Presuppositions 9
            Historical-critical Approaches to the *Megillot* 9
            Literary Approaches to the *Megillot* 10
            Advocacy Approaches to the *Megillot* 11
    Reading the *Megillot* 12

A Method of Reading the *Megillot* 13
    Biblical Performance Criticism 13
    Performance as Creativity, Commentary, Connections 16
        Creativity in the *Megillot* 16
        Commentary on the *Megillot* 19
        Connections with the *Megillot* 19

The Scroll of the Song of Songs 21
    Introduction 21
        The Scroll and the Festivals of Passover and Sabbath 23
        The Background of the Scroll 24
        History of Interpretation 25

Poetry in the Scroll	27
The Purpose of the Scroll	29
Creativity in the Song of Songs—A Greek Play	30
Commentary on the Song of Songs	47
Players	47
The Woman	47
The Man	49
The Chorus of Men	50
The Chorus of Women	51
Pace	52
Playfulness	55
Connections with the Song of Songs	58
The Scroll of Ruth	**63**
Introduction	63
The Scroll and the Festival of *Shavuot*	63
The Background of the Scroll	65
The Literary Artistry of the Scroll	67
The Purpose of the Scroll	68
Creativity in Ruth—The Miniseries	69
Commentary on Ruth	88
Characters	88
Naomi	88
Ruth	90
Boaz	92
P'loni Almoni	93
Orpah	94
Young Man	94
Townsfolk	94
Elimelek, Mahlon, Chilion	94
Voiceover Narrator	95
YHWH	95
Correlations	96
Ruth and David	96
Ruth and Tamar	96
Ruth and the Matriarchs	97
Ruth and the "Woman of Valor" (Prov 31:10-22)	97
Ruth and Esther	98
Ruth and the Postexilic Community	98
Conundrums	99

Contents   xiii

      What happened on the threshing floor? (Ruth 3:6-15) 99
      What happens with the laws? 101
      What happens to Ruth? 102
  Connections with Ruth 103

The Scroll of Lamentations 107
  Introduction 107
      The Scroll and the Fast of *Tishah B'Av* 108
      The Background of the Scroll 109
      Poetry in the Scroll 111
      The Purpose of the Scroll 113
  Creativity in Lamentations—Performance Poetry 115
      Lamentations Poem 1 118
      Performance Poem 1 120
      Lamentations Poem 2 125
      Performance Poem 2 128
      Lamentations Poem 3 132
      Performance Poem 3 135
      Lamentations Poem 4 139
      Performance Poem 4 142
      Lamentations Poem 5 145
      Performance Poem 5 146
  Commentary on Lamentations 148
      Crafting 148
      Constraining 154
      Keening 158
  Connections with Lamentations 160

The Scroll of Ecclesiastes 165
  Introduction 165
      The Scroll and the Festival of *Sukkot* 167
      The Background of the Scroll 168
      The Literary Character of the Scroll 169
      The Purpose of the Scroll 172
  Creativity in Ecclesiastes—A Television Talk Show 173
  Commentary on Ecclesiastes 199
      Panelists 199
          Qohelet 199
          The Optimist 200
          The Pietist 201

       Role Models? 202
     Performative Aspects of the Scroll..202
       Ready-mades 202
       Wordplay...205
       Embodiment 207
     Prevailing Wisdom 208
  Connections with Ecclesiastes...210

The Scroll of Esther 215
  Introduction 215
     The Scroll and the Festival of *Purim* 215
     The Background of the Scroll 217
     History of Reception 220
     The Literary Character of the Scroll...221
     The Purpose of the Scroll...223
  Creativity in Esther—A Pantomime 224
  Commentary on Esther 249
     Cast..249
       Ahasuerus 249
       Vashti 251
       Mordecai 252
       Esther...254
       Haman 256
       Zeresh...257
     Comedy 257
     Chiaroscuro...260
  Connections with Esther..261

The *Megillot*—Concluding Comments...267
  Reading the *Megillot* as a Collection...267
  Reenacting the *Megillot*...270

Works Cited...273
Notes 283

Editor's Foreword

The *Reading the Old Testament series* shares many of the aims and objectives of its counterpart, *Reading the New Testament*. Contributors to the current series, like those to its predecessor, write with the intention of presenting "cutting-edge research in [a form] accessible" to a wide audience ranging from specialists in the field to educated laypeople. The approach taken here, as there, focuses not on the minutiae of word-by-word, verse-by-verse exegesis but on larger literary and thought units, especially as they function in the overall conception of the book under analysis. From the standpoint of method, volumes in this series will employ an eclectic variety of reading strategies and critical approaches as contributors deem appropriate for explicating the force of the text before them. Nonetheless, as in RNT, "the focus [will be] on a close reading of the final form of the text." The overarching goal is to provide readers of the commentary series with an aid to help them become more competent, more engaged, and more enthusiastic readers of the Bible as authoritative Scripture.

The title of the series prompts several comments. For the editor, at least, the term "Old Testament" is a convenient convention, since any alternative seems either awkward or provocative. The Hebrew Bible is the shared heritage of Judaism and Christianity, the body of believers whom Paul once described as branches from a wild olive tree who have been "grafted contrary to nature into a cultivated olive tree" (Rom 11:24). Since the beginnings of Christianity, questions concerning how and in what sense the Hebrew Bible/Old Testament functions as Christian Scripture have perpetually confronted the church. Nonetheless, throughout its history, in the spirit of Paul, the church has insisted that the God of Abraham, Isaac, and Jacob is the God of the New Testament. Rather than impose a detailed doctrine of the unity of the two Testaments or specify a particular hermeneutical approach, the editor and the publisher have chosen to invite contributions to the series from scholars selected because of their learning and insight, again in the spirit of Paul, we hope, without regard to faith tradition or denominational identity.

The books of the Hebrew Bible were the fountainhead for the faith of both Paul and Aqiba. May it be that, through the scholarship presented in the pages of this series, the books of the "Old Testament" water the faith of another generation.

—Mark E. Biddle, General Editor
Richmond, Virginia

Introduction to the *Megillot*

What is the *Megillot*?

Five intriguing and quite different compositions are gathered together in the Hebrew Bible under the name *Megillot*, the Hebrew word for "scrolls." They are the Song of Songs, Ruth, Lamentations, Ecclesiastes, and Esther. The Song of Songs is a collection of love poems; Ruth is a charming short story of a Moabite widow who becomes integrated into the Israelite community; Lamentations is also a collection of poems but focused on grief and loss in response to the destruction of Jerusalem and its temple; Ecclesiastes is a philosophical rumination on human existence; and Esther is a satirical tale of one man's threat to wipe out the Jewish population of Persia that is thwarted by the Jewish Queen Esther, the tale that gave rise to the annual Jewish *Purim* festival. In many Old Testament canons these five compositions are found in a different order and are scattered among other books rather than collected in one group. Ruth comes first, placed between Judges and 1–2 Samuel; Esther is found after the "historical" books of Chronicles, Ezra, and Nehemiah; Ecclesiastes and the Song of Songs follow Proverbs in the "Wisdom" section of the Old Testament; and Lamentations comes after the prophetic book of Jeremiah. Contemporary Jewish Bibles, however, always group them together, despite their different subject matter.

The order of biblical books in the Old Testament canon was settled at an earlier time for Christian communities than for Jewish communities. This is predominantly due to the different format in which they were preserved. The Christian faith that arose during the Roman era quickly adopted the codex that enabled separate documents to be bound between covers. With this technology, the order of books in a collection was no longer as flexible. By contrast, Jewish communities largely maintained the tradition of preserving their writings in scrolls made of parchment. Even now, synagogues have collections of scrolls from which Scriptures are read. Notably, the *Torah* is always preserved on one scroll, thus the order of the first five books in the Bible has long been set. The second group of books in the Hebrew Bible, the Prophets (*Nevi'im*) is also well established in terms of content, and there are only minor variations in their order. But the last division, the Writings (*Ketuvim*), was fluid for much longer. The individual scrolls were kept in baskets or cabinets from which they were brought out for reading. It is not until the tenth century CE that there is evidence for the *Megillot* as a set collection in codices, and around this time the term *ḥamesh megillot* ("Five Scrolls") began to be used.

The Babylonian Talmud from the sixth century CE does not have a *Megillot* collection. The five books are included in the *Ketuvim* (Writings), but not as a group. The books of the *Ketuvim* seem to be ordered on the basis of their historical setting as well as their content. Ruth came first, set in the time of the judges and providing a genealogy for King David. It was followed by Psalms (the book associated with King David); Job; Proverbs, Ecclesiastes, and Song of Songs (the latter three associated with King Solomon); Lamentations (the fall of Jerusalem); Daniel and Esther (both from the Persian era); Ezra/Nehemiah and Chronicles (also from the postexilic period). Job is anomalous, as it was thought Job lived in the days of Moses, but the rabbis did not want to begin the *Ketuvim* with a book about suffering. Though Ruth begins with suffering ("There was a famine in the land"), it ends with happiness and points directly to David, so its placement was deemed appropriate.

The Masoretic Text, the oldest authoritative version of the Hebrew Bible with its earliest surviving codices from the tenth century CE (the Aleppo Codex) and the eleventh century CE (the Leningrad Codex), preserves a *Megillot* collection that is ordered slightly differently, based on a historical schema and assumption of authorship. Ruth, purportedly written by Samuel in the time of Judges, comes first; the Song of Songs, thought to be authored by a young King Solomon, is next; followed by Ecclesiastes, authored by an older Solomon; then Lamentations from Jeremiah's hand in the late monarchic period; and finally, Esther, written by Mordecai in the Persian era.

The placement of these five books within Christian Old Testaments follows the order in the Septuagint, the Greek translation of the Hebrew Bible that was used by the early church. The same assumptions were made regarding authorship, but the placement of books in the Septuagint is different from the three-part division of the Hebrew Bible. The Septuagint was divided into four sections: *Torah* (the basic text), Historical books (dealing with the past), Wisdom and Poetic books (dealing with the present), and Prophetic Books (focused on the future). The location of the books of the *Megillot* gives some indication of how they were interpreted within later

Christian tradition: Ruth and Esther as "historical"; Ecclesiastes as "wisdom"; the Song of Songs also understood as "wisdom" or at least associated with Solomon, the traditional founder of wisdom in Israel; and Lamentations as "prophetic."

Authorship and date of composition will be discussed in later chapters for each individual scroll. Suffice to say, their placement in the *Ketuvim* of the Hebrew Bible indicates that they reached their final form *after* Israel's monarchic period even if the subject matter and implied author belong to earlier times. It is worth noting at this point that, despite the difficulties posed by the individual scrolls that means they do not always sit comfortably within Scripture, their status as inspired writings has long been recognized. By at least the second century CE, both Jewish and Christian canons included these scrolls. As we will see, rabbis and church fathers debated their *value*, but the debates were over how they related to other canonical books and how they should be used rather than whether they belonged to Scripture.

Chronological ordering sits well with contemporary readers due to a "modern obsession with history" (Strawn 2020, 124), but, as other biblical collections demonstrate, chronology is not the sole ordering principle or interpretive key for understanding biblical books. Medieval Judaism reordered the *Megillot* collection according to the festival calendar beginning with the spring new year (Exod 12:2), and most Jewish Bibles since then have preserved the same order based on the annual liturgical cycle: Song of Songs is associated with Passover (April); Ruth is read at *Shavuot* (May/June); Lamentations is read on the fast day of *Tishah B'av* (July/August), Ecclesiastes is read on the third day of the *Sukkot* festival (September/October); and Esther is the basis for *Purim* during the month of Adar (March). These are not the only Jewish festivals, so other principles must have been at work to determine the collection. Notably, the number five connects the *Megillot* with the *Torah* (Pentateuch) and the five-part division of the Psalter. A few Hebrew manuscripts even place the *Megillot* after the *Torah* (Strawn 2020, 140). These relatively short compositions can be preserved on one physical scroll (hence "The *Megillot*"). The editors of this Reading the Old Testament series have chosen to consider these five Old Testament books under this grouping, so my discussion will follow the liturgical order that is preserved in all contemporary Jewish translations.

The Scrolls and the Festivals

Jewish practice is bound to time, whether seasonal or daily. Time-bound rituals "give expression to the idea that godliness is not limited to the spiritual realm but can be found in our physical world, defined by time and space" (Brawer 2008, 181). As we can see in the opening chapter of Genesis with its rhythmic ". . . and there was evening, and there was morning, the first/second/third etc. day," the Jewish conception of the day is that it begins at nightfall, specifically at the moment of *tzeit ha-kokhavim*, or when at least three stars can be seen (Brawer 2008, 182). This simple observation forms a link between nature and time. It is also a reminder that even on occasions when observation and worship are demanded in special measure, Sabbath and festivals included, the period begins with a time of inactivity and surrender to sleep, signifying trust in God's care and protection.

It is said that most Jewish holidays as practiced today can be summed up in nine words: "They tried to kill us. We won. Let's eat." This saying is certainly true for Passover, celebrating the exodus from Egypt and its tyrannical Pharaoh, and for *Purim*, the name given to the feast that commemorated the overturning of Haman's edict to annihilate the Jews in the story of Esther. The Jewish *fasts* are summed up with a similar saying: "They tried to kill us. They managed it. Let's *not* eat." *Tishah B'av* is an annual fast day remembering the destruction of the Jerusalem temple and other occasions when enemies defeated the Jews. The remaining festivals connected to the *Megillot* have their origin in the agricultural calendar: *Shavuot* for the early summer wheat harvest and first fruits and *Sukkot* for the autumn harvest. Passover (*Pesach*) is also connected to an agricultural event, incorporating the festival of unleavened bread held at the start of the barley harvest. *Pesach*, *Shavuot*, and *Sukkot* are collectively known as *shalosh regalim*, the "three feet," because in biblical tradition they were to be observed as pilgrimages to the temple in Jerusalem (Lieber 2012, 158). After the destruction of the second temple in 70 CE, sacrificial rituals that had been linked to the festivals could no longer be carried out, requiring modification to almost all the biblical festivals. They were transformed into practices that could be performed in homes and synagogues, and they continue to be celebrated in the cycle of Jewish worship to this day.

Each of the Jewish festivals, regardless of its ancient roots, has historical memory in the biblical tradition. Passover, as mentioned, remembers the exodus. *Shavuot* celebrates Moses receiving the Torah on Mount Sinai during the wilderness wanderings following the exodus, and *Sukkot* also remembers the time in the wilderness when the Israelites slept in temporary accommodations on their journey. *Tishah B'av* focuses on the destruction of the temple and *Purim* on the attempted destruction of the Jews in Esther's story. As we will see when we revisit each of these festivals in connection with individual scrolls, the rituals combine elements of nature, cultic practices including prayers and recitation of Scripture, and special foods (or fasting in the case of *Tishah B'av*). Seasons of the year are therefore linked with key moments in Jewish history to create continually renewed spiritual meaning for participants. Practical elements such as spring cleaning (Passover), hospitality (*Sukkot*), and charity (*Purim*) are welcome benefits of the customary observances. Understood as divinely mandated occasions, Jewish festivals (like those of any culture) dramatize the ideals of the community and impart joy and color to its everyday life. The spiritual life is thus ordered around regular festival celebrations that remember the faithfulness of God in history and call for ongoing faithful response.

Reading the *Megillot* Intertextually

The order of the scrolls in the *Megillot* was discussed above at some length because I agree with Marc Zvi Brettler when he claims, "The ordering matters because it alters the context in which we understand the text; a book's meaning can shift depending upon which books we read before and after it" (2005, 9). Removing Ruth and Esther from the "historical" books of the Old Testament and Lamentations from "prophetic" literature, for example, allows us to appreciate their literary character more freely without first making assumptions about their historicity. As a collection these scrolls inform each other and form linkages with each other. When we read the Song of Songs with its sexually explicit love poems prior to the scroll of Ruth, we are primed to view the ambiguous action at the threshing floor in the third chapter of Ruth as having an intimate quality. The scroll of Ruth ends with a celebration of birth that brings new life and hope to widows, and the scroll of Lamentations begins with the mourning cry of the city envisaged as a widow seeing the death of her children. The questioning of God's justice in Lamentations is continued in the sceptical view expressed by the author of Ecclesiastes—that God is uninterested in human affairs. The contrary exhortation to enjoy life by feasting and drinking also found in Ecclesiastes becomes a prominent motif in Esther, which records no less than seven drinking parties. The Song of Songs and Esther bookend the collection and share the distinction of not once referring to God. And as we will see, although the other three scrolls mention the name of God, God does not speak directly in *any* of the five scrolls. This give us an overarching theological framework for reading the *Megillot*, suggesting that human experience is the key theme in the collection. The *Megillot* gives us glimpses into the common experiences and dilemmas of human life—romance and love, birth and death, meaning and values in social and political relationships—yet their collection as *Scripture* enables us to view those ordinary aspects of life as revelatory. Precisely *because* the books are preserved for use in Jewish festivals, we can infer a connection between human activity and the numinous. When God is silent, as Christian Brady evocatively suggests, "life becomes interpretation" (2005, 224).

Interpreting the Scrolls

Ever since the scrolls of the *Megillot* came into existence, they have been interpreted in a myriad of ways. I am going to approach them via the lens of Biblical Performance Criticism, outlined below, but for now I will briefly survey how they have been understood by Jewish and Christian readers across the centuries.

Early Jewish and Christian Interpretation—Literal, Allegorical, and Transformational

Up until the Enlightenment, readers of the Bible tended to take the books at face value, accepting their claims of authorship and assuming the events happened as described. The Bible was understood as cryptic but perfect, divinely inspired, and above criticism or reproach. If texts appeared to contradict each other, they were harmonized by interpreters so that they agreed.

Where a literal interpretation was especially challenging, early interpreters turned to allegory. Allegorical interpretation was practised across the ancient world as a means of smoothing over problematic texts. For example, Hellenes confronted by myths of deities engaging in immoral behavior were able to allegorize the myths to retain their value in their traditions. Jewish scholars such as Philo of Alexandria and Christian leaders of the early church such as Origen used allegorical exegesis to affirm that all parts of the biblical tradition were morally and spiritually uplifting. If a "literal" reading of the text was found to be wanting, it could be redeemed by allegory and retain its relevance for readers' moral lives.

The scroll that is most open to allegorizing in the *Megillot* is that of the Song of Songs. The relationship between the man and the woman was understood variously as God's relationship to God's chosen people; the relationship between divine and human intellect; an ecclesiastical reading of a description of Christ and his bride, the church; or Christ as the bridegroom of the individual soul.

Jewish tradition understands the interaction between the word of God and human interpretation of it in the light of receiving the Torah at Sinai. There Moses received both the written law (*mikra*) and the oral law (*mishnah*). The name *Mishnah* comes from the Hebrew verb *šnh* ("to repeat" or "to study something handed down"). Although the name signifies that it was handed down orally, the *Mishnah* was transcribed by the end of the second century CE. The *Talmud* forms the documents that commented on and expanded the *Mishnah* over time. In Jewish practice, then, biblical traditions are repeated, discussed, and expanded. New significance for the *Megillot* is given in the building up of these traditions. For example, according to the Jerusalem *Talmud Hagigah*, King David was born and died during the festival of *Shavuot*, adding a layer of meaning to the scroll of Ruth. The *Mishnah Taanit* records five specific events that occurred on the ninth of *Av* that warrant fasting on that day, including the destruction of both Solomon's Temple and the Second Temple begun by Ezra and Nehemiah. The scroll of Lamentations is thus used in the commemoration of that day.

A rabbinic parable explains the significance of this interpretive tradition when it describes a king leaving two servants equal measures of wheat and flax:

> The wise one of them took the flax and wove a beautiful cloth and took the wheat and made it into fine flour, and sifted it, and ground it, and kneaded it, and baked it, and set it on the table, and spread the beautiful cloth over it, and left it there until the king should come. And the fool of them did nothing. After some time, the king came into his house, and said to them, to his two servants, "My sons, bring to me what I gave you." One of them brought out the bread of fine flour, on the table, with the beautiful cloth spread over it. And the other of them brought out the wheat in a pile and the bundle of flax upon it. Woe for that shame! Woe for that disgrace! Which one is more favored? You must admit it is the one who brought out the bread on the table with the beautiful cloth spread over it (*Seder Eliyahu Zuta*, Chapter 2).[1]

As discussed by Karin Zetterholm (2012, 5–6), the parable shows that interpretation was an ongoing process that transformed the meaning of the biblical text. The wise servant actively engaged with the materials given, transforming them into new and useful products. Interpretation and adaptation for new circumstances, according to this parable, is what is *desired* by God. The oral law was necessary to give new meaning to old traditions. Moreover, Jewish rabbinic tradition allows different interpretations to sit side by side, demonstrating a freedom for dissent and an openness to multiple readings.

The early Christian church adopted the Jewish Scriptures (in the Greek translation, the Septuagint) but reread the traditions in the light of their faith that Jesus of Nazareth was the Messiah foretold by the Jewish Bible. Due to King David's lineage spelled out at the end of the scroll of Ruth, Ruth's name is included in the genealogy of Jesus in the Gospel of Matthew. Otherwise, there are no direct quotations from the *Megillot* in the New Testament. A number of allusions, however, show that the New Testament writers knew of the scrolls. For example, Jesus is likened to a bridegroom in several parables and the church to a bride in the book of Revelation, picking up the allegorical interpretation of the Song of Songs that was favored by early church fathers. Barry Webb argues that Paul's epistle to the Corinthians and Mark's account of the passion of Jesus are informed by suffering expressed in Lamentations (2000, 79–80). I will suggest below that the "daily gratitude" wisdom of Ecclesiastes is echoed in Jesus' Sermon on the Mount. The scroll of Esther was largely ignored by the early church, although a comment by Clement of Alexandria about Esther's clothing indicates an allegorical interpretation. It seems that a lack of specifically messianic references in the *Megillot*, other than mention of King David in Ruth, meant that this part of inherited Jewish Scripture was marginal for early Christian faith.

By the medieval period, identifying the scrolls of the *Megillot* with annual festivals had given a clear focus for the meaning and use of each scroll within Jewish interpretation. Christianity transformed or discarded Jewish festivals over time and did not have the same interpretive key for the *Megillot*, although allegorical readings persisted. The rise of scholarly study of the Bible after the Enlightenment brought new interest in the individual scrolls for both Jewish and Christian interpreters.

Modern Interpretation—Historical-critical, Literary, and Advocacy Approaches[2]

Presuppositions. Contemporary interpretation of biblical texts by faithful readers begins with some presuppositions. First, the authors of this material were human beings using human language to create human documents that can be studied like any other literary works. Studying the Bible is not quite as simple as that because it was written in ancient languages across a long period of time, and we have no direct access to original documents or living informants to guide us. We must continually ask questions of the texts in order to make discerning judgments about what the original authors were intending to convey, a method of study usually referred to as the historical-critical approach.[3]

Many of us have had a lifelong relationship with Scripture and have been interpreting it, perhaps unconsciously, by listening to sermons, studying with small groups, and reading devotionally. Critical interpretation of Scripture overlaps with but also differs from devotional interpretation. Let me take the first chapter of the scroll of Ruth by way of example.

A devotional approach to this chapter might involve reflection on how an experience of grief or hardship has affected my faith. I might ask myself if I, like Naomi, have ever felt bitter towards God, and what would be needed to change that. I may be aware of a community in which *I* would feel safe and supported after a time of loss. I might ask if I would be willing, like Ruth, to step into new territory in support of a loved one.

By contrast, critical analysis might include considering what I will learn by reading the text in ancient Hebrew. I might ask who the likely author of the story was and when it was first written. Or, indeed, did it exist as an oral tradition before being written? When did the scroll of Ruth become part of the canon of sacred Scripture? I might think about the relationship between the Israelites and Moabites, and the distance between Moab and Bethlehem. What was the status of women in the time of ancient Israel, and what security was offered to widows? What lies behind Naomi's strange reason for asking her daughters-in-law to return to Moab in verses 11-13? Do other names in the first chapter have the same significance as Naomi/Mara? What is the literary context of the book in my Bible, and does that shed any light on its meaning? My Bible includes a part of the chapter as poetic verse—why? The latter set of questions are helpful in interpreting the scroll beyond my own subjective experience.

The second presupposition guiding interpretation is that the canonical status of the human documents included in the Bible lifts them above other human documents as the inspired word of God. As faithful readers, we approach Scripture with the expectation that God is speaking. Even the *Megillot*, where God is either absent or *not* heard speaking, can be celebrated as a collection of works that speak to our relationship with the divine.

Finally, the canonical status of Scripture means that these documents have been reinterpreted by communities of faith across history in different settings, resulting in layers of meaning that have built up over time. Some layers have been discarded along the way but will have been valid for a particular time. As Brettler comments, "the Bible, like any ancient text, has been read differently in different periods, because readers read the Bible using their own conventions or rules . . . the validity of any reading depends on its time period and the conventions of that period" (2005, 14).

***Historical-critical Approaches to the* Megillot.** In the seventeenth century CE, with the rise of European rationalism, biblical study became dominated by "critical" methods that moved away from viewing the text as perfect and divine in origin. The Dutch philosopher Baruch Spinoza wrote, "I hold that the method of interpreting Scripture is no different from the method of interpreting nature, and is in fact in complete accord with it" (1670, trans. Shirley 1991). Such sentiments gave rise to "scientific" study of the Bible. The primary focus was seeking to understand the background of the text and how it came into being. In other words, the world "behind" the text such as authorship and historical context are of interest rather than the world "of" the text—the ideas, characters, and events described in it. The term "historical-critical" signifies that the context for interpretation is the place and time in which the texts were composed, and they are to be read "objectively," independently of prior religious commitment or traditions. These approaches look for clues in the texts about when they were written, by whom, for which audiences, against which socio-politico-economic context, and with which literary or historical influences. When applying these sorts of questions to the *Megillot*, it is apparent that the individual origins or the works were quite different. Historical-critical studies of the *Megillot* have thus tended to read the works separately rather than as a group.

Attention to the historical origins of individual biblical books enables us to appreciate the diversity of voices and contexts that have come together in the Bible to address profound issues of faith and identity. It has limitations, however, since it has shown that few definitive answers are possible for any book in the Hebrew Bible, including the *Megillot*. From the 1960s onwards there was a migration from the "scientific" to the "literary" in Biblical Studies, partly due to dissatisfaction with the lack of secure results from historical-critical methodology and partly in renewed appreciation for the Bible as outstanding world literature.

***Literary Approaches to the* Megillot.** It is remarkable that the books that have been collected together as canonical Scripture cover such a wide range of literary styles, including narrative, law, prophecy, psalms, wisdom, memoirs, genealogies, blessings and curses, proverbs, parables, and more. The *Megillot*, as already noted, is found in the *Ketuvim*, or "Writings." This last division of the Hebrew Bible is especially marked by a diversity of styles and subjects. Within the *Megillot* itself we find erotic poetry, stories of two diametrically opposite women—one a foreigner in Israel and the other an Israelite in a foreign land—told with entertainment as a primary motive, poetry that functions as lament, and a poetic-prose treatise on the meaning of life.

Although I will be demonstrating that each of the scrolls in the *Megillot* makes a unique contribution to the Hebrew Bible as a whole, all have affinity with literature and traditions from the ancient Near East. Love poetry has been found in Mesopotamia and Egypt and even India that bear similarities to the Song of Songs. The "city lament" genre is known in Mesopotamia in the second millennium BCE and may have informed the writer of Lamentations. Parallels have been noted between parts of Ecclesiastes and the Gilgamesh Epic. The plot of Ruth with a key device of a relationship developing on the threshing floor during harvest time is evocative of fertility rites connected to grain in some cultures of the ancient Near East. The tale of Esther has parallels to other documents that have been discovered, including a neo-Assyrian description of honor bestowed on Necho by Ashurbanipal and Greek Herodotus's tale of the Lydian Candaules. Taking all of these parallels into account, we can see that the authors of the scrolls in the *Megillot* creatively adapted traces of existing genres from the literary world of the ancient Near East whilst placing their unique Israelite stamp on them.

Appreciation for the literary qualities of the *Megillot* includes analysis of their narrative or poetic structure. Much attention has been given to narrative analysis of the Bible in recent decades, and fruitful insights have been applied to the narratives of Ruth and Esther. Robert Alter notes that there are stylistic differences between early (First Temple) and late (Second Temple) compositions but observes that the author of the scroll of Ruth "consciously archaized" his writing, "seeking to make [it] sound as though it were produced in the period of the Judges" (2019b, xliv). The scroll of Esther, on the other hand, has a "loose" and "ragged" narrative style (Alter 2019b, 715). Both compositions demonstrate typical Hebrew narrative features, however, such as the use of a narrator, differing points of view, significance in time and place, character development, emphasis on dialogue, and use of repetition, themes, and key words. Hebrew poetry also has typical features including terseness, parallelism, heightened use of metaphor, personification, and rhetorical devices evidenced in wordplay and audience engagement. The Song of Songs and Lamentations are entirely poetic in structure. The scroll of Ecclesiastes combines prose and poetic forms. Alter describes the composition of Ecclesiastes as "evocative rhythmic prose that occasionally scans as poetry" (2019b, 673). Notably, literary readings of the scrolls in the *Megillot* have drawn out the humor inherent in them.

Attention to the literary character of each of the scrolls in the *Megillot* has resulted in new and influential ways of understanding them, drawing out dramatic, satirical, dialogical, metaphorical, and artistic features that enhance appreciation for them as carefully constructed literary creations.

***Advocacy Approaches to the* Megillot.** A third group of approaches to studying the *Megillot* could be described as focusing on the world "in front of" the text. Readers bring their own experiences, perspectives, and concerns to the text and expect it to engage with these questions. What a biblical passage meant for its original reader and what it means for a contemporary reader could be quite different. Advocacy approaches interpret and critique the ideology present in texts and reread them in light of new experiences.

Feminist readers, for example, have noticed that the experience of women is highlighted in all of the scrolls except Ecclesiastes, where, if anything, a chauvinistic attitude is apparent in its explicitly negative comments about women (7:26-28). Women's stories are the focus of Ruth and Esther as reflected in their titles. The scrolls of Esther, Lamentations, and the Song of Songs commence with women's voices. Ruth, Lamentations, and the Song of Songs highlight the woman's point of view. In addition to feminist concerns, advocacy studies of the *Megillot* that I have come across in the preparation of this book have included attention to violence and war, suffering and trauma, treatment of foreigners, terrorism, climate change, and the arts.

Reading the *Megillot*

In the analysis of each scroll that forms the major chapters of this book, I will draw from each of these methodological approaches as well as offer unique insights from Biblical Performance Criticism. Each chapter will give brief comments on the background of the scroll (historical-critical analysis) as well as its literary character (literary analysis) before applying my own Performance Critical lens. A section at the end of each chapter will bring the concerns of the individual scroll into conversation with concerns of our own time, thus adding an "advocacy" focus for each scroll.

The five scrolls have been preserved as a collection, yet their distinctiveness in style and content demands that any reader of each individual scroll must take its specific genre into account as the first step in interpretation. It also reminds us that good Bible study begins by noticing what is actually there in the text rather than what we expect to find in the text. By analysing each scroll separately, I will attend to its unique compositional characteristics and draw out historical and theological issues underlying its original context as well as consider its ongoing impact in new settings. The final chapter of this book will step back again to comment on their status as a collection and why it is helpful to read them together. As we will see, the diversity of genres in the *Megillot* will open up a range of interpretations about how one should live faithfully—interpretations that will surprise, intrigue, and delight their audiences.

A Method of Reading the *Megillot*

Biblical Performance Criticism

My method for reading the *Megillot* is drawn from the relatively new discipline of Performance Criticism in Biblical Studies. This way of approaching the Bible is still developing and moving in diverse directions, but its proponents share a conviction that the biblical worlds were predominantly oral-aural cultures in which messages were conveyed orally by embodied communicators to audiences in shared spaces. All biblical scholars are committed to the interpretation of ancient written texts, but Biblical Performance Criticism (BPC) reminds interpreters that these texts are better understood as "scripts." Ancient scribes, prophets, teachers, and evangelists were "performers" who re-presented traditions for audiences in specific settings. A message conveyed in this manner has significant components that are not present in the individualistic silent reading that typifies engagement with the biblical traditions in many contemporary settings. One major emphasis is that scripts were performed before a gathered audience. An audience is influenced by the sound of the words, the performer's tone of voice, the use of gestures and props, and even silence. The reactions of others around them and the context—emotional, social, political—all play a part in interpretation. Biblical Performance Critics argue that meaning-making emerges from the dynamic relationship of performer, audience, text, and setting.

The broader secular discipline of Performance Studies is an interdisciplinary field including theater studies, cultural anthropology, linguistics, sociology, social psychology, ethnomusicology, and literary theory, amongst others. The common thread is the study of performance and the use of performance as a lens to study the world. To coin Shakespeare's phrase, all the world is a stage, after all (not a text!). Themes that are found across the field of Performance Studies are self-reflexivity (the performer's awareness of the separation between the self and the role); universality (communication that is holistic and relevant to a broad range of experience); embodiment (interactions between performers and audience in a shared space rather than abstract words on a page); dynamic process (the actual activity of the performance is as valid as the completed event); and reenactment (recognizing that all performance is based on preexisting models, scripts, or patterns). Finding these themes in biblical texts enables us to recognise their essentially performative foundation.

Biblical Performance Criticism began with New Testament studies where the oral foundation of Scripture was readily evident. The letters of the apostles were recited publicly to different congregations in different places (1 Thess 5:27), and the book of Revelation, given to John for the churches, began with the statement "Blessed is the one who reads aloud the words of the prophecy, and blessed are those who hear . . ." (Rev 1:3, NRSV). We know that access to written materials was only available to an elite group in ancient communities, so it was likely that the Gospels were spread by being performed regularly for appreciative audiences keen to know more about Jesus of Nazareth to whom they had committed themselves. The Gospels themselves portray Jesus teaching disciples and crowds in a variety of locations, often by reciting and expanding Jewish Scriptures in the manner of the oral tradition of the rabbis.

Scholars of the Hebrew Bible also began to consider the foundation of orality when describing transmission of those traditions. It seems obvious to view prophets in the Hebrew Bible as performers who spoke publicly before audiences, often using symbolic actions and embodying their own message. Hebrew narrative has a characteristic paratactic and repetitive style that has been recognized as aiding both storyteller and audience in oral delivery. The paramount example of Hebrew poetic composition is the Psalter, and superscriptions with instructions for musicians and so forth demonstrate that this material was used in performative ways from ancient times until now.

By recognizing that communication, human interaction, and interpretation are interconnected, proponents of BPC have welcomed interdisciplinary approaches to biblical texts. Insights from historical-critical methods, literary methods, and advocacy methods in Biblical Studies all contribute to meaning-making. A major strength in the approach of BPC, arising from its interest in embodiment and audience response, is its explicit intention of integrating theory and praxis. Its scholars deliberately look for relationships between biblical traditions and contemporary settings and issues.

Such a holistic, dynamic approach has the potential to transform our interaction with Scripture. It reminds us that the original traditions were developed with any number of possible motives: to entertain, create beauty, determine or change identity, develop or foster community, teach or persuade, and speak of the sacred. Scripture was presented via performance to audiences in its first iterations and continues to be reenacted with new audiences down through the centuries. Since performers, settings, and audiences are constantly changing and adjustments are inevitable when transmitting traditions in new circumstances, a focus on Scripture as performance opens the possibility of new and differing interpretations of the same script. BPC reminds us that there was no "original text" and therefore no definitive interpretation. As Peter Perry has commented,

> Performance criticism also exposes the unreality of a search for an "original" version. Even if we assume that a manuscript has all the words and letters that an author penned, we can't reproduce the embodiment that the author envisioned. Even if the exact words are used in the same language, every performer of that text will say the words slightly differently based on their own preferences and interpretation. Every audience will hear it differently based on their preconceptions and the situation. (2016, 148)

BPC has followed oral-tradition scholars such as Albert Lord (1960) and John Miles Foley (2002) in recovering clues of underlying performance that can be found in written literature. The texts are viewed as scripts and examined for their oral imprint and their intrinsic potential for theatricality. Scholars look for the characteristics, formulas, patterns, rhythms, and lexemes that give evidence for the original oral communication of the text, along with any "stage directions" that are built into them, giving clues about time, space, movement, costume, props, lighting and so on.[4]

Another approach of scholars engaged in BPC is to internalize and perform biblical texts for contemporary audiences in order to better understand what original audiences may have experienced. Rhetorical features such as the use of repetition are more readily noticed, as are humor and other emotive triggers. Such "practice-based research" gives the performer greater insight into the text's world, noticing the kinetic, emotive, and rhetorical dimensions from the inside. It also encourages the audience to make connections between what they are experiencing in hearing the biblical text with issues and events of their own world. In other words, the interface between ancient performances and contemporary performances, informed by scholarly insights, are deeply explored in this practice-based method.

Some critics of Biblical Performance Criticism argue that there is no evidence for ancient forms of Hebrew theater. The modern Hebrew word for theater, *bamah*, derives from the biblical word meaning "high place." Since these "high places" were critiqued in biblical laws and traditions, it is unlikely that such a modern concept of theater would have been tolerated in ancient Israelite society. Moreover, Jewish attendance at Greek and Roman theaters was discouraged as these were places associated with idolatry and pagan festivals. To view biblical texts through the lens of performance, however, one need not assume that they were staged theatrical dramas in their original iteration. We can appreciate the performative qualities of a text understood as a script at a theoretical level and gain new insights about biblical traditions from that imaginative exercise. By the same token, scripts of biblical texts that are "performed" in contemporary settings can shed new light on familiar material and bring greater connection between our world and the biblical world.

Performance as Creativity, Commentary, Connections

In this book I intend to approach the scrolls of the *Megillot* via the three-fold paradigm of creativity, commentary, and connections. I have been influenced by the work of the late professor of Performance Studies at Northwestern University, Dwight Conquergood, who established the Department of Performance Studies in 1984 and was determined to overcome the growing divide between academics and practitioners. In advocating for learning as a synthesis of research and practice, he used his own alliterated terms for describing the work of Performance Studies: imagination, inquiry, intervention; creativity, critique, citizenship; artistry, analysis, activism (2002, 152). Each triad celebrates the artistic nature of performance, uses it as a lens to analyse aesthetic and everyday behavior, and seeks intentional connections with the issues and concerns of contemporary society.

I do not aim to reproduce a drama as it may have played out in ancient Israel but, with imagination and creativity, to exploit the dramatic and theatrical qualities of the biblical material by translating and analysing it through the lens of performance. In doing so I aim to highlight the artistry of the original composition (creativity), explain its meaning (commentary), and raise issues of relevance for our own times (connections).

Creativity in the *Megillot*

To focus on creativity in Scripture is to be alert to both the underlying oral foundation and the compositional skill of the literary scribe. The way that we can most readily access these are through performance-sensitive translations of the Hebrew texts.

The starting point for my method, therefore, is my own translation of the scroll from the Hebrew text. I have worked with a critical edition of the

Masoretic Text (MT). The name Masorete is from an Aramaic word meaning to transmit or hand down. The Masoretes, working in the tenth century CE, were the transmitters of the ancient Hebrew Bible, which had reached its final form by the second century CE. In antiquity Hebrew was written in consonantal form, and the Masoretes added vowel pointing and accents on the basis of the received oral tradition to aid ongoing recitation. They also noted any variations between the textual and oral traditions that were passed on. Whilst the MT is my basic text for translation, like other translators I have at times needed to consider other ancient witnesses such as the Greek translation (Septuagint) and Latin translation (Vulgate) when the text is unclear.

Translations of biblical texts fall on a spectrum between "formal" or "literal" (word-for-word) and "dynamic equivalence" (thought-for-thought). Formal translations attempt to translate each word based on usage of that word at the time of writing. Since Hebrew omits some words commonly used in English (such as pronouns) and includes words that would translate into several English words due to the addition of conjunctions, articles, pronouns, and so on as prefixes and suffixes to words, it is impossible to create an actual word-for-word translation.[5] Another difficulty for word-for-word translations is the presence of words that appear only once in the Hebrew Bible, technically referred to as *hapax legomena*. Without comparable data it can be difficult to know how to translate such words. Nonetheless, in my translations I have attempted to stay at the formal end of the spectrum in order to hear something of what the original audience may have heard when the traditions were conveyed orally.

Within the Hebrew Bible there is a basic division between prose and poetry. While these categories could once again be viewed as being on a spectrum, with debate about where the dividing line falls, poetry and prose/narrative are distinguished by their characteristic features, as discussed in the previous chapter. As we have noted, the scrolls that make up the *Megillot* include literature from both categories. One of the advantages of Biblical Performance Criticism is that it is a holistic method that can be applied to both prose and poetry. Moreover, reading the scrolls as scripts for performance will continue to blur the distinctions between these categories.

In translating for performance, I have tried to draw out clues to the oral imprint of the texts by focusing on the following features: I look out for linguistic patterns such as parallel lines in poetry, the use of acrostics, and chiastic structures. I generally replicate the order of sentences in Hebrew, even though this can sound unnatural in English expression. In Hebrew the verb usually precedes the subject. The effect of translating this way is that action is stressed prior to the subject of the action. It enables us to see times when this usual pattern is interrupted, technically called "fronting," which allows us to hear an emphasis in the original script that we would otherwise miss if we consistently translate according to English grammatical patterns. I take notice of the distinction between male and female, singular and plural. Although it is not always possible to replicate this distinction in the translation, I will comment on it in my commentary when it is significant for interpretation. Use of plural verbs, for example, may signify audience involvement. I aim for lexical consistency within each scroll by translating the same Hebrew words and roots with the same English word. This better allows us to hear what original audiences would have heard and will highlight repeated words and themes. The Hebrew verbal system has some unique features to which I draw attention in my translation. A narrative form of the verb that occurs at the beginning of many clauses incorporates the conjunctive *waw*, and I have consistently translated this "and" to convey the movement in the script. Hebrew verbal stems that determine nuances of meaning can be significant, such as the use of the causative *hifil* stem. Some recurring Hebrew expressions have a contemporary sound when translated literally, especially the preposition "like." Yet there is also value in retaining archaic language such as the common particle *hinnēh* ("behold") or idioms that are not commonly used (such as "burning" for anger). Such expressions remind us that we are dealing with ancient literature, after all, and we are far removed from it in time and cultural perspective. I have tried to notice wordplay and soundplay and at times attempted to replicate similar patterns in translation. Finally, I am aware of the diacritics in the Hebrew text, particularly the *athnach*—a pause marker in the middle of most verses, the *setumah* (ס)—a short pause between verses, and the *petuchah* (פ)—a longer pause between verses or chapters. Since these maks were added by the Masoretes to aid in recitation, they can also act as guides for the use of silence in a script, in making assumptions about which ideas belong together, and in determining where there may be scene divisions.

    I have translated the five scrolls of the *Megillot* in the company of a Hebrew translation group that meets weekly, and together we have noticed many of these features during those sessions. Another influential source has been the work of Robert Alter, especially his book *The Art of Bible Translation* (2019a) where he describes the principles he followed as he translated the Hebrew Bible over many decades, now published as *The Hebrew Bible: A Translation and Commentary* (2019b).

    My appreciation for the artistry of each scroll has spilled over to creatively imagine each work as a different type of performance, based on the content and style of the material. Others may envisage these scrolls differently, but the lens of performance allows for and even encourages diversity of reception.[6]

Commentary on the *Megillot*
Commentary is undertaken in order to highlight performative features embedded in the scripts along with common themes of performance literature as identified above. The script of each of the scrolls guides the questions that arise for discussion in my commentary. What is the nature of the performance? How are characters presented? Do characters serve as models for faithful reenactment? What performative techniques are employed to influence the audience? Is there innovative use of traditions that causes audiences to reassess their views? Are there gaps that need to be filled in order to understand what was intended in the original? Are there ready-mades being employed that will engender surprise, humor, or disquiet for an audience? I have adopted this term—"ready-mades"—from improvised performance as shorthand for terms or phrases that have connection to other parts of Scripture. When utilized in a new performance, they may evoke other settings and reshape the meaning in this new setting. Is the material open-ended as is the case in the dynamic nature of much performance? Does it invite the audience to become involved in the action or respond to it in any way?

In short, my commentary will investigate the scrolls as performances, asking whether this lens adds insights for meaning-making.

Connections with the *Megillot*
As noted above, a tenet of Biblical Performance Criticism is its desire to overcome the gap between theory and practice. BPC also aims to transform audiences from objective spectators to engaged practitioners faithfully reenacting biblical traditions in our own settings. Such faithful reenactments come from insights gained from analysing the scripts of the *Megillot*, especially when they address issues of our own day. When they do, are they open to faithful reenactment, or do they serve as warning bells asking us to critique these faith traditions in the light of new knowledge and perspectives?

In his book *Interested Parties*, David Clines is critical of traditional historical-critical methodology that aimed only to understand the original context and thereby screened out the present. Clines encourages us to critique and judge ancient literature by the standards of our day (2009, 107–109). John Collins similarly reminds us that not all Scripture is morally edifying but adds, "there is no reason in principle why a text that is shocking might not be inspired . . . can we learn something from it about human nature or about the way the world works?" (2004, 601). Both of these authors remind us that biblical interpretation is more than just an academic exercise; it shapes faithful action in our own time.

Each of the scrolls of the *Megillot*, even if only obliquely, addresses issues that are relevant in our own time. Because we view this material as inspired Scripture, it is ethically responsible for us to engage with these issues by bringing our perspective into dialogue with the world of the scroll. Each of my chapters, therefore, concludes by addressing an area where the content of the scroll connects with contemporary experience, allowing us to bring our experience into dialogue with Scripture itself.

Biblical traditions already function as ready-mades for contemporary audiences due to familiarity with their content through long use in church settings and academic study. Through performance-sensitive translations we can better engage with ancient audiences by hearing more of what they heard, being similarly surprised and challenged as these traditions connect with our own time. BPC invites contemporary hearers of these traditions to make them their own: upholding, transmitting, and reenacting them in our own times and places.

The Scroll of the Song of Songs

Introduction

An opinion often expressed about the Hebrew Bible is that it is infused with violence and vengeance. To any holding this view, the scroll of the Song of Songs comes as a surprise. It is a book of love poems that express desire, longing, admiration for the physical beauty of the lover, and celebration within a bucolic natural world that arouses senses and ignites passion. It invites us into a private world of sexual intimacy, opening with the words of a woman who craves her lover's kiss.

Robert Alter has described this strange biblical book where God is never directly mentioned as "the most consistently secular of all biblical texts" (1985, 185). There is no reference to the Jewish themes of Torah, covenant, salvation history, wisdom, or priesthood. There is no glimpse of the ideal Israelite that we see in Psalms and wisdom traditions: a well-aged man, blessed by offspring, offering charity to his fellow man, obedient to the law, fearing God (for example, Pss 15; 128; Job 1; Prov 3–4). The lovers do not conform with typical roles of men and women that we see elsewhere in the Hebrew Bible or even in the five scrolls. Female and male voices are both heard, and the female voice dominates. She has the first and last word and more than half of the total number of lines. Whereas elsewhere in the Hebrew Bible marriage and the sexual union of men and women are intended for procreation, children are never mentioned in this book.[7] There is no hint of the purity rituals that underlie other references to sexuality in the Hebrew Bible. The couple does not fit into the grand narrative of the Israelite people by being connected to the family of Abraham or other prominent characters of Scripture. The Woman is named "the Shulammite" twice in the scroll, but this name is not found elsewhere in the Hebrew Bible.[8] Neither of the lovers in the scroll can be identified. King Solomon is named in the superscription and tradition has linked him as a character within the scroll, but even those who argue in favor of Solomon as a protagonist infer from the poetry that the Woman chooses her anonymous lover over the king. How is it that this strange scroll has been incorporated into the Hebrew Bible?

The name of the scroll gives us some insight about its inclusion. "Song of Songs" is typical of the Hebrew way of expressing the superlative, familiar to us in phrases such as "King of kings" and "Lord of lords." Some of the English translations try to capture this superlative meaning: "The Song—best of all songs" (*The Message*); "The Ultimate Song" (Complete Jewish Bible); "This song of songs, more wonderful than any other" (Living Bible); "The greatest song" (New International Reader's Version). Why should it surprise us that the Israelites wanted to preserve the greatest of all songs?

The name of Solomon is another hint. Like in the books of Proverbs and Ecclesiastes, reference to one of the greatest of Israel's kings lends legitimacy to the composition. The preposition before Solomon's name in the superscription, however, offers some ambiguity since it could be validly translated "which is Solomon's," "belonging to Solomon," "of Solomon," or "for Solomon." Solomon is named in the scroll (1:5; 3:9, 11) and there are references to "the king" (1:4, 12) and "a king" (7:5 [MT 7:6]), but, as we will see when examining the poetry more closely, most of these references are used figuratively or illustratively in the poem rather than in order to identify the male protagonist as Solomon. Whether or not Solomon can be linked to the scroll, it was a known practice to attribute biblical books to famous figures from earlier Israelite history.

The most likely explanation for the inclusion of this scroll with its focus on human, erotic love as Holy Scripture was that from an early time it was understood allegorically as expressing the great love between Israel (the bride) and God (her groom). The marriage metaphor was used by several of the prophets to describe the relationship between God and Israel, showing us that speaking of that relationship in love language was not unusual (for example, Hos 1–3; Jer 3; Ezek 16; 23). Around the year 100 CE, Jewish rabbis at Jamnia were debating which books should be included as holy. Two books, in particular, were under discussion: the Song of Songs and Ecclesiastes (Qohelet). Canonicity was described with the concept of "defiling the hands":

> When a person held and read what was really a holy book, holiness was held to pass to the person's hands; this kind of holiness could be a dangerous thing, and the hands therefore needed to be cleaned afterwards. So when a rabbi said that [a scroll] does not defile the hands, he meant

that he did not feel that he had to clean his hands after reading it. (Fuerst, 1975, 3–4)

Rabbi Akiva ben Joseph famously claimed, "No one in Israel ever disputed that the Song of Songs defiles the hands. For all the whole world is not as worthy as the day on which the Song of Songs was given to Israel, for all the writings are holy, but the Song of Songs is the holy of holies" (Mishnah Eduvot, cited in Scolnic 1996, 55). Benjamin Scolnic suggests that for Rabbi Akiva the Song of Songs *completed* the metaphor of the marriage covenant used by the prophets: "the prophets may have denounced infidelity but the Song of Songs spoke of reunion and love" (1996, 56).

The Scroll and the Festivals of Passover and Sabbath
It is fitting, therefore, that the scroll of the Song of Songs is read at the Festival of Passover. As Brent Strawn evocatively comments, the Passover is "the beginning of the courtship between God and Israel" (2020, 140). The historical link between Passover and the Song of Songs is found in *Song of Songs Rabbah*, a collection of midrashim from the seventh or eighth century CE. Detailed interpretation of each verse in the Song of Songs is linked to the book of Exodus, especially the crossing of the Red Sea and the covenant at Sinai. As Scolnic notes, "The Song of Songs, according to the rabbis, is a text which describes the very events that Pesah [Passover] celebrates and commemorates. To read the Song of Songs Rabbah, therefore, is to read a kind of Haggadah for Pesah" (1996, 60). The rabbis are especially aware of the mutual, dialogical character of the Song where, in the allegorical interpretation, both God, represented by the male, and Israel, represented by the female, praise each other. Ilana Pardes suggests that "Not only modern readers cherish the rare egalitarian bent of the Song. It must have been alluring for the rabbis as well, given their reading of the Shulamite as representing a more elevated and appealing role for the Community of Israel" (2019, 30–31).

In contemporary Judaism, influenced by current Hebrew Bible scholarship that is more inclined toward a literal reading than an allegorical interpretation of the Song of Songs, the springtime setting of the poetry (e.g., 2:10-13) is given as an explanation for reading the scroll at Passover: ". . . on the Sabbath of the festival [of Passover] it is customary to read the Song of Songs with its description of spring. This constitutes our recognition that the forces in the physical environment which make for physical survival and well-being have a divine source" (Klein 1979, 104). This connection is understandable if we consider that Passover had its historical origins in the Levant as an agricultural spring festival. It has even been suggested that early Israelites celebrating Passover adapted songs from Canaanite fertility rituals, vestiges of which can be found in the scroll of the Song of Songs. On this basis, T. J. Meek claims that the festival and the book "belong together because they have always been together" (quoted in Pardes 2019, 158).

In addition to its use at Passover, the scroll of the Song of Songs makes an appearance in most Jewish communities at the weekly Sabbath celebration. The practice of welcoming the Sabbath (*Kabbalat Shabbat*) has its origins in the sixteenth century in Safed when Jewish mystics (Kabbalists) would go into the fields at sunset to sing and welcome in the Sabbath as a Queen. They would sing six psalms representing the days of the week, concluding with a seventh psalm that honored the Sabbath (Brawer 2008, 138). One of their number composed a hymn called the *Lekhah Dodi*, literally "come, my beloved," using the vocabulary of Song of Songs 7:11 (MT 7:12) as its point of departure and refrain:

> Come, my beloved
> Let us go forth into the fields,
> And lodge in the villages. (NRSV translation)

Ilana Pardes describes the way these verses in the Song of Songs inspired this Sabbath ritual:

> If in the Song the Shulamite urges her lover to go out to the fields, here the amorous imperative is a spiritual one: the *dod*, the divine lover, is urged to greet the Shekhinah, the glorious bride, as she returns from exile with the coming of the Sabbath . . . every Friday, the flow of divine bounty is restored through this ritualistic welcoming of the Shekhinah by both God and the congregation of worshippers. (2019, 96–97)

This *Kabbalat Shabbat* service is still popular today in many Jewish communities, although it usually takes place within the synagogue. It includes a performative ritual element when the entire congregation stands and turns towards the setting sun while singing the hymn, embodying the moment of the Sabbath's commencement as the sun sinks below the horizon.

The Background of the Scroll

Commentators debate the origin of the poems that make up the Song of Songs. As mentioned above, some suggest a cultic foundation on the basis of similarities to hymns found in ancient cultures that practiced rituals of sacred marriages between gods or myths of a dying and rising god, emulating the natural seasonal cycle. Others argue for a background of wedding celebrations, which would have continued for several days and included singing and dancing. This suggestion is supported by poems in the Song of Songs describing the physical appearance of the lover—three describing the Woman (4:1-7; 6:4-7; 7:1-8) and one describing the Man (5:10-16), corresponding to a Syrian tradition of lauding the beauty of bride and groom during a wedding ceremony known by the Arabic term *wasf*. This term is now commonly used by commentators when referring to those sections of the scroll. Only one other example of a *wasf* has been found in ancient Jewish literature. The Genesis Apocryphon found amongst the Dead Sea Scrolls includes a description of Sarai's beauty as an expansion of Genesis 12:14-15: "When Abram entered Egypt the Egyptians saw that the woman [Sarai] was very beautiful. When the officials of Pharaoh saw her, they praised her to Pharaoh."[9]

Occasionally, commentators include the Song of Songs amongst the wisdom literature of the Hebrew Bible, due to its canonical placement in the Septuagint and the Christian Old Testament after Proverbs and Ecclesiastes. Kirsten Nielsen suggests this positioning of the composition "makes it possible to see the Song of Songs in the light of the wisdom traditions and their reflections about how God made the world and what is good for humanity" (1998, 181). Poems about love between humans, she argues, can be understood as integral to the goodness of God's created world.

Debates of origins naturally influence ideas on the dating of the Song of Songs. Based on references to Solomon in the scroll, there are suggestions that it was composed at the time of Solomon, either by the king himself, by poets and scribes within his court, or as a polemic against his many foreign marriages (Pope 1977, 24). Theories based on cultic origins for the Song of Songs would also date the material to an early period when Canaanite influence was still strong. A mixture of archaic language and postexilic vocabulary suggests that, even if the original composition is from an older period, it has been edited later. Elsie Stern concludes, "Contemporary scholarly consensus hypothesizes that the poem probably had its roots in early folk and literary traditions but was composed or redacted in the 4th or 3rd century BCE" (2004, 1565).

History of Interpretation

In *The Song of Songs: A Biography*, Ilana Pardes thoroughly examines the ways in which this scroll has been interpreted through history. As discussed above, the allegorical interpretation was prominent from an early time by Jewish readers, and early Christian reception was similar except the lovers were envisaged as the church (the bride) and Christ (the groom). There were also mystical readings by both Jewish and Christian exegetes, focusing on God/Logos and the soul, or male and female aspects of the divine.

Prominent Christian mystics in the medieval period include Bernard of Clairveaux (c. 1090–1153) who wrote eighty-six sermons on the Song of Songs, most of them focusing on the first two chapters! Another was Teresa of Avila (1515–1582) whose ecstatic writings on her union with Christ based on passages in the Song of Songs inspired a Bernini sculpture depicting a swooning Teresa receiving shafts of love. Such Christian mystical interpretations, as Pardes points out, are hardly surprising given that, prior to the Reformation, most religious writing was carried out by celibate monks and nuns. This period was also the context for the rise of the genre of courtly love literature: "love was in the air in a new way, creating an urgent need to redefine the relationship between body and soul, as well as between earthly and spiritual amorous pursuits" (2019, 100).

Another medieval scholar worth mentioning is Fray Luis de León (1527–1591), a Spanish Augustinian friar who translated the Song from the original Hebrew to Spanish: a vernacular translation that occasionally deviated from the Vulgate (the accepted Latin translation). When it landed in the hands of the Inquisition, it was one of the offences for which he was imprisoned for four years along with his familiarity with Hebrew and Jewish exegetes and his appreciation for the work as literal love poetry.

During the Enlightenment period, many more scholars interpreted the poetry in literal rather than spiritual terms. Johann Gottfried Herder (1744–1803) was a founding figure of literary approaches to the Bible. He understood the Song as "Volkslied" (folk poetry) and encouraged readers to appreciate the ancient oriental setting of the original poetry. This led to the influential work of J. G. Wetzstein (1815–1905), who was the first to find connections between the Song of Songs and the Syrian *wasf* as described above. Amongst scholars of the Jewish Enlightenment, Shlomo Löwisohn (1789–1821) envisaged the book as a dramatic love triangle between King Solomon, the Shulammite, and a Shepherd (an idea proposed much earlier in the twelfth century by Jewish commentator Ibn Ezra). Scholarship that focused on connections between Israelite and other comparative traditions from the ancient Near East found similarities between the scroll and Egyptian love poems as well as Canaanite or Babylonian fertility ritual hymns. Although little evidence for direct connections exists, such hymns could have been "a source of inspiration for Hebrew poets who were eager to celebrate the pleasures of earthly love" (Pardes 2019, 161).[10]

Contemporary scholarship is more inclined to accept the Song of Songs at face value as erotic love poetry and has placed a greater focus on the aesthetic qualities of the book. Robert Alter led the way in appreciating the beauty of the poetry, and most contemporary commentaries, including this one, emphasize that aspect of the book. It has been a source of interest and debate for biblical feminist scholarship due to the prominence of a female protagonist and her apparent equality alongside her male companion. Phyllis Trible interpreted the book as a "reversal" of the myth of the fall in the Garden of Eden. In the Song of Songs there is "no male dominance, no female subordination, and no stereotyping of either sex . . . Throughout the Song [the Woman] is independent, fully the equal of the man. Although at times he approaches her, more often she initiates the meetings" (Trible 1978, 161). Some feminist interpreters and recent masculinist readings have drawn attention to "thorns" in Trible's "garden of delight" (1978, 144), such as abusive watchmen (5:7) and overprotective brothers (8:8-9).[11] We will return to this critique in the connections section of this chapter.

By way of summary, in the history of scholarly approaches to this scroll the allegorical interpretation was dominant until the Enlightenment, but since then there has been a dual emphasis on the cultural context that gave rise to such literature and appreciation for its aesthetic qualities.

Poetry in the Scroll
Although the poetry of the scroll of the Song of Songs shares aspects with other Hebrew poetry, such as parallelism, terseness, and a lack of narrative particles, it stands out from other biblical poetry for several reasons. First, it is admired for the beauty and breadth of metaphors and similes used. The natural world of flora and fauna, vineyard work, the domestic sphere, and the urban domain, even royal imagery, are all probed for descriptors of the realm of love.

Second, the poetry uses this imagery with great freedom, reveling in ambiguity and double *entendre*, yet maintaining a delicacy that hints at the erotic without becoming pornographic (Strawn 2020, 139). Commenting on the "playfulness" of Hebrew poetry, Robert Alter reminds us,

> . . . the literary art of the Bible, in both prose narrative and poetry, reflects many more elements of playfulness than might meet the casual eye. Only in the Song of Songs, however, is the writer's art directed to the imaginative realization of a world of uninhibited self-delighting play, without moral conflict, without the urgent context of history and nationhood and destiny, without the looming perspectives of a theological world-view. (1985, 203)

Third, it is frequently noted that the poetry in the Song of Songs evokes all five senses, using each to draw the lovers ever nearer to each other. Sight can cross a long distance, whereas hearing requires a closer proximity for sounds to be audible. Touch requires direct contact, but the senses of smell and taste are by far the most intimate.[12] By stressing these senses, the audience is invited to participate imaginatively and emotionally alongside the lovers.

Fourth, there seems to be deliberate wordplay that emphasizes particular sounds through repetition or evokes key words and ideas. For example, the repeated "sh" sound in the Hebrew opening lines evokes a "sensual celebration" (Pardes 2019, 1), while an alliterated series of "k" and "s" sounds in 8:6 may reflect the hardness of passion followed by the hiss of flames. The final word in that verse, *šalhevetyāh*, uses the *-yāh* ending as a grammatical intensifier, but it undoubtedly intentionally evokes Yah, the shortened form of the divine name (Linafelt 2016, 52–53).[13]

The final notable feature is the high proportion of *hapax legomena* in the scroll. There are nearly fifty of these words, a high proportion within the hundred or so verses in the scroll. Without corresponding material elsewhere in the Hebrew Bible for comparison, such words can only be speculatively translated.

Commentaries evidence much debate about the division of the poems, noting that there is repetition across the scroll in both wording and leitmotifs. Within these debates, views of composition of the scroll range from those who advocate that it is an anthology of originally separate love poems to those who believe there was authorship or careful editing by a single individual. The observable repetition attests to the title of the composition as a "song" since refrains and reprised material are typical in musical composition. Tod Linafelt is helpful here:

> So much of what constitutes poetry can be found in what is sometimes referred to as the "musicality" of its language: the sounds, the rhythms, the structure of its syntax, the way particular words echo other meanings. It is true that nearly all of these aspects of poetry are lost in translation . . . But of course, not *all* is lost. (2016, 50)

Even if English translations are not able to convey the exact artistry of the original Hebrew of the Song of Songs, we can appreciate the features noted above: the beauty of the figurative language, the playful ambiguity between speech and intended meaning, and the appeal to the senses. I have made a few poor attempts to replicate wordplay when it seems especially prominent in the Hebrew, but exposure to the original Hebrew itself is highly commended![14]

The Purpose of the Scroll

What purpose does a series of poems on human love that express a desire for sexual intimacy have as part of Scripture? At a basic level, it reminds us that romance and sexual attraction are part of what it means to be human and are a gift from a good Creator. The fact that this poetry is part of the canon suggests that these things were valuable to communities of faith in the ancient world and down through the ages just as they are in our time.

This scroll becomes more significant when viewed intertextually against other writings in the Hebrew Bible. As we have noted, it recreates the garden of Eden where a man and woman are created to be together, bone of bone and flesh of flesh (Gen 2:23). It forms a contrast to other stories of love and passion that do not demonstrate such egalitarian relationships and result in conflict: stories such as Jacob and Rachel (Gen 29); Samson and Delilah (Judg 16); Amnon and Tamar (2 Sam 13). On the other hand, a focus on the word "love" (*ʾhv*) in the scroll recalls the covenant relationship between God and the Israelite community, in which "loving the Lord with all one's heart, soul, and might" implies complete devotion (Deut 6:5). Similarly, the connection of love with "passion" (*qnʾ*) at the end of the scroll (8:6) echoes God's self-disclosure—"I am a passionate God"—at the introduction to the Decalogue (Exod 20:5). Human love becomes a metaphor for God's love. Allegorical and/or metaphorical readings of the scroll are therefore as compelling as literal readings because they attest to a God who loves creation as passionately as lovers long for each other. Prophetic discourse regularly took up this language of love to condemn their communities for flouting that relationship (e.g., Isa 5:1-7). The scroll of the Song of Songs reminds us that love is a powerful force, as powerful as death, and in the wrong circumstances it can become dangerous.

Interpreters often comment on the lack of apparent conclusion to the scroll. The last exchanges between the man and woman are invitations to each other to continue their tryst, "picking up old themes and whirling on with them into new love" (Fuerst 1975, 199). It takes us back to the beginning of the poems again to appreciate afresh the playful and equal interplay between the lovers. The poems therefore attest to the fact that true love never ends (1 Cor 13:13).

Creativity in the Song of Songs—A Greek Play

While there is no direct evidence that the Song of Songs was ever staged as a drama in ancient Israel, a comment by Rabbi Akiva suggests it was sung in public settings in ancient times: "Whoever sings the Song of Songs with a tremulous voice in a banquet hall and (so) treats it as a sort of ditty has no share in the world to come" (Tosefta to Sanhedrin, cited in Clines 2009, 100 n8). We have already noted Rabbi Akiva's high view of the Song of Songs, but his dismissive comment reveals the wide appeal of the composition and the breadth of possibilities in its performance and interpretation. The reference to a "tremulous voice" is especially intriguing: were men taking the female parts as is familiar to us in theatrical performance from the time of ancient Greece until relatively recently?

Even if ancient Israel did not produce theatrical productions, many ancient and modern interpreters have commented on the dramatic quality of the Song of Songs, with its alternating voices using feminine and masculine verbs and pronouns and occasional interruptions by a group of plural voices. Two of the earliest Greek translations (the Sinaiticus and Alexandrinus texts of the Septuagint) added marginal notes indicating the different speakers, and a number of contemporary translations follow suit, including my own translation.

The early Christian father Origen claimed that the Song of Songs was written in the form of a drama, and poet John Milton in the seventeenth century agreed: "Scripture affords us a Divine pastoral Drama in the Song of Solomon consisting of two persons, and a double chorus, as Origen rightly judges" (quoted in Pope 1977, 35). Some have argued against the genre of drama on the lack of evidence for drama in ancient Israel. Moreover, although there are alternating speakers in dialogue, the identity of the speakers is, at times, ambiguous and there is no clear plot line. This is the nature of performance in script form, however, and whilst divisions of translations do not always strictly agree, one of the benefits of viewing Scripture through the lens of performance is acknowledging the inherent innovation and variation that performance makes possible (Mathews 2020, 5).

When translating the Song of Songs I was reminded of classic Greek plays. These were shown at the time of festivals and were presented in competition with others. They had minimal sets and stage directions. There was no narrator but instead a chorus was used to articulate important aspects of the material presented. In Greek plays the choral odes were spoken in unison and the chorus wore the same masks, distinguishing them from other characters but not from each other. It is probable that short interludes of incidental music would mark the passage of time or transition between chorus and dialogue.[15]

The Song of Songs, as discussed above, has long been associated with Jewish festivals. Its title "the Song of Songs" is suggestive of a competition.[16] Although a variety of settings can be inferred and some props are identifiable, there are no real stage directions outside of the imagination of the hearer. Furthermore, spoken movement is more often than not using double *entendre* (consider "he is grazing in the lilies," "he sent his hand through the hole," "I went to the mountain," "let him come," "I came"). The Hebrew text uses the *setumah* (ס) as a division marker several times, and once a *petuchah* (פ), marking a longer break. One could imagine short musical interludes at these points in a performance of the script as they sometimes indicate a change of scene but other times suggest a break in time. The Song of Songs has no narrator, but the dialogue between the Woman and the Man is occasionally interrupted by plural voices that suggest two choruses—a female chorus is identified as "daughters of Jerusalem" and a male chorus implied by plural verbs and the content of the speech, such as references to their sister (8:8-9). I have divided one verse where plural verbs are used into two separate choruses, based on the subject matter of the verse (6:13 [MT 7:1]). The inclusion of choruses invites an audience into this performance of love poetry and encourages movement between private and public realms. In presenting the Song of Songs in the form of a Greek play, I am inspired by Philip Vellacott's description of the plays of Euripides:

> Euripides was the first playwright to use the chorus as a commentator; the first to put contemporary language into the mouths of heroes; and the first to interpret human suffering without reference to the wisdom of gods . . . his daring interpretations of ancient myths are enhanced by his brilliance as a lyricist, for Euripides' choral odes are among the most beautiful ever written. (Euripides 1963, cover)

As will be discussed in more detail in the "Commentary" section below, the chorus of women has an important role in the Song of Songs as they draw attention to key aspects of the lovers' relationship. The language of this ancient Hebrew book sounds contemporary, no doubt because of our culture's obsession with love and physical beauty and greater exposure to sexual activity in present-day popular media. The Song of Songs is the only book in the Hebrew Bible that expresses love as a mutual and reciprocal sentiment, mirroring a modern Western notion more accurately than in other parts of Scripture (van Wolde 2008, 19). We have already noted the lack of direct reference to God in this scroll, either as a source of love or a means of salvation. And the beauty of the poetry has been stressed above.

In my script presented below I have allocated speeches to characters based on verbal forms and pronominal suffixes. As in much Hebrew poetry, speeches can shift between first- and third-person address, but gendered forms and pronouns aid us in deciding who is speaking and to whom. The two main actors refer to each other with characteristic terms of endearment: the Woman most often refers to the Man as *dôdî*, the masculine noun *dôd* with a first common singular pronominal suffix ("my" *dôd*). The word *dôd* has the same root letters as the proper name David, a name usually interpreted to mean "beloved." When the word occurs without the pronominal suffix I have translated it "loving," but otherwise I have used the original Hebrew "Dodi" as if it is the Woman's favorite pet name for her lover. The Man addresses the Woman with a greater number of terms, but the most common one is *ra'yāti*, a noun meaning "female companion" with a first common singular pronominal suffix. Since it is used as a term of endearment I have translated this word "my darling."

The scenes that I propose move between public and private areas. In most cases the chorus speaks in the public areas, while the bedroom is reserved for the two lovers. The performance opens and closes in a vineyard and the central section describes a garden. Hebrew composition is often structured to focus on the center, and it is notable that at the center of this composition is what could be understood to be a climax, underscored by the double *entendre* of the language (see 4:16–5:1). A lack of *setumah* breaks between 5:2 and 6:9 encourages us to hurry through this section despite the disturbing report of abuse in the street (5:7). Many commentaries also ignore, race past, or marginalize this verse, but my connections section below considers it carefully.

For the most part the Song of Songs is a playful, enjoyable script. Audiences will respond to it in different ways, but in order to remind us that Scripture, while serious, can also be fun, I have added a subtle winking emoticon where I have noticed innuendo in the speeches of the Woman and the Man.

I am hopeful that the creativity of this appealing script will be evident in its offering as a Greek play.

¹THE SONG OF SONGS
Which is for Solomon

CHARACTERS
The Woman (THE SHULAMMITE)
CHORUS of women
THE MAN (DODI)
CHORUS of men, the Shulammite's brothers

Scene: In the Vineyard (1:1-17)

THE WOMAN:	²Let him kiss me from the kisses of his mouth
	For better is your loving than wine . . .
	³For fragrance your oils are better.
	Fresh oil is your name,
	therefore young maidens love you!
	⁴Draw me after you, let us run!
	He made me come—the king—into his rooms ;)
CHORUS of women (to the man):	Let us rejoice and be glad in you
	Let us make remembered—your loving— beyond wine.
THE WOMAN:	Rightly they love you!

ס

THE WOMAN: (to the chorus):	⁵Black am I and lovely
	O daughters of Jerusalem,
	Like tents of Qedar,
	Like the curtains of Solomon.
	⁶Do not look at me because I am black,
	Because she scorched me—the sun—
	The sons of my mother were burning over me,
	They set me as keeper of the vineyards,
	My vineyard for me I did not keep ;)

(to the chorus):	⁷Tell to me, the one whom she loves—my very being— How will you graze? ;) How will you make yourself lie down at noon? Why should I be like one covered Near the flocks of your companions?
THE MAN:	⁸If you do not know for yourself O beautiful among the women Go out yourself in the tracks of the sheep And graze your young goats ;) Near the tabernacle of the shepherds. ⁹To my mare among the chariots of Pharaoh I compare you my darling. ¹⁰Lovely are your cheeks with earrings, Your neck with beaded strings.
CHORUS *of women*:	¹¹Earrings of gold we make for you, With beads of silver.
THE WOMAN:	¹²As long as the king is on his couch My nard will give its fragrance. ¹³A purse of myrrh is my Dodi to me Between my breasts he lodges. ¹⁴A cluster of henna is my Dodi to me In the vineyard of En-Gedi.

ס

THE MAN:	¹⁵Behold you, beautiful my darling. Behold you, beautiful, your eyes are doves.
THE WOMAN:	¹⁶Behold you, beautiful my Dodi. Indeed, desirable!
BOTH:	Indeed, our bed is green ¹⁷The beams of our house are cedar Our rafters are cypress.

Scene: In the Bedroom (2:1-17)

THE WOMAN:	¹I am the crocus of the plains, The lily of the valleys.

THE MAN:	²Like a lily among the thorns,
	Thus is my darling among the daughters.
THE WOMAN:	³Like a quince in the trees of the forest,
	Thus is my Dodi among the sons.
	In his shadow I crave and I stay,
	And his fruit is sweet to my taste. ;)
	⁴He brought me to the house of wine,
	And his banner over me was love.
	⁵Sustain me with raisin cakes,
	Support me with the quinces,
	For faint with love am I.
	⁶His left is under my head
	And his right embraces me.
(to the chorus):	⁷I will make you swear, you daughters of Jerusalem
	By the gazelles or by the does of the field,
	Do not awaken and do not arouse the lover
	Until she is ready.

ס

THE WOMAN:	⁸A voice! My Dodi! Behold this one coming,
	Leaping on the mountains, bounding on the hills. ;)
	⁹Likened, my Dodi, to the gazelle,
	Or the fawn of the deer.
	Behold this one standing behind our wall,
	Gazing through the windows
	Looking through the lattices.
	¹⁰He answers, my Dodi, and says to me,
THE MAN:	Stand yourself up, my darling, my beauty, and go!
	¹¹For behold, the winter has passed,
	The rain is over and gone.
	¹²The flowers can be seen in the land
	The time of singing has arrived,
	And the voice of the turtledove can be heard in our land.
	¹³The fig tree ripened her buds,

              And the vines! Blossoms are giving fragrance.
              Stand yourself up, my darling, my beauty, and
              go!

                              ס

              ¹⁴My dove in the clefts of the rock,
              in the hiding place of the cliff,
              Make me see your countenance,
              Make me hear your voice,
              for your voice is pleasant
              and your countenance is lovely.
BOTH: ¹⁵Catch for us foxes,
              foxes in soxes,
              Poxes in our rootstockses . . .¹⁷
              And our vineyards blossom.
THE WOMAN: ¹⁶My Dodi is for me and I am for him,
              The one grazing in the lilies. ;)
              ¹⁷Until it sighs—the day—
              And they flee—the shadows—
              Turn round! Liken yourself, my Dodi, to a
              gazelle,
              Or to a fawn of the deer on the mountains of
              ravines. ;)

                              ס

              Scene: In the Bedroom (3:1-2a)

THE WOMAN: ¹On my bed in the night-time
              I sought the one she loves—my very being—
              I sought him and I did not find him.
              ²Let me rise, now, and let me go around in
              the city,
              In the squares and in the streets,
              Let me seek the one she loves—my very
              being—

Scene: In the Street (3:2b-5)

THE WOMAN: I sought him and I did not find him.
³They found me—the watchmen—
the ones going round in the city.
"the one she loves—my very being—
Have you seen?"

⁴Like hardly I had passed by them
I found the one she loves—my very being—
I held him and I did not let go of him
Until I brought him to the house of my mother
And to the room of the one who conceived me.

(to the chorus): ⁵I will make you swear, you daughters of Jerusalem
By the gazelles or by the does of the field,
Do not awaken and do not arouse the lover
Until she is ready.

ס

Scene: On the Outskirts of the City (3:6-11)

CHORUS *of women*: ⁶Who is this coming up from the desert,
Like pillars of smoke?
Perfumed with myrrh and frankincense
From all the powders of the merchants?

THE WOMAN: ⁷Behold! His litter—the one belonging to Solomon—
Sixty mighty men around it
From the mighty men of Israel.
⁸All of them skilled of sword
Trained in warfare.
Each his sword along his thigh
From the dread of the night.

ס

⁹A palanquin he made for himself—King
Solomon—
From the trees of Lebanon.
¹⁰Its pillars he made silver,
Its back gold, its chariot purple
Its inside was fitted with love,
By the daughters of Jerusalem.
¹¹Go out and look, daughters of Zion, upon
King Solomon
In the crown with which she crowned
him—his mother—
on the day of his wedding,
and on the day of joy of his heart.

ס

Scene: In the Bedroom (4:1-5:1)

THE MAN: ¹Behold you beautiful, my darling,
behold you beautiful.
Your eyes are doves
from behind your veil.
Your hair is like a flock of goats
That came down from Mount Gilead.
²Your teeth are like the flock of shorn ewes,
That came up from the washing—
All of them bear twins
And bereaved? Not one of them!
³Like the thread of scarlet are your lips
And your mouth is lovely.
Like half of the pomegranate is your cheek
From behind your veil.
⁴Like the tower of David is your neck,
Built in layers:
A thousand shields hang on it,
All quivers of the warriors.
⁵Your two breasts are like two fawns—

	Twins of a gazelle,
	Grazing among the lilies.
THE WOMAN:	⁶Until it sighs—the day—
	And they flee—the shadows—

THE MAN: I will go myself, to the mountain of myrrh,
                    To the hill of frankincense.
                    ⁷All of you is beautiful, my darling
                    And a blemish? There is not one in you!

ס

⁸With me from the land of frankincense, bride
With me from the land of frankincense you
should come.
You should travel from the top of Amanah,
From the top of Senir and Hermon,
From the dens of lions,
From the mountains of leopards.
⁹You have captured my heart, my sister,
bride,
You have captivated my heart with a single
glance from your eyes,
With a single bead from your necklace.
¹⁰What beauty is your loving, my sister, bride,
What better is your loving than wine
And the fragrance of your oils than all spices!
¹¹Nectar drips from your lips, bride,
Honey and milk are under your tongue,
And the fragrance of your garments
Is like the fragrance of the land of frankin-
cense.

ס

¹²A garden locked is my sister, bride,
A spring locked, a fountain sealed.
¹³Your shoots are a paradise of pomegranates
With fruits of choice,

	Henna with nard.
	¹⁴Nard and saffron, reed and cinnamon,
	With all trees of frankincense,
	Myrrh and aloes,
	With all top shelf spices.
	¹⁵A fountain of gardens,
	A well of waters,
	And streams from the land of frankincense.
	¹⁶Arise, North Wind!
	And come, South Wind!
	Sigh on my garden
	Let its spices flow ;)
THE WOMAN:	**Let him come**, my Dodi, to his garden
	And let him eat the fruits of his choice. ;)
THE MAN:	¹**I came** to my garden, my sister, bride ;)
	I plucked my myrrh with my spice,
	I ate my honeycomb with my honey,
	I drank my wine with my milk.
CHORUS *of women:*	Eat, friends!
	Drink and be drunk with loving!

ס

Scene: In the Bedroom (5:2-6)

THE WOMAN:	²I am sleeping and my heart rouses,
	A voice! My Dodi knocking.
THE MAN:	Open to me my sister, my darling,
	My dove, my perfect one,
	For my head is full of dew,
	My locks with drops of the night ;)
THE WOMAN:	³I had stripped off my tunic,
	how can I dress?
	I have bathed my feet,
	How could I soil them?
	⁴My Dodi sent his hand through the hole ;)

And my belly stirred because of it.
⁵I got up to open to my Dodi,
And my hands dripped myrrh,
And my fingers—myrrh everywhere
Upon the handles of the bolt ;)
⁶I have opened myself to my Dodi,
—My Dodi had gone away, had passed by.
My very being went out when he spoke.
I sought him and did not find him,
I called him and he did not answer me.

Scene: In the Street (5:7—6:3)

THE WOMAN:	⁷They found me—the watchmen— the ones going round in the city. They struck me, they bruised me, They lifted my veil from over me, The watchmen of the walls.
(to the chorus):	⁸I will make you swear, you daughters of Jerusalem, If you find my Dodi, What you must tell to him, That faint with love am I.
CHORUS of women:	⁹What is your Dodi more than any lover, O most beautiful among women? What is your Dodi more than any lover, That thus you make us swear.
THE WOMAN:	¹⁰My Dodi is radiant and ruddy, Distinguishable from thousands! ¹¹His head is gold—pure gold— His locks are wavy, Black like the raven. ¹²His eyes are like doves On channels of water, Washed in milk, Sitting in fullness. ¹³His jaws are like precincts of spices Towers of aromatics,

	His lips are lilies,
	Dripping myrrh everywhere.
	¹⁴His hands are rounds of gold,
	Filled with beryl.
	His belly is a work of ivory,
	Bedecked with sapphires.
	¹⁵His thighs are columns of alabaster,
	Set on pedestals of gold.
	His countenance is like frankincense,
	Choice as the cedars.
	¹⁶His mouth is sweet,
	And all of him desirable.
	This is my Dodi, and this is my friend,
	Daughters of Jerusalem.
CHORUS *of women:*	¹Where has he gone—your Dodi—
	O most beautiful among women?
	Where has he turned—your Dodi—
	Let us seek him with you.
THE WOMAN:	²My Dodi has gone down to his garden,
	To the precincts of spices,
	To graze in the gardens ;)
	And to gather lilies.
	³I am for my Dodi and my Dodi is for me:
	The one grazing in the lilies ;)

Scene: In the Bedroom (6:4-9)

THE MAN:	⁴Beautiful are you, my darling, like the city of pleasure,
	Lovely like the city of peace,
	Daunting like banners lifted.
	⁵Turn your eyes away from me,
	The ones which overwhelm me!
	Your hair is like the flock of goats
	That came down from Gilead.
	⁶Your teeth are like the flock of ewes
	That came up from the washing—
	All of them bear twins
	And bereaved? Not one of them!

⁷Like half of the pomegranate is your cheek
From behind your veil.
⁸Sixty—they are queens
And eighty—concubines
And maids without number.
⁹Just one is she, my dove, my perfect one,
Just one is she to her mother,
Pure is she to the one who bore her.
Daughters saw her and called her happy.
Queens and concubines—they praised her.

ס

Scene: In the Street (6:10-13 [MT 6:10—7:1])

CHORUS *of women:*	¹⁰Who is this seen like dawn, Beautiful like the moon, Daunting like banners lifted?
THE WOMAN:	¹¹To the gardens of nuts I went down, ;) To see the freshness of the river, To see the sprouting of the vines, The blooming of the pomegranates. ¹²I did not know where my very being set me. Chariots? My kinsman is a prince!
CHORUS *of men:*	¹³Turn, turn, Shulammite!¹⁸ Turn, turn, and let us gaze on you.
CHORUS *of women:*	Why should you gaze upon the Shulammite, Like the dance of two camps?

Scene: In the Bedroom (7:1 [MT 7:2]—8:4)

THE MAN:	¹How beautiful are your feet in sandals, Daughter of nobility. The curves of your thighs are like jewels From the work of the hand of a master! ²Your naval is a bowl of roundness, No lack of mixed wine. Your stomach is a heap of wheat

Fenced in with lilies.
³The two of your breasts are like two fawns,
Twins of a gazelle.
⁴Your neck is like a tower of ivory,
Your eyes are pools in Heshbon
By the gate of Bath-rabbim.
Your nose is like a tower of Lebanon,
Watching the faces of Damascus.
⁵Your head over you is like the Carmel,
And the hair of your head like purple,
A king is bound in the tresses.
⁶How beautiful and how desirable are you?
Lovely! With waves of pleasure! ;)
⁷This is your stature—like a date palm,
And your breasts for clusters,
⁸I say, let me climb on the date palm,
let me hold onto its branches. ;)
May they be—your breasts—like clusters of the vine,
And the fragrance of your breath like quinces.

THE WOMAN:
⁹And your mouth is like wine—the best—
Going down to my Dodi smoothly,
Gliding over sleeping lips.
¹⁰I am to my Dodi
and over me is his desire.

ס

THE WOMAN:
¹¹Come here, my Dodi,
Let us go out to the field,
Let us spend a night in the henna. ;)
¹²Let us start out early for the vineyards,
Let us see if they have flowered—the vines—
Opened—the blossoms—
Bloomed—the pomegranates.
There I will give my love to you.
¹³The love-plants give fragrance
And over our openings ;) all the choice things.
New things, also old things.

	My Dodi, I have treasured them for you.
	¹Who can set you like a brother for me,
	Suckling at the breasts of my mother? ;)
	I will find you in the open,
	I will kiss you,
	And they will not scorn me.
	²I will lead you,
	And bring you to the house of my mother
	who taught me.
	I will make you drink from the spiced wine,
	From the crushed juice of my pomegranates.;)
	³His left is under my head,
	And his right embraces me.
(to the chorus):	⁴I will make you swear, you daughters of Jerusalem,
	By the gazelles or by the does of the field,
	Do not awaken and do not arouse the lover
	Until she is ready.

ס

Scene: On the Outskirts of the City (8:5-7)

CHORUS *of women:*	⁵Who is this coming up from the desert,
	Leaning against her Dodi?
THE WOMAN:	Under the quince tree I aroused you,
	There she labored you—your mother—
	There she labored and birthed you.
	⁶Place me like the seal over your heart,
	Like the seal over your arm.
	For strong like death is love,
	Fierce like Sheol is passion,
	Its sparks are sparks of fire—
	A flame of Yah!
	⁷Waters—many—are not able to quench the Lover,
	And floods cannot drown her.
	If he gave—a man—all the wealth of his

house for the Lover,
Despising, they would despise him.

ס

Scene: In the Vineyard (8:8-14)

CHORUS *of men:*	⁸There is a sister for us—a little one—
And breasts? Not any to her.
What shall we do for our sister
On the day on which she is spoken for?
⁹If a wall is she,
We will build upon her a battlement of silver.
And if a door is she,
We will bind over her a board of cedar.
THE WOMAN:	¹⁰I am a wall,
And my breasts are like the towers.
Then I was in his eyes like a finder of peace.

פ

CHORUS *of women:*	¹¹A vineyard Solomon had in Baal-Hamon,
He gave the vineyard to the keepers.
Each would bring from his fruit
A thousand pieces of silver.
THE MAN:	¹²My vineyard, which is for me, for myself. ;)
The thousand for you, Solomon
And two hundred for the keepers of his fruit.
(to the woman):	¹³The ones who stay in the gardens,
The companions listening for your voice,
Make it be heard to me!
THE WOMAN:	¹⁴Fly, my Dodi
And be like a gazelle or the fawn of a deer,
Upon the mountains of spices. ;)

Commentary on the Song of Songs

My commentary section of this chapter considers aspects of the script that are highlighted when viewing it as performance. The discussion will cover three areas: the *players* in the script (the two main characters and the two choruses), the *pace* of presentation (how the script divides into scenes and maintains its dynamic movement), and the *playfulness* of the poetry (including wordplay, innuendo, and intertextual connections).

Players

In contrast to most Greek plays, there is a small cast in this performance. The size of the chorus of women and chorus of men is not specified but could be any number from just a few to a sizable group.[19] Some have argued for three main players: a shepherdess, a shepherd, and Solomon the king, forming a love triangle of sorts.[20] My own translation infers only one couple, neither of whom is conclusively identified. References to King Solomon provide the context for the poetry, and other royal imagery is part of the rich metaphorical texture. The lack of concrete identification of players makes this poetry accessible to any reader who is inspired to place themselves within the drama.

The Woman. In one verse of the scroll the Woman is twice addressed as *šûlammît*, and both times the definite article is used ("*the* Shulammite"). This implies a geographical designation as we see with other women in the Hebrew Bible, such as Ruth the Moabite. A similar-sounding name is attributed to Abishag the Shunammite (1 Kgs 1:3), the young woman found to lie with the aging King David to keep him warm. The name Shunammite comes up again in 2 Kings 4 when the prophet Elisha interacts with a Shunammite widow. The location Shunem is mentioned as belonging to the tribe of Issachar (Josh 19:18) and may be identified as the small Muslim village in the Jezreel Valley of Israel that is the location for the archaeological site Tel Shunam. By contrast, the place name Shulam is not known in the Hebrew Bible.[21] It is more likely that "the Shulammite" is a name that deliberately evokes the names Solomon and Jerusalem, both of which have etymological roots in the word *šālôm* (peace, wholeness). Indeed, towards the end of the scroll the Woman refers to herself as "a finder of peace" (8:10). As Israelite poetry that invites allegorical interpretation, a hint in the name that identifies the female protagonist with the ideal city Jerusalem would not be surprising.

Significantly, however, she is only named the Shulammite by the male and female choruses (6:13 [HB 7:1]). Her male lover uses other titles, more descriptive and affectionate: we have already noted the most common appellation "my darling" (1:9; 2:2, 10, 13; 4:1, 7; 5:2; 6:4), but he also calls her "beautiful" (1:8, 15; 4:1, 7), "my dove" (2:14; 5:2; 6:9), "bride" (4:8, 9, 10, 11, 12; 5:1), "my sister" (4:9, 10, 12; 5:1, 2), "my perfect one" (5:2; 6:9), "daughter of nobility" (7:1 [MT 7:2]), "my garden" (5:1), and "my vineyard" (8:12). In addition to these titles, the Man describes the Woman with metaphors and similes drawn from the worlds of nature and architecture. Some of these imply colors so we can picture her with dark flowing locks, grey eyes, rosy cheeks, white teeth, and scarlet lips, sweetly scented and fresh-breathed. She is shapely with well-rounded breasts and curvy thighs. She is wearing jewels and is perhaps only scantily dressed in his imagination, with only one brief mention of garments (4:11), but several references to her veil delicately preserve her modesty in his descriptions (4:1, 3; 6:7).

The Woman's self-description "Black am I and lovely" (1:5, my translation) has been the subject of much debate. Although it is the Woman commenting on her own appearance, does the word "black" describe her ethnicity, or is it better explained by her exposure to the sun in the vineyards as implied in the following verse? In some ancient and even in more recent interpretations, the word "black" was equated with inferiority and sinfulness. When the phrase is translated "I am black, but comely" (KJV) or "Dark am I, yet lovely" (NIV), there is an implication that the beauty of the Woman is *in spite of* her darkness. Such translations have been challenged by interpreters who have been conscientized by a history of slavery, racism, and terrorism. The "black is beautiful" slogan has been influential on the NRSV and other modern translations and it is now more common to see a translation such as "I am black and beautiful" (NRSV).[22] The conjunctive particle *uʼ* can validly be translated "and" or "but" depending on the context. In my deliberately literal translation where I aim to translate the same Hebrew word or particle with the same English word, I have consistently translated this word "and." My assumption, however, is that the darkness is due to the sun's effect since descriptions of the Woman by her lover imply that her skin is light enough to be described as lily-like (2:2; 4:5; 7:2 [MT 7:3]) and the hue of pomegranates can be seen in her cheeks (4:3; 6:7).

In the man's references to his beloved we can infer her strong personality, since he describes himself as "captivated" (4:9), "daunted," and "overwhelmed" (6:4-5) by her. He also refers to her as one whom others should admire (2:2; 6:9).

Though describing herself as "faint with love" (2:5; 5:8), she comes across as confident and proactive. Her self-descriptions are never self-effacing: she introduces herself as "black and lovely" (1:5), "*the* crocus of the plains, *the* lily of the valley" (2:1)—we see her special emphasis in using the definite article when the Man responds that she is like "*a* lily among the thorns" (2:2). She draws attention to herself, sometimes by speaking of herself in the third person (1:7; 2:7; 3:1-5; 6:12; 8:4, 7); she initiates conversations; she invites trysts with her lover; and she ventures out into the public arena to search for him. As Alice Ogden Bellis describes,

> She is a strong young woman demanding that the daughters of Jerusalem do as she bids them and implicitly that her brothers and the broader community allow her to live her own life . . . . She is her own person, the mistress of her body, and the master of her destiny. No one will dictate the terms of beauty, class, or honor and shame to her. (Bellis 2021, 111)

In this scroll we view events most often from the perspective of the Woman. Many could relate to her subjective experience of being in the first flush of love, when lovers perceive that the world is centered on themselves. When the Woman uses the metaphor of royalty to describe her lover (1:4, 12; 7:5 [MT 7:6]) she is signalling that, whatever her social and economic circumstances, she knows herself a queen in the company of her king. By appreciating and extolling each other's beauty and worth, the lovers impart a sense of well-being that applies equally to themselves and to the world around them. In such a context, she can rightly claim to be a "finder of peace" (8:10).

The Man. The Hebrew Bible does not characteristically describe the physical appearance of its protagonists. This scroll, however, celebrates the physical features of the Man and the Woman. When challenged by the chorus of women to explain the attractions of her Dodi, the Woman gladly does so (5:9-16). In her description of him she uses similar imagery of architecture and spices that the Man has used for her, but the overall imagery contrasts his chiselled hardness with her curvy softness. His belly, for example, is "a work of ivory bedecked with sapphires" (5:14), while hers is "a bowl of roundness . . . a heap of wheat fenced in with lilies" (7:2 [MT 7:3]). In the Woman's description, the Man shines: she calls him "radiant and ruddy" (5:10) and uses three different Hebrew words for "gold" within five verses to describe parts of his body. Arms, legs, and feet are equated to precious worked materials of ivory and columns of alabaster. Value and hardness are thus the ideals of manly beauty exploited in her description. He, too, has dark hair and grey eyes and is pleasingly scented with spices. The scroll begins with the Woman desiring his kisses, and she refers to enjoyment of his mouth in two other poems (5:16; 7:9 [MT 7:10]). The dark hair, good teeth, and overall pleasantness and freshness of the descriptions suggest that both the Man and the Woman are still young!

Recalling that we are viewing events predominantly through the Woman's eyes, we wonder if the Man is fully reliable. He has a wide experience of the world, seen in his references to Egypt, Lebanon, and the mountains on the edges of Israel, and he seems to be constantly on the move. He knocks on her door to rouse her but is gone by the time she opens to him (4:2-6), leading the daughters of Jerusalem to offer to help look for him (6:1). Yet the Man seems capable of mesmerizing the Woman with his poems of love and appreciation for her, and he is not shy about using overtly suggestive descriptions of how he would like to enjoy her body (e.g., 7:7-8 [MT 7:8-9]). Is his elusiveness a form of affectionate teasing, or is he perhaps aware that anticipation is integral to lovemaking and heightens the moments of consummation?

The Chorus of Men. Although this group does not play a large role in the drama, it does add some dramatic tension. These men are portrayed as the brothers of the Shulammite. On two occasions they have a speaking role, but they are in the background of other parts of the action. Different interpretations are possible, but it is likely that the Watchmen (3:3; 5:7) and the Brothers (1:6; 8:8-9) are the same players. In the context of a Greek play, changes of masks would allow differentiation between the roles even if acted out by the same group of players.

It seems clear that this group has not contributed to the Woman's sense of self-worth. She complains of their mistreatment of her in an early scene, explaining that her dark skin is due to her work in the vineyard. By running two thoughts together she likens the "scorching of the sun" to the "burning" of her brothers—notably she distances herself from a close relationship with them by referring to the brothers as "sons of my mother" (1:6). Even at this point, however, the Woman's sense of humor is apparent as she cheekily claims that they did not have control over her body:

THE WOMAN:	They set me as keeper of the vineyards, My vineyard for me I did not keep ;) (1:6b)

Twice the Woman searches by night for her lover and is found by "watchmen"—a group that seems to be identifiable as her brothers. The first time (3:3-4) the appearance of her lover enabled her to flee with him and remain safe from the men, but on the subsequent occasion (5:7) they beat and bruise and disgrace her. Nonetheless, she is not cowed by their view of her, and when they speak disparagingly of her as their "little sister" without breasts (8:8) and boast about their plans to keep her confined (8:9), she responds with defiance:

THE WOMAN:	I am a wall,
	And my breasts are like the towers. (8:10)

The Chorus of Women. This group is addressed by the Woman as "daughters of Jerusalem" (1:5; 2:7; 3:5; 5:8, 16; 8:4).[23] When they and the male chorus refer to the Woman as the Shulammite (6:13 [MT 7:1]) they may be suggesting that she is one of them since *šûlam* (Shulam) could be understood as a shortened form of *yerûšālayim* (Jerusalem).

Attention to plural verbal forms suggests that they speak early in the scroll, addressing the same Man that the Woman addresses in the opening lines:

CHORUS *of women:*	Let us rejoice and be glad in you
	Let us make remembered—your loving—
	beyond wine (1:4b).

Their role akin to a Greek chorus is immediately obvious. Right at the outset they are providing commentary on the drama, offering to share the joy of the lovers and to "make remembered" their love.[24] They validate the Woman's admiration for her lover by agreeing with her, and she in turn agrees with them when she speaks again to the man: "Rightly they love you!" (1:4c).

At the critical halfway point of the scroll they again exhort the lovers, affirming the joy of their relationship:

CHORUS *of women:*	Eat, friends!
	Drink and be drunk with loving! (5:1b)

The chorus continues to "make remembered" the Man by asking key questions about him: what is so special about him (5:9), and where is he (6:1)? They also "make remembered" the Woman when they draw attention to her beauty by echoing the Man's words of admiration:

THE MAN:	Lovely are your cheeks with earrings,
	Your neck with beaded strings. (1:10)
CHORUS *of women:*	Earrings of gold we make for you,
	With beads of silver. (1:11)

THE MAN:	Beautiful are you, my darling, like the city of pleasure,
	Lovely like the city of peace,
	Daunting like banners lifted. (6:4)
CHORUS of women:	Who is this seen like dawn,
	Beautiful like the moon,
	Daunting like banners lifted? (6:10)

Four times the Woman repeats an adjuration to the female chorus. This vow serves as a refrain in the Song, and all except one are followed by a *setumah*, marking the end of a section (2:7; 3:5; 8:4). The mandate "Do not awaken and do not arouse the lover until she is ready" serves as a reminder that love need not be hurried, again affirming that anticipation is a significant part of lovemaking. The other time the refrain is heard is after the most disturbing incident of the scroll—the abuse of the Woman by the watchmen. The lack of *setumah* implies that the performance should continue right on. It is followed by the chorus of women's question about the Man's appearance, suggesting that the chorus is intent on distracting the Woman and aiding her in forgetting her unpleasant experience. This seems to be successful. Notably, however, the chorus of women goes on to have a protective function for the Woman in the aftermath of this incident. When exhorted by a group of men to "Turn and let us gaze on you" (6:13a), the Shulammite is defended by the chorus of women who retort, "Why should you gaze upon the Shulammite?" (6:13b).

The chorus of women serves their function well in this performance. They draw the attention of the audience to the main theme of the Song of Songs, aid us in admiring the lovers, and recognize the need for protection when the Woman becomes vulnerable. At the end of the script they disappear and leave the lovers to their own world. The inconclusive ending of the scroll of the Song of Songs tells us something of the nature of love: it is ultimately a private realm inhabited by the lovers alone, and it has no real beginning and no real end.

Pace

Objections to a dramatic reading of the Song of Songs especially focus on the lack of discernible plot. Without a narrator to provide exposition and commentary, we rely on the dialogue alone to identify characters, their relationship to each other, and their movement and locations. We have a tendency to fill in gaps in order to make linear sense of the material, as evidenced already by discussions above as to why the Woman refers to herself as "black" or why the Masoretes chose not to provide a pause marker after the abuse of the Woman. As can be seen from the division of scenes in my script, the Masoretic diacritics are helpful but not conclusive.

In *The Art of the Play*, Alan Downer refers to the scene as the basic unit of dramatic construction: "a portion of the total play in which the stage is occupied by an unchanging group of players" (1955, 170). In my view, changes in time and location can also be indicators for a change of scene. All of these criteria, however, are difficult to discern in the Song of Songs.

The speakers have been identified on the basis of grammatical cues. A basic distinction between singular and plural can be made when first-person speech is used, distinguishing the Man and the Woman from the chorus, except for the occasions where the Man and Woman may be speaking together (1:16b-17; 2:15). Second-person speech in Hebrew is gender- and number-bound (unlike English), and so it is usually possible to decide who is being addressed. Occasional use of vocatives ("O daughters of Jerusalem") also aids in identifying the target audience of a speech. Some interpreters refer to only one chorus, but again, based on verbal forms, I have identified a chorus of women and a chorus of men. Nonetheless, comparing my translation to others will reveal different interpretations of who is speaking when.

References to locations such as vineyards (1:6, 14; 2:15; 7:12 [MT 7:13]; 8:11-12), a tabernacle of shepherds (1:8), a bed (3:1), the squares and the streets of the city (3:2-3; 5:7), and the house of my mother (3:4; 8:2) allow for changes in scenes, yet other locations—the king's rooms (1:4) or couch (1:12), Solomon's palanquin (3:9), a tree house (1:16b-17)—are as likely to be metaphorical as real in this performance. The many references to natural locations—mountains, forests, gardens—arguably straddle the gap between reality and metaphor. Love has its natural home in beautiful surroundings, but love can also make surroundings beautiful, as Rodolfo and Mimi in Puccini's *La Boheme* would attest when they proclaim their love for each other in a freezing garret.

Those who interpret the Song of Songs from a literary rather than dramatic perspective also have difficulty determining the literary units. Though divided by the Masoretes into eight chapters, some poems that seem to be spoken by the same voice straddle chapter divisions or pause markers. There is also debate as to whether one hand or many are responsible for the material. Proposals range from one author who composed six poems in three pairs to multiple authorship of over thirty individual poems (Nielsen 1998, 184).

The fluid nature of the players and scene changes in this performance is well recognized:

> [Some readers] define the Song as a drama with identifiable scenes. Such readings are attuned to the performative dimension of the Song's language of love, but any attempt to find a coherent line of action or a clearly defined drama in this ancient anthology of love poems is ultimately strained. The division into eight chapters is quite arbitrary and does not rely on clear poetic demarcations. Poems emerge out of nowhere, merge with one another, or end abruptly. And the lovers, like their poems, appear and disappear unexpectedly. (Pardes 2019, 7)

Due to the lack of clarity surrounding scene divisions and entrances and exits of players I decided not to include the stage directions "enter" and "exit" as one would normally find in scripts of Greek plays.

One of the ways interpreters make sense of the material is to describe it as "dreamlike," supported by references to sleeping, beds, and nighttime. Song 5:2 is cited as evidence for this dreamlike state: "The exquisite verse 'I was asleep but my heart was awake' underscores the paradoxical experience of dreams, split as they are between passive sleep and a wakefulness that may exceed daytime" (Pardes 2019, 9). My translation of this verse ("I am sleeping and my heart rouses") recognizes that there is an adjective in the original Hebrew rather than a verb and takes into account the Vulgate's use of the word *vigilate* along with the Greek Septuagint's translation of "I am asleep but my heart is fully awake." Such translations convey an anticipatory rather than dreamy state.[25] Furthermore, beds and nighttime are the very contexts for physical love under ordinary circumstances. What is unusual in this performance of love is the extension of those romantic encounters to include daytime and outdoor settings!

A key theme in performance is that of process or dynamic movement. Henry Bial, an important figure in Performance Studies, writes, ". . . a performance is not a static finished product. Performances are always in-process, changing, growing, and moving through time" (2004, 215).[26] Although a part of canonical Scripture, the Song of Songs continues to be interpreted anew down through the ages. Elsie Stern describes its dynamic and fluid aspects that lend themselves to new readings as "oscillation among the different spheres and modes." She speaks of shifts in the poetic voices in both grammar and mood: "The poetic voices shift repeatedly from praise to adjuration, from playfulness to violence, and from third-person to second-person address" (2004, 1564). The shifting between first-, second-, and third-person address is evident right from the first few verses where the Woman speaks *about* her lover, then directly *to* him, then *about* him in figurative terms, then includes herself *with* him, then again speaks *to* him. This shifting of perspective invites us as audience to participate in the performance. If we only ever heard the lovers speaking directly to each other, our involvement would be voyeuristic. Instead we are drawn in to admire them and share in their joy. Frequent use of volitive verbs has a similar effect, whether through requesting our permission with cohortatives ("let me seek him") or demanding our attention or compliance with imperatives ("Eat, drink, and be drunk with love").

The multitude of settings and fluidity of players in those settings suggest for Ilana Pardes that the two lovers are engaged in "a flirtatious hide-and-seek" (2019, 8). Just as love is grasped it is gone again. The final verses in the scroll embody this fluid ambiguity. Fittingly, it is a dialogue between the lovers. The Man speaks first, reiterating a line from earlier in the scroll, "make me hear your voice." In response the Woman says, "fly my Dodi." Both speak with the urgency of imperatives, but it seems that where he pulls she pushes. Her final words echo earlier words of his, though, as she demands that he "Be like a gazelle or the fawn of a deer upon the mountain of spices." When he has grazed like a deer or gazelle before, it has been within her arms. If she is now sending him away, it is in order for him to return to her embrace.

The pace of this performance, then, is erratic and cyclical. Like love, it has no end. Like love, it cannot be contained. Like love, it triumphs over adversity to fly on to new heights. Within the *Megillot* this scroll exhibits unique freedom and open-endedness. As we will see presently, this scroll is a stark contrast to the scroll of Lamentations in which grief *must* be contained.

Playfulness

I have referred a number of times to the broad range of metaphors and similes employed in the script of the Song of Songs. The *wasf* passages describing the physical beauty of the Woman and the Man are especially lively. On occasion one comes across attempts to portray a visual image of the literal features as described, with goats for hair, sheep for teeth, a tower for a neck, gazelles or fawns for breasts, and so on. While amusing to contemplate, such attempts miss the power of metaphorical language. Not only have the words retained their "lovely expressiveness" for over two millennia, but they also "enable the poet to speak candidly of sexual gratification without seeming to do so" (Alter 2019b, 585). The language is highly playful, inviting us both to enjoy the images at their face value and to read into them an underlying eroticism.

Vineyard and garden thus represent the Woman's body—places full of sensual pleasures where the Man is invited to spend time grazing and enjoying ripe fruits. Of all her body parts, the Woman's breasts receive the most attention, being likened to clusters of dates, hills of spices, and twin fawns. When the Man speaks of his intention to go to the "mountain of myrrh, the hill of frankincense" (4:6b), an ancient connection between hills and women's breasts is evoked.[27] The image of twin fawns or gazelles grazing among lilies evokes a delightful vision of a perfect pair of rounded hind parts of young animals poking up from the long grass. The Woman draws on another characteristic of gazelles when she speaks of her Dodi "leaping on the mountains, bounding on the hills" (2:8). If he is coming to her breasts, he is coming with speed and grace! She also describes him as "a 'purse of myrrh' between my breasts" (1:13). Not only is there wonderful wordplay in the rhyming phrase *tserôr hammor* (poorly conveyed in my translation of rhyming vowel sounds), but the image is also playful as we imagine a miniaturized lover nestling in her cleavage.

Names in the Hebrew Bible can often be etymological, hence the choices I made with some of my translations. "Lebanon" (*lebānôn*) is used as a place name frequently through the scroll, but since it was the origin of the spice frankincense (*lebônāh*) I have usually translated "the land of frankincense" (4:8, 11, 15). The woman is likened to Tirzah and Jerusalem in 6:4, names that I have translated "city of pleasure" and "city of peace" respectively as it seems their reputation is what is in mind. Other place names are listed like a travelogue. This is another hint that the original poetry was intended to be viewed on multiple levels. It is a celebration of the wonders of the poet's homeland as much as a celebration of love.[28]

Each of the lovers speaks of the other with the imagery of food and drink, highlighting the intimacy of taste and smell that is only possible when there is no distance between them. The Man refers to various liquids when speaking of the woman: wine, oil, nectar, milk, honey; but both use verbs suggesting the flow of moisture, conveying a subtle innuendo. Again, there is repetition of sounds in the phrase "nectar drips from your lips" (*nofet tittofnāh śiftôtayik*), followed by "honey and milk are under your tongue" (4:11). The inversion of this well-known biblical word pair "milk and honey" suggests that the Shulammite herself is the promised land! We have already noted the connection between her name and "shalom." The sensual "sh" sound is prominent in certain parts of the script, including the title *shir ha-shirim*. The *sounds* of words in the Song of Songs thus contribute to the overall impression of languid lovemaking.

I have mentioned some examples of rhyme found in the script. Another striking, and more playful, example can be found in the original Hebrew in 2:15. The Hebrew transliteration is

eḥezû lānû šû'ālîm
šû'ālîm qᵉṭanîm mᵉḥabᵉlîm qᵉrāmîm/
ûkrāmēnû sᵉmādar

The NRSV translates the lines this way:

> Catch us the foxes
> The little foxes
> That ruin the vineyards—
> For our vineyards are in blossom

The plural verbs and pronouns suggest that this is spoken by the lovers together, with the first section sounding like a nonsense nursery-rhyme phrase with its five rhyming words in sequence. The second part of the verse returns to a normal tone. One can imagine lovers recollecting a familiar childish rhyme when contemplating a minor irritation and then returning to their usual blissful awareness of each other. I have accordingly translated it thus:

> Catch for us foxes,
> foxes in soxes
> Poxes in our rootstockses . . .
> And our vineyards blossom.

For original Israelite audiences to this performance, references to vineyards and gardens could have evoked memories of other well-known traditions. As already noted, several prophets made use of the marriage metaphor. Isaiah's vineyard love-song (Isa 5:1-7) shares significant vocabulary with the Song of Songs, even in its name *šîrat dôdî* ("the song of my Dodi")! Ezekiel includes a passage about Jerusalem as a personified bride, bejeweled and beautiful like a queen. There is a partial *wasf* in his description of the woman's breasts, hair, arms, neck, nose, ears, and head (Ezek 16). Hosea also describes a wife, whether real or metaphorical, by referring to her breasts and her nakedness (Hos 2). Both Ezekiel and Hosea refer to grain, wine, oil, and honey as gifts for the woman they describe. Ezekiel also speaks of a garden filled with precious stones as a gift for a king (Ezek 28). The writer of Genesis places a human couple in a garden that provides good gifts for their well-being. The Man in that story speaks of his female partner as "Bone of my bone and flesh of my flesh" (Gen 2:23), exhibiting the sort of mutuality between the couple that is evident in the Song of Songs. Each of these traditions shares vocabulary and themes that are found in the Song of Songs. In every one of these alternate traditions, however, human failing spoils the vineyards and gardens and gifts become curses. If the prophetic and Genesis traditions were ready-mades for the original audience of the Song of Songs, they would have been surprised and delighted by the fact that there is no turning from paradise here. No judgment, no punishment, no expectation of confession, and no need for divine redemption. The performance begins in bliss and concludes in expectation of continued bliss for the human couple. Only one brief incident reminds us that no perfect world exists, and to this we must now turn.

Connections with the Song of Songs

One verse seems out of place in the Song of Songs:

> THE WOMAN: They found me—the watchmen—
> the ones going round in the city.
> They struck me, they bruised me,
> They lifted my veil from over me,
> The watchmen of the walls. (5:7)

The verbs here describe serious action. "Struck" (*nkh*) is the act of beating someone or something in violence, often translated "smited" when referring to violence coming from God's hand. "Bruised" (*ptz'*) is a less common verb, only used two other times in the Hebrew Bible, but those occurrences also indicate significant damage (Deut 23:2; 1 Kgs 20:37). Three times in the performance the Man refers to the Woman's veil, using it to protect her modesty as has been noted above. Here it is taken from her by the watchmen in order to shame her. The Woman who has been reveling in the love and admiration of her lover is now abused and humiliated by a group of men. The linguistic structure of the verse with "watchmen" at the beginning and end shows how the Woman is suddenly surrounded by watchmen, hemming her in so that she cannot escape their violence. Since the Woman describes her brothers' anger towards her (1:6) and the brothers themselves boast of closing her in (8:9), it seems reasonable to equate this group of violent men with the Woman's own family members. It is well known that a significant percentage of women who suffer violence at the hands of men know their perpetrators, most often partners or family members.[29] Early on the Woman seems to laugh off the disapproval of her brothers, and later she defies their intentions, but here she is victim to their abuse. It is a shocking scene. Perhaps for this reason it tends to be ignored or trivialized in commentaries or, more insidiously, interpreters blame the woman herself for her abuse.[30]

The fact that this is just one verse amongst one hundred and thirteen in the Song of Songs mitigates its marginalization to some extent, but ignoring or refusing to draw attention to abuse when it occurs contributes to perpetuating the cycles of violence that exist in our societies. So often victims of abuse refer to the shame-induced silence surrounding their experience—a silence that has kept the issue of the abuse of women out of public scrutiny until relatively recently.

A significant factor in breaking down this silence surrounding violence against women in recent years is this is the global Me Too movement initiated by American activist Tarana Burke in 2006, who encouraged women who had been sexually assaulted to make their experience known. A decade later, in the wake of sexual abuse allegations against Hollywood producer Harvey Weinstein, actress Alyssa Milano posted a statement on Twitter: "if all the women who have been sexually harassed or assaulted wrote 'Me Too' as a status, we might give people a sense of the magnitude of the problem." The #metoo social media movement was initiated and has continued to be a powerful force in drawing attention to the issue. It has encouraged more women to speak publicly about their experiences of abuse in the media, in the workplace, in religious institutions, and in the home. This attention has brought pressure on governments to investigate issues relating to women's safety and to bring recommendations that will engender change. Recognizing that violence stems from attitudes that develop early in life, awareness campaigns and education of children and youth about respect and equality between sexes are underway in many jurisdictions.[31] In 2021, sexual abuse survivor Grace Tame was awarded Australia's highest honor, Australian of the Year, in recognition of her advocacy work for survivors of sexual assault including raising public awareness and pushing for legal reform. When Grace Tame speaks of the power that abusers hold over their victims, keeping them in shame-induced silence, she challenges the community to combat that power with the "power of love" that enables victims to speak out, be heard, and begin to heal.[32]

Unfortunately, theological institutions, churches, and other religious communities are no safer for women. Across the globe it has been found that the incidence of violence against women, especially in the context of domestic abuse, occurs within religious institutions at similar rates to the general population. This is an issue that cannot and should not be ignored.

In his book *Interested Parties*, biblical scholar David Clines offers a reading of the Song of Songs that runs counter to most other commentaries. He argues that the Song of Songs is no different from other books in the Hebrew Bible in that it was written by an Israelite male author "to meet the desires and needs of other Israelite males" (2009, 99). For Clines, the Woman in Songs:

> does not exist . . . she is a figment of the poet's imagination . . . he is a certain kind of man who wants a certain kind of woman, a type that is not generally available in his culture. He fantasizes such a woman, he writes his dream, he finds an audience of like-minded men, his poem becomes a best-seller. (2009, 106)[33]

The argument made by Clines is compelling, not least because he is correct in seeing how differently this woman behaves when compared to most other "heroic" women in the Hebrew Bible (who are contrasted with "loose women" whose wanton behavior elicits warnings by prophets and sages). The reading posed by Clines raises another issue of concern when considering the safety of women in our society and our religious institutions. Under the "male gaze" the Woman becomes "the other," one to be watched for male pleasure (2009, 118–19). Indeed, this male gaze is explicit in the Song of Songs when the Woman comes to the attention of "watchmen" (*haššomerîm*—a masculine plural participle from the verb *šmr*, to watch, keep, preserve, 3:3; 5:7) who later demand, "Turn and let us gaze on you" (6:13 [MT 7:1]). The male chorus also comments on their young sister (8:8), drawing attention to her breasts (if only to assert that she has none!) Our societies, especially in the advertising industry but also in other forms of media, routinely objectify women and sexualize girls.[34] Attention to these verses in the Song of Songs reminds us that such exploitation has been occurring for millennia.

An advantage of approaching biblical books via Performance Criticism is its openness to appreciating different performances of the same script. We have already noted that some interpreters best understood the Song of Songs as an allegory of the relationship between the divine and humanity while others preferred a literal reading of the material as human love poetry celebrating sexual relationships. The reading of Clines is straightforwardly historical, positing the likely circumstances for authorship and readership of this ancient Israelite scroll that has been transmitted as *the* Song of Songs. Yet Clines is also concerned about the effect of the Song of Songs on its readers, whether in the past or the present. When ethical considerations arise from reading Scripture, he argues, we must notice them and respond to them:

> To be truly academic, and worthy of its place in the academy, biblical studies has to be truly critical, critical not just about lower-order questions like authorship of the biblical books or the historicity of the biblical

narratives, but critical about the Bible's contents, its theology, its ideology. (2009, 109)

I am challenged by David Clines's perspective and share his concern in bringing attention to problematic aspects that have become evident within the script. Nonetheless, I continue to be inspired by the literary beauty of the Song of Songs and the portrait it paints, even if only an idealistic fantasy, of true mutuality between a human couple. The speeches of the Man, rather than objectifying the Woman, invite her to participate *with* him in his appreciation of her ("make me see your countenance, make me hear your voice," 2:14). On the other hand, the scroll *does* raise issues that we need to face. The Woman in the Song of Songs is independent, self-assured, and in a relationship with someone who treats her as an equal, yet other men still abuse her. The overall message of the Song of Songs is that the power of love is stronger than forces that try to separate the lovers, but the scroll does not shy away from the violence in its midst. In recognizing that this reality is present even within scrolls held as sacred Scripture, we may be inspired to engage in conversations, education, and structural change to ensure that all women feel safe in our cities and especially within our religious institutions.

The Scroll of Ruth

Introduction

The scroll of Ruth is named for its heroine, a widowed Moabite accompanying her widowed Israelite mother-in-law Naomi as she returns to Israel. Arriving in Naomi's hometown of Bethlehem impoverished and grieving, the women's fortunes change due to a chance meeting with Boaz, a relative of Naomi's husband Elimelek. He takes them under his wing, initially providing food for them and later negotiating to "redeem" the land that had belonged to Elimelek, as well as taking on Ruth as his wife.

The Scroll and the Festival of *Shavuot*

The literary setting of Ruth is a time of harvest, and this setting determines the role of the story within the festival scrolls. It is read at the Festival of *Shavuot* (the Hebrew word for "weeks"), also known as "Weeks" and "Pentecost" as it comes fifty days (seven weeks) after Passover. The story in the book of Ruth spans about seven weeks—the same period as the festival. Originally Shavuot was one of the three pilgrimage festivals when, according to the Torah, Israelites were expected to travel to Jerusalem to celebrate before YHWH at the Jerusalem temple (Deut 16:16). It was the first of the harvest festivals, a spring season of seven weeks between the harvests of barley ("first fruits") and wheat, with Shavuot concluding the grain harvests. Some months later the Autumn Festival of *Sukkot* (Booths/Tabernacles) is a celebration of the fruit harvest. Shavuot was given a historical grounding in the story of the Israelites by Jewish sages as the anniversary of Moses receiving the Law at Mount Sinai (Exod 19–24). According to this tradition, Moses received the oral law, and the written Law was recorded during the forty years of wilderness wanderings. Passover celebrates freedom from slavery, but at Shavuot the Israelites became a nation committed to the Law of YHWH.[35]

During the medieval period an observance developed of studying the Torah all night during the festival of Shavuot, a ritual known as *Tikkun Leyl Shavuot*, more commonly simply referred to as *Tikkun* (Lieber 2012, 165). The weekly practice of parading the Torah and other scrolls around the synagogue is especially associated with this festival that commemorates the Law. Symbolically, the history of Israel is reenacted in this ritual. The scrolls are taken from the cabinet known as the Holy Ark (*Aron haKodesh* or *Teivah*)[36] in memory of the tablets received by Moses that were housed in the holy of holies in the tabernacle and later the Jerusalem Temple. The congregation stands before the *Teivah* representing the original community of Israelites at the base of Mount Sinai (Exod 19:17). They chant verses from Scripture as the scrolls are marched around the synagogue, recalling the march through the wilderness with the Torah housed in the ark in their midst, the conquering of the land of Canaan, and the establishment of Jerusalem and the temple. Ornamental coverings on the scrolls recall the vestments used by priests, connecting the study of the Torah to the historical worship rituals. One who is called on to read from the Torah is described as "receiving an *Aliyah*" (literally, "going up"), recalling the pilgrimage to Jerusalem's high elevation. This involved and highly participatory ritual demonstrates the sense of connection between Jewish history and contemporary religious practice.[37]

The scroll of Ruth is read during morning services of the festival of Shavuot. According to Yael Rosenberg, the story is read at this festival for many traditional reasons:

- Just as Torah learning is acquired through pain and poverty, so did Ruth endure pain and sorrow in order to become part of the Jewish nation.
- Just as Ruth was converted and accepted by YHWH, so did the Israelite nation enter into covenant with YHWH by accepting the Torah on this day.
- The numerical value (gematria) of the name Ruth is 606. The Torah comprises 606 *mitzvoth* (commandments) that are added to the seven laws of Noah to reach the total of 613 commandments.
- Ruth was the great-grandmother of King David, who died at the age of seventy on the holiday of Shavuot. Ruth is known as *Em Hamlchut* ("Mother of the Kingdom").
- The central theme of the story of Ruth is *ḥesed* ("loving kindness"). Not only does the Torah instruct Israelites to accept converts; it also commands that they be treated with loving kindness.
- The setting of the harvest in Ruth connects her story with the harvest festival Shavuot.

- The book of Ruth validates the oral Torah by reinterpreting the law excluding Moabites from the community.[38]

The Background of the Scroll
The plot of the scroll of Ruth hinges on fulfilment of Torah laws, in particular provision for the poor while gleaning (Lev 19:9-10; Deut 24:19-21) and laws concerning redemption of property (Lev 25:24-25) and levirate marriage (Deut 25:5-10). The law of redemption is based on the principle that YHWH is the owner of the land and has distributed it as an inheritance among the tribes of Israel. The land for each tribe should not be sold outside of the tribe, and if it is sold due to poverty, a family member should "redeem" the land. The practice of levirate marriage provides for a widow, enabling her remarriage within the family in order that her children retain the parental heritage of her deceased husband. This latter theme is a prominent one in the scroll of Ruth. Naomi alludes to it first when trying to convince her daughters-in-law to return to their homes (Ruth 1:11-13). Frequent references to kinsmen, near relatives, and redeemer-kinsman (*go'el*) keep the possibility of a levirate marriage for Ruth alive throughout the story (Ruth 2:1; 2:20; 3:2; 3:9; 3:12-13; 4:1; 4:3-6; 4:8-10; 4:14). In addition, Boaz's ancestor Perez was conceived by Tamar, also a foreigner, who, when denied the right of levirate marriage, took surreptitious action herself to bring it about (Gen 38).

This emphasis on Torah fulfilment in Ruth's story suggests she is an ideal proselyte, committed to the Law and acting in accordance with it, working hard but resting when appropriate, caring for the needy, taking positive action to ensure the continuation of her dead husband's line. Remembering Ruth on the festival dedicated to observation of the Law seems most appropriate. Whilst there is a Deuteronomic law (Deut 23:3) forbidding access of the Ammonite or Moabite to the assembly of YHWH, it is conveniently ignored in this scroll (see below for more on this).

The location of the book of Ruth in the Christian Old Testament mirrors that in the Septuagint, the Greek translation of the Hebrew Bible, and makes contextual sense for the story. It follows the book of Judges, giving logic to its opening words "In the days when the judges ruled" (Ruth 1:1, NRSV). The book of Judges ends with the words "In those days there was no king in Israel; all the people did what was right in their own eyes" (Judg 21:25, NRSV). The last few verses in the book of Ruth herald the monarchy that will shortly become established by listing the genealogy leading from Perez (one of the five sons of the eponymous Judah) to David, who marks the tenth generation of Judah (Ruth 4:18-22). Ruth's story takes place in Bethlehem in the land of Judah, which will be the birthplace of David. Along with this

Genesis-like genealogy,[39] the author has drawn on patriarchal traditions by focusing on the wife of an ancestor: a woman of good character who meets her future husband at a well (Ruth 2:9; cf. Gen 24). Unlike Sarah, Rebekah, and Rachel, however, Ruth had no difficulty in conceiving a son. As has already been mentioned, Ruth is more closely connected to Tamar's story in Gen 38 than to the earlier matriarchs. This will be further elaborated in the commentary below. The complication in the story came instead from her foreign status and the obligation of redemption falling to a nearer kinsman than Boaz. The setting within the time of Judges and the style of the book with its flavor of the patriarchal traditions locates it convincingly within the early Israelite writings. The concrete location (Bethlehem of Judah) and names that appear in genealogical lists elsewhere in the Hebrew Bible give it the nature of a historical narrative.

Despite this veneer of historicity, however, it seems evident that Ruth is preeminently a novella, written both for entertainment and to address, albeit with a light touch, the serious issue of xenophobia. The placement of the scroll of Ruth within the Writings of the Hebrew Bible gives the first clue to its late dating, since the Writings constitute the latest of the collections of books in the Hebrew Bible that were accepted as canonical. The focus on Judah is another clue. The latter part of Israel's history in the Hebrew Bible is confined to the southern kingdom, predominantly consisting of the tribe of Judah. A narratorial aside in the fourth chapter (Ruth 4:7) that explains the legal practice of redemption and levirate obligations for a later audience is another indication of late transmission. There is also the presence of words that exhibit Late Biblical Hebrew, as pointed out by Robert Alter:

> The writer took pains to create a narrative prose redolent of the early centuries of Israelite history, but it is very difficult to execute such a project of archaizing without occasional tell-tale slips . . . Here, there are at least a dozen terms that reflect distinctive Late Biblical usage . . . and another ten idiomatic collocations occur that never appear in earlier biblical texts. (2019b, 621)[40]

Finally, it belongs to the genre of historical fiction, a category of writing that blossomed during the Second Temple period. Such books are set against historical backgrounds but are narratives that have no discernible connection to any historical events recorded elsewhere. The books of Esther, Daniel, Tobit, Judith, Susanna, and Bel and the Dragon could also be included in this category. They undoubtedly had didactic purposes, such as encouraging those of Jewish faith to stand steadfast in the face of hostility or encouraging readers to see that they can be successful even in foreign settings when faithful to beliefs and practices, but the aesthetic appeal of this genre is also undeniable.

The Literary Artistry of the Scroll
The story of Ruth can be appreciated as carefully crafted literature. Many scholars have highlighted a chiastic structure in the scroll of Ruth, in which parallel themes are arranged that pivot at the center of the story (Bertman 1965).[41] Even without focusing on a chiastic arrangement, however, we can see how contrasting themes are used to drive home the movement from death and emptiness to new life and fulfilment. Disaster and loss make way for blessing and abundance. Bitterness is replaced by sweetness. Names are important clues also, as will be expanded on in the commentary below. Bethlehem—house of bread; Elimelek—my god is king; Mahlon—sick; Chilion—annihilation; Naomi—my sweetness; Mara—bitterness; Orpah—back of the neck; Ruth—companion; Boaz—strength; *P'loni Almoni*—nonsense; Obed—worshipper; David—beloved. Despite some negative connotations seen here, there are no truly evil characters in the story. The whole story exhibits a key quality of kindness (*ḥesed*) where the actors treat each other with respect, obedience, politeness, and generosity. Due to this quality, adjectives commonly used in commentaries on this story are "charming" and "beguiling." It's been called an idyll, a gem, a cameo, a gracious and lyrical short story, and its dramatic quality as "performed story" has also been noted (Queen-Sutherland 2016, 38; Alter 2019b, 622).

In this drama the agricultural and the personal are intertwined. Famine in the "house of bread" that drives away a family from their homeland turns to harvest that welcomes back the remnant of that family at a time when bread is again plentiful. The successful gleaning allows for generosity and provides opportunity for subtle references to seed and fertility. Daring, risky strategies at the threshing floor are delicately conveyed with the aim of retaining honor for all involved. Age and experience count for more than youth and spontaneity. And in cultures where the forces of nature that determine production are more closely intertwined with women's business, this story is predominantly a woman's story. Men's business is necessary, but women are agents in every scene, especially underlined in the first chapter where men are introduced only to report their deaths while women take the lead in speech and action. We might also note that throughout the story women only speak to women and men only speak to men with the exception of Ruth and Boaz alone breaking that pattern.

The Purpose of the Scroll

This story is not about wars or issues of politics, nor are its main actors any of the great leaders of Israel. If there is divine intervention, it is subtle rather than miraculous. There is no mention of the exodus or Jerusalem. Faith is explicit at the beginning of the story but becomes less obvious as the scenes unfold. Several coincidences, nevertheless, suggest that there is a God working behind the scenes. And so a story that has little direct connection with the cult of Israel and no emphasis on prayer or sacrifice instead celebrates God's providence in times of need through the experiences of just a few representative individuals.

If a larger purpose for this book is warranted, it may be found in the xenophobic politics of a postexilic Jewish community characterized by books such as Ezra and Nehemiah, where the purity of Jewish identity was a very real concern. The postexilic period was a testing time for the Israelites. Forced exposure to other cultures provided new worldviews and temptation to move away from ancestral traditions. More insidiously, expansion of empires from the east and west across the whole of the known ancient world resulted in pressure for assimilation to the dominant culture, both in language and practices. Indeed, during the Greek Empire this assimilation was enforced on pain of death. Closer to home, returning exiles found themselves at odds with Israelites who had remained in the land ravaged by destructive armies, resulting in tension over priorities and leadership as the community sought to reestablish itself in the postexilic period. In this context there was a particular emphasis on genealogy where proof of legitimacy could be found (see Ezra 2:62) and explicit advice for Jewish men to rid themselves of foreign wives and children (Ezra 10:10-11). The foreigners in view in those traditions are likely to be Babylonians or Persians, but the traditions of the Hebrew Bible betray a long-held prejudice against the nearer neighboring kingdom of Moab. Ancestral narratives place the origins of Moab in the incestual relationship between Lot and one of his daughters (Gen 19). The prophet Balaam was hired to bring curses against Israel by the king of Moab (Num 22–24). One of the oppressors of Israel in the book of Judges was King Eglon of Moab (Judg 3), and the monarchic period was characterized by hostilities with the Moabite nation.

Against such teaching the story of the Moabite Ruth celebrates a foreign wife, a "woman of valor" (Ruth 3:11), who chooses to turn her back on her own heritage in order to adhere to the laws of the Israelites and who produces an heir for her Israelite husband that gives her a place in the genealogy that leads to the great King David, no less!

Creativity in Ruth—The Miniseries

In reading the scroll of Ruth as a performance, I have imagined the material as a televised miniseries of four episodes, mirroring the traditional division of the Hebrew scroll into four chapters. The first few verses of the book are expository and do not lend themselves to performance. Instead, I envisage the information provided in Ruth 1:1-7 as a rollup script that sets the scene for the action, accompanied by atmospheric musical score that becomes an iconic aspect of the miniseries. This material with its accompanying theme music is repeated at the beginning of each episode, and snippets from the previous episode(s) would follow to remind the audience of key characters and events between episodes.

Given the tragic nature of the beginning of the scroll of Ruth, the theme music should be melancholic but with a note of hopefulness. An ideal candidate, in my view, is Ennio Morricone's score for the 1972 spaghetti western *Once Upon a Time in the West*. Fittingly, the main theme forms the *leitmotif* for the newly widowed homesteader Jill McBain, coming to claim the property Sweetwater following the murder of her husband and his children. Despite her dubious background of prostitution, Jill maintains a dignified presence throughout the film's action. Her theme with its wordless vocals sung by Edda Dell'Orso is hauntingly sad but set in the key of D Major, swelling to an optimistic high note of G before returning to the opening phrases.

The first episode of the miniseries thus begins at verse 8 of chapter 1. Each episode is divided into scenes on the basis of changes of location. As in all biblical narrative, characters are driven by what they say and what they do. I have thus presented the episodes as a screenplay, with stage directions and dialogue. A narratorial voiceover is present when necessary, but redundant narrated phrases such as "she said to her" are omitted. YHWH is a behind-the-scenes character in this series, referred to by others but never appearing in person. Interestingly, Ellen van Wolde points out the large number of direct speeches and concomitant few indirect narrator's texts in this story in comparison to other Hebrew Bible narratives, describing it as "almost a script for a theatre play: dialogues are lined up by short narrator's texts" (1997, 16).

The script is based on my own translation of the scroll of Ruth. This translation is highly iconic, even more focused on word-for-word equivalence than one would normally find in formal translation, with word order usually mirroring the Hebrew and consistency in translation of the same Hebrew word or root with the same English word. This includes literal translation of cognate accusative forms. English translations often avoid repetition for stylistic reasons, but a literal translation is simple and effective and retains the intended emphasis in the original Hebrew (see Ruth 1:1; 2:3; 2:11; 2:16).

I have translated several idioms literally from the original Hebrew.[42] It does not take much effort to imagine the meaning of such idioms for the original audience of the scroll, but we cannot be fully certain given the distance between us and them. There is value, moreover, in making clear in our translation that Hebrew is an archaic language that can never be fully confidently translated into contemporary English.[43]

With a similar aim, I have occasionally used transliteration rather than translation, especially when the wordplay of the original Hebrew is evident in Hebrew but difficult to capture in an English translation. The character *P'loni Almoni* (Ruth 4:1) is a case in point, as will be discussed in the commentary section below. The term *go'el*, often translated "kinsman redeemer," has also been transliterated throughout (Ruth 3:9; 3:12; 4:1; 4:2; 4:6; 4:8; 4:14), as has *shalom* (2:12).

When I have noticed an affinity between Hebrew words and an equivalent English expression, I have replicated this. For example, the Hebrew *halo'* is usually translated with some form of a negative rhetorical question, but I have just kept the expression "hello?!," knowing that vocal tone would convey the intended meaning (see Ruth 2:8, 2:9; 3:1, 3:2). The Hebrew preposition k^e can be translated "like" and makes perfect sense when done so, instilling a contemporary flavor to the dialogue akin to conversing with young people who sprinkle their conversation with the filler "like" (see Ruth 1:4; 2:13; 2:17; 3:6).

Robert Alter (2019b, 626) suggests that the story turns on four thematic key words: the three verbs *lashuv* ("to go back or return"), *lalekhet* ("to walk"), and *lidboq* ("to cling") and on the noun *ḥesed* ("kindness").[44] Each of these words has significance in the broader Hebrew Bible and Jewish faith. The verb *lashuv* ("to go back or return") is a favorite word of the prophetic literature, as it is linked with repentance. The term "Halakhah" which is based on *lalekhet* ("to walk") is shorthand for Jewish law: the "way" a Jew is expected to behave in every aspect of life. When Ruth "clings" to Naomi, this English translation of *lidboq* is not strong enough. The same word is used for flesh sticking to bones (Ps 102:5) or Adam and Eve becoming one flesh (Gen 2:24). In this context it denotes fierce commitment, even between in-laws! Finally, *ḥesed* ("kindness") implies love, faithfulness, and loyalty. It is a word used nearly 250 times in the Hebrew Bible and in most instances has God as the subject.

Given the significance of these thematic key words, I have included each of them as titles for the four episodes of the Ruth Miniseries. The sole *petuchah* that occurs after 4:17 is the only major break in the narrative suggested by the Masoretes. I have removed the following material (the genealogy of David) from the action of the miniseries and included it as fallout information on a rollup script against fading music and a lingering image of a young shepherd boy.

Ruth—The Miniseries
FADE IN

EXT: DRONE VIEW OF THREE WOMEN WALKING ALONG A DESERT ROAD

Background music is Jill's Theme (Morricone) while a **ROLLUP** slowly crawls (Ruth 1:1-7)

> [1] And it happened in the days of the judging of the judges, and it happened a famine in the land, and he went—a man from Beth-lehem the house of bread of Judah—to sojourn in the fields of Moab, he and his wife and the two sons of his. [2] And the name of the man was Elimelek, meaning "my god is king" and the name of his wife was Naomi, meaning "sweetness," and the names of two sons of his were Mahlon (sick) and Kilion (annihilation); they were Ephrathites from Beth-lehem the house of bread of Judah. And they came to the fields of Moab and they were there.
>
> [3] And he died—Elimelek—husband of Naomi and she was left—she and the two sons of hers. [4] And they took up for themselves wives—Moabites—the name of the one was Orpah, meaning "back of the neck," and the name of the second was Ruth, meaning "companion," and they stayed there, like, ten years.
>
> [5] And they died also, the two of them—Mahlon and Kilion—and she was left—the woman—without the two lads of hers and without her husband.
>
> [6] And she got up—she and her daughters-in-law—and she returned from the fields of Moab, for she had heard in the field of Moab that he had visited—YHWH—his people to give to them bread. [7] And she went out from the place where she had been there, and two daughters-in-law of hers with her, and they walked on the road to return to the land of Judah.

EPISODE 1—THE RETURN

CHARACTERS:
Voiceover Narrator
Naomi (Israelite widow of Israelite Elimelek)
Orpah (Moabite widow of Israelite Kilion)
Ruth (Moabite widow of Israelite Mahlon)
Women of Bethlehem

SCENE 1: RETURN TO YOUR MOTHERS (Ruth 1:8-18)

EXT: ON THE ROAD FROM THE FIELDS OF MOAB TO THE LAND OF BETHLEHEM—CONTINUOUS

> NAOMI
> [8]Walk, return each to the house of her mother. Let him—YHWH—do with you kindness like you have done with the dead and with me. [9]Let him give—YHWH—to you both, and find rest, each in the house of her husband.

Naomi kisses them and they lift their voices and weep.

> RUTH AND ORPAH
> [10]Surely with you we will return to your people.

> NAOMI
> [11]Return my daughters, why walk with me? Is there still for me sons in my belly to be for you husbands? [12]Return my daughters. Walk. Surely I am too old for a husband, surely I would say 'is there hope that even tonight with a man I would bear sons,' [13]but can you wait until they grow up? But can you be shut off from a husband? No my daughters. For far more bitter to me than to you for it went out against me—the hand of YHWH.

[14]*They lift their voices and weep again. Orpah kisses Naomi and Ruth clings to her.*

NAOMI
[15]Behold, she has returned—your sister-in-law—to her people and to her gods. Return after your sister-in-law.

RUTH
[16]Don't urge me to leave you, to return from following you. For wherever you walk I will walk, and inever you lodge, I will lodge, your people my people and your gods my gods, [17]inever you die, I die, and there I will be buried. Thus may he do—YHWH—to me and thus may he do it again if even the death would separate between me and between you.

VOICEOVER NARRATOR
[18]And Naomi saw that determined was she to walk with her and she ceased to speak to her.

SCENE 2: RETURN TO THE WOMEN OF BETHLEHEM (Ruth 1:19-22)

EXT: ON THE OUTSKIRTS OF BETHLEHEM—CONTINUOUS

VOICEOVER NARRATOR
[19]And they walked, the two of them, until coming to Beth-lehem the house of bread. And it happened when they came to Beth-lehem the house of bread, it was stirred up—the whole city—about them.

WOMEN OF BETHLEHEM
Is this Naomi?!

NAOMI
(sarcastically)
[20]Do not call me "my sweetness." Call me Bitter Mara for he caused bitterness—*Shaddai* the sufficient—to me—far more. [21]I was full when I walked away and empty he made me return—YHWH. Why call me Sweet Naomi and YHWH answers against me, and *Shaddai* the sufficient makes evil for me!

VOICEOVER NARRATOR

²²And she returned—Naomi—and Ruth the Moabite her daughter-in-law with her, the one who returned from the fields of Moab. And they came to Bethlehem the house of bread at the beginning of the harvest of barley grains.

FADE OUT

END OF EPISODE 1

EPISODE 2—THE WALK

FADE IN

EXT: DRONE VIEW OF A SMALL DWELLING ON THE OUTSKIRTS OF A SMALL JUDEAN VILLAGE

ROLLUP with text of Ruth 1:1-7 against background music of Jill's Theme (Morricone)

CHARACTERS:
Voiceover Narrator
Naomi/ Mara (Israelite widow of Elimelek)
Ruth (The Moabite)
Boaz (A kinsman of Elimelek, owner of the field of barley)
Young Man (The one standing over the reapers)
Male Reapers
Female Reapers

SCENE 1: LET ME WALK (Ruth 2:1-2)

INT: NAOMI'S SMALL DWELLING IN BETHLEHEM—CONTINUOUS
The small, spartan dwelling with a fireplace for cooking but no ingredients. Two women sit, radiating a dejected air, the older barely noticing the younger.

> VOICEOVER NARRATOR
> ¹And for Naomi a kinsman to her husband, a man mighty of valor from the clan of Elimelek and his name was Boaz, meaning "in him is strength."

> RUTH
> ²Let me walk please the field, and let me glean amongst the grains, after whoever I will find favor in his eyes.

> NAOMI
> Walk my daughter.

Ruth gets up and walks out, heading for the barley-fields.

SCENE 2: WATCH ME WALK (Ruth 2:3-18)

EXT: BARLEY FIELDS OF BOAZ—CONTINUOUS

> VOICEOVER NARRATOR
> ³And she walked. And she came and she gleaned in the field after the reapers. And she chanced to chance upon the portion of the field belonging to Boaz who was from the clan of Elimelek. ⁴And behold! Boaz came in from Beth-lehem the house of bread.

> BOAZ
> YHWH be with you!

> REAPERS
> May he bless you—YHWH!

> BOAZ
> *(addressing the young man overseeing the reapers, pointing to Ruth seated near a shelter)*
> ⁵To whom belongs this young woman?

YOUNG MAN

⁶A young woman, a Moabite is she. She returned with Naomi from the field of Moab. ⁷And she said, "Let me glean, please, and I will gather amongst the sheaves after the reapers." And she came and she stood from the morning and until now, this one is resting herself in the house a little.

BOAZ

⁸Hello?! Listen, my daughter. Do not walk to glean in another field and also do not cross over from this one, and here cling to my young women, ⁹keep your eyes in the field in which they are reaping and walk after them. Hello?!, I have ordered the young men to leave from molesting you. And when you get thirsty, and you can walk to the vessels and drink from them which they have drawn—the young men.

¹⁰*Ruth falls on her face and bows down on the land, then addresses Boaz playfully:*

RUTH

Why have I found favor in your eyes to notice me for I am one that is noticed.

BOAZ

¹¹The telling has been told to me everything that you did with your mother-in-law after the death of her husband, and you left your father and your mother and the land of your birth and you walked to a people who you did not know three days ago. ¹²May he make *shalom*—YHWH—your works and may your reward be *shalom* from YHWH the God of Israel whom you have come for refuge under his wings.

RUTH

¹³Let me continue to find favor in your eyes, my lord, for you have comforted me, and for you have spoken

to the heart of your slavegirl, and I am not like one of your slavegirls.

> BOAZ
> [14]At the time of the eats, draw near here and eat from the bread and dip your bit in the vinegar.

> VOICEOVER NARRATOR
> Ruth sat beside the reapers and Boaz passed to her grain, and she ate and she was sated and left some over.

[15]*Ruth gets up to continue gleaning*

> BOAZ
> *(addressing his reapers)*
> Even between sheaves she can glean, and do not cause her any humiliation. [16]And also pulling, pull out for her from the bundles and leave them and she will glean and do not rebuke her.

> VOICEOVER NARRATOR
> [17]And she gleaned in the field until the evening, and she beat out what she had gleaned, and it was, like, an ephah of barley. [18]And she lifted it up and came into the city, and she saw—her mother-in-law—that which she had gleaned, and she brought out and gave to her what was left over after being sated.

SCENE 3: IT WAS WORTH THE WALK (Ruth 2:19-23)

INT: NAOMI'S SMALL DWELLING IN BETHLEHEM—CONTINUOUS

> NAOMI
> [19]Where were you gleaning today and where did you work? Let it be the one who noticed you is blessed!

> VOICEOVER NARRATOR
> And she told her mother-in-law who it was she worked with.

> RUTH
> The name of the man who I worked with today is Boaz.

> NAOMI
> [20]Blessed is he by YHWH who has not taken away his kindness with the living and with the dead. A near relative to us is the man, one of our *go'el* is he!

> RUTH
> [21]Also, for he said to me "with the young men who are with me, cling to them, until when they have finished all the reaping that is for me."

> NAOMI
> *(ironically)*
> [22]Better, my daughter, that you go out with his *young women*, and not let them harass you in another field.

EXT: DRONE VIEW OF RUTH GLEANING IN THE FIELDS THEN RETURNING TO NAOMI'S HOUSE

> VOICEOVER NARRATOR
> [23]And she clung to the young women of Boaz to glean until the end of the reaping of the barely and the reaping of the wheat, and she returned to her mother-in-law.

FADE OUT
    END OF EPISODE 2

EPISODE 3—THE CLING
FADE IN

EXT: DRONE VIEW OF A SMALL DWELLING ON THE OUTSKIRTS OF A SMALL JUDEAN VILLAGE

ROLLUP with text of Ruth 1:1-7 against background music of Jill's Theme (Morricone)

CHARACTERS:
Voiceover Narrator
Naomi/ Mara (Israelite widow of Elimelek)
Ruth (The Moabite)
Boaz (A kinsman of Elimelek, owner of the field of barley)
Extras sleeping at the threshing floor

SCENE 1: HOW TO CLING (Ruth 3:1-5)
INT: NAOMI'S SMALL DWELLING IN BETHLEHEM—CONTINUOUS

The same small, spartan dwelling belonging to Naomi but now the fire is lit and a pot of stew bubbles over it. Naomi and Ruth are sitting together contentedly, gazing into the fire. Naomi stirs and turns suddenly to Ruth.

> NAOMI
> ¹My daughter—hello?! Should I not seek for you a resting place that is good for you? ²Now hello?! Boaz is known to us, the one who you were with his young women. Behold he is a scatterer at the threshing floor of the barley this night. ³And you should wash, and you should anoint, and you should put your mantle on yourself and you should go down to the threshing floor. Do not be known to the man until he is finished eating and drinking. ⁴And it will be in his lying down you know the place where he lies down there and you should come and uncover from his feet and you should lie down and he will tell you what you should do.

RUTH
⁵Everything that you say to me I will do.

SCENE 2: WHERE TO CLING (Ruth 3:6-15)
INT: THRESHING FLOOR IN BETHLEHEM AT NIGHT—CONTINUOUS

Pan over a scene dimly lit of many people carousing, men fondling passing women and so forth. Focus in on Boaz eating and drinking and laughing, then on Ruth waiting near the door in the deeper shadows.

VOICEOVER NARRATOR
⁶And she went down to the threshing floor, and she did, like, everything that she had commanded her—her mother-in-law. ⁷And he ate—Boaz—and he drank and it was good—his heart—and he came to lie down at the end of the grainheap. And she came in secret, and she uncovered from his feet and she lay down. ⁸And it happened in the middle [half] of the night and he was startled—the man—and he turned himself over, and behold! A woman lying from his feet.

BOAZ
⁹Who are you?

RUTH
I am Ruth your maidservant, and you should spread out your wing over your maidservant for a *go'el* are you.

BOAZ
¹⁰Blessed are you to YHWH my daughter. You have made better this last kindness of yours than the first to not go after the choice young men whether poor or rich. ¹¹And now my daughter, do not be afraid. Everything that you say I will do for you, for they are knowing—all at the gate of my people—that a woman of valor are you. ¹²And now (er) truly (er) if a

go'el am I, and also there is a nearer relative than me.
¹³Lodge here tonight and it will be in the morning
if he redeems you, good! Let him redeem, and if
he does not delight to redeem you, I will redeem
you—I—by the life of YHWH. Lie down until the
morning.

VOICEOVER NARRATOR
¹⁴And she lay down from his feet until morning and
she arose before a man could notice his neighbor,
and he could say to let it be known that she came—
the woman—the threshing floor.

BOAZ
¹⁵Bring the garment which is on you and hold it.

VOICEOVER NARRATOR
And she held it, and he measured six barleys and he
set it on her and he went to the city.

EXT: OUTSIDE THE THRESHING FLOOR

Pan out as the dawn begins to break, Boaz heading in one direction and Ruth in the other. Follow Ruth to Naomi's dwelling.

SCENE 3: CLINGING TO HOPE (Ruth 3:16-18)

INT: NAOMI's small dwelling in Bethlehem—continuous

NAOMI
¹⁶Who are you my daughter?

VOICEOVER NARRATOR
And she told to her everything that he did to her—the
man.

RUTH
¹⁷Six barleys—these ones—he gave to me, for he said
"do not return empty to your mother-in-law."

NAOMI

[18]Sit, my daughter, until you know how it will fall out—the matter—for he will not rest—the man—for he will finish the matter today.

FADE OUT

END OF EPISODE 3

EPISODE 4—KINDNESS

FADE IN

EXT: DRONE VIEW OF AN IRON-AGE GATEWAY COMPLEX OF A SMALL JUDEAN VILLAGE

ROLLUP with text of Ruth 1:1-7 against background music of Jill's Theme (Morricone)

CHARACTERS:
Voiceover Narrator
Boaz (A kinsman of Elimelek, owner of the field of barley)
P'loni Almoni
Naomi/ Mara (Israelite widow of Elimelek)
Ruth (The Moabite)
Elders of Bethlehem
Women of Bethlehem

SCENE 1: THE KINDNESS OF BOAZ (Ruth 4:1-18)

EXT: DRONE VIEW OF AN IRON-AGE GATEWAY COMPLEX OF A SMALL JUDEAN VILLAGE, BOAZ AND *P'LONI ALMONI* APPROACHING THE GATE AS NARRATED

> VOICEOVER NARRATOR
> [1]And Boaz went up to the gate and sat down there, and behold the *goʾel* was passing by of whom he had spoken

EXT: IRON-AGE GATEWAY COMPLEX WITH BENCHES AROUND THE EDGES—CONTINUOUS

BOAZ
Turn aside, sit here, "P'loni Almoni"

P'loni Almoni turns aside, and sits beside Boaz.

VOICEOVER NARRATOR
²And he took ten men from the elders of the city

BOAZ
Sit here.

The ten men sit beside Boaz and P'loni Almoni. Boaz turns to P'loni Almoni. Others from the village gradually drift over and form an interested crowd to proceedings.

BOAZ
³The portion of the field which belongs to our brother to Elimelek, she will sell—Naomi—the one returning from the field of Moab. ⁴And I said to myself "I will redeem your ear to say buy in front of the ones sitting and in front of the elders of my people, if you will redeem, redeem! And if no other redeemer, tell me and let me know, for there is no-one except you to redeem and I after you."

P'loni Almoni
I will redeem.

BOAZ
⁵In the day of your acquiring the field from the hand of Naomi, together with Ruth the Moabite, wife of the dead one you will acquire to make stand the name of the dead one over his inheritance.

P'loni Almoni
⁶I am not able to redeem for myself lest I impair my inheritance. Redeem yourself—you—my redemption for I am not able to redeem.

The Scroll of Ruth

> VOICEOVER NARRATOR
> ⁷And this in former times in Israel over the redemption and over the exchange to make stand every word, he drew off—a man—his sandal and gave to his neighbor, and this the testimony in Israel.

> P'loni Almoni
> (to Boaz)
> ⁸Acquire yourself.

P'loni Almoni draws off his sandal.

> BOAZ
> (To the elders and all the people who have gathered to watch)

> ⁹Witnesses you all are this day that I have acquired everything that belonged to Elimelek and everything that belonged to Kilion and Mahlon from the hand of Naomi. ¹⁰'And also Ruth the Moabite, wife of Mahlon, I acquired for myself for a wife to make stand the name of the dead one over his inheritance, and not be cut off the name of the dead one from among his brothers and from the gate of his place. Witnesses are you this day.

> ELDERS AND ALL GATHERED AT THE GATE
> ¹¹Witnesses! And may he give—YHWH—the woman—the one coming to your house—like Rachel and like Leah who built, the two of them, the house of Israel. And do valor in Ephrathah and proclaim the name in Beth-lehem house of bread. ¹²And let it be—your house—like the house of Perez whom she bore—Tamar—to Judah, from the seed that he will give—YHWH—to you from this young woman.

SCENE 2: THE KINDNESS OF YHWH (Ruth 4:13-17)

EXT: DRONE VIEW OF A PROSPEROUS HOUSE, BOAZ AND RUTH ENTERING THE HOUSE HAND IN HAND

> VOICEOVER NARRATOR
> ¹³And he took—Boaz—Ruth and she was for him for a wife, and he went in to her, and he gave—YHWH—to her a pregnancy and she bore a son.

EXT: FRONT OF BOAZ'S HOUSE—CONTINUOUS

Women congregating at the front of the house as Naomi comes out showing them the new-born child.

> WOMEN OF BETH-LEHEM
> (to Naomi)
>
> ¹⁴Blessed be YHWH, who did not deprive you of a *go'el* today! And let it be known—his name—in Israel. ¹⁵And he will be for you for a restorer of life and will sustain your grey hair, for your daughter-in-law who loves you—she bore him—she who is better to you than seven sons.

> VOICEOVER NARRATOR
> ¹⁶And she took—Naomi—the lad and she set him in her lap and she was for him a nurse. ¹⁷And they called for him—the neighboring women—a name:

> WOMEN OF BETH-LEHEM
> Born is a son to Naomi.

> VOICEOVER NARRATOR
> And they called his name Obed which means worshipper. He was the father of Jesse, the father of David, the beloved.

פ

FALLOUT SCRIPT AND CLOSING CREDITS

ROLLUP with text of Ruth 4:18-22 against background music of a triumphant rendition of Jill's Theme (Morricone)

[18]And these are the generations of Perez: Perez begat Chezron. [19]And Chezron begat Ram; and Ram begat Amminadab. [20]And Amminadab begat Nachshon; and Nachshon begat Salmon. [21]And Salmon begat Boaz; and Boaz begat Obed. [22]And Obed begat Jesse, and Jesse begat David.

EXT: DRONE VIEW OF A YOUNG LAD WATCHING OVER SHEEP, PRACTISING WITH HIS SLING

FADE OUT

Commentary on Ruth

In providing a brief commentary on Ruth from the perspective of Biblical Performance Criticism, I am approaching the script in the role of Director. A director must know who her *characters* are, including their backstory, and how their words and actions can be engaged to portray believable performances.

Elsewhere I have discussed the nature of "ready-mades" in biblical performances as "any word or phrase that relies on the audience's stored knowledge and expectations in order to engender elements of surprise or disquiet when heard in new or unexpected situations" (2020, 86–87). In this commentary, I discuss "ready-mades" as *correlations* between Ruth's story and other stories in the Hebrew Bible. Past and present audiences of the miniseries of Ruth would typically have these implicit or explicit links within their own stored knowledge.

A director should also be aware of gaps or inconsistencies in the plot and decide how to portray such *conundrums* in the performed script. Three such questions are addressed below: What happened on the threshing floor? What happens with the laws? What happened to Ruth?

Characters

The major characters in this scroll are Naomi, Ruth, and Boaz. Minor characters include Orpah, the youth overseer, and P'loni Almoni. Extras include Elimelek, Mahlon, Chilion, the reapers, and the townsfolk (women of Bethlehem, elders). Offstage are the Voiceover Narrator and YHWH. As is typical in biblical narratives, characters are determined by what they say and what they do. In this story there is a particular focus on the names of the characters that lends significance to their role.

Naomi. Naomi is the first and last woman named in the story, preceded by her husband's name and followed by the list of male ancestors leading from Perez to David. When a child is born from the marriage of Boaz and Ruth, it is Naomi who is acknowledged and congratulated. Due to this prominence, some commentators suggest that it is Naomi who is the main character in the story.

Naomi's first speech while returning to Jerusalem (1:8-9) shows her kindness and solicitude for her daughters-in-law. She urges them to return to their own mothers, probably assuming that they would have a greater chance of future security in their own homeland of Moab than as foreigners in Israel. Their mutual kisses and weeping indicate an affectionate and close relationship that is borne out by Ruth's determination to "cling" to her mother-in-law.

The second speech of Naomi (1:11-13), where she tries again to convince her daughters-in-law of the wisdom of her advice, betrays a sarcastic edge that is even more apparent when she meets the women of the town upon her return. She alludes to the practice of levirate marriage, in which a brother would take on his widowed sister-in-law in order to provide offspring for the dead husband. Naomi points out the impossibility of providing further sons for the two women. After Orpah turns back, Naomi tries a third time to persuade Ruth (1:15), but she is silent in the face of Ruth's impassioned speech of commitment. Whether the silence is one of frustration or resignation is hard to tell, but in her final speech of the first episode (1:20-21), Naomi refers to the "bitterness," "emptiness," and "evil" with which she is returning to Bethlehem, so it is possible she is implying that Ruth's unacknowledged presence with her is included in that misfortune. If this assumption is correct, it is clear that the relationship later returns to their earlier affection and is obvious to others around. When Boaz meets Ruth, he has heard of her high level of commitment to Naomi (2:11-12), and the townswomen at the end remind Naomi of the worth of Ruth as "better than seven sons" (4:15).

Naomi is the only character who refers specifically to her own name, asking the townswomen to call her "Mara" (bitter)—the opposite of sweet. She refers several times to YHWH, indicating an active, if troubled, faith. Her return from Moab is prompted by hearing of YHWH visiting his people, yet in her speech on return she indicates that she is the recipient of divine curse rather than blessing. Her reference to the divine as *Shaddai* in this speech is another indication of her sarcasm: *Shaddai* (Almighty) can be translated "the sufficient one," but the Almighty has not been sufficient for her. The birth of the child at the end of episode 4 prompts the townswomen to pronounce a blessing on Naomi, and we assume she also recognizes the hand of YHWH in that event. In the second episode, Naomi recognizes divine providence when hearing that Ruth has met with the kinsman Boaz, but she is not content to leave the situation in divine hands alone. It is her plan that Ruth follows when making a daring appearance on the threshing floor, and its details reveal a calculated strategy pointing to a cunning and imaginative woman (3:1-4). Ruth is to make herself attractive but not reveal her identity until Boaz is off his guard: sated and prone. While her instruction to Ruth to uncover his feet and lie down and wait for him to "tell you what you should do" suggests that she is putting Ruth at great risk, the beginning of this speech indicates that her motivation is for Ruth's security and well-being. This concern had already been shown when Naomi advised Ruth to cling to the young women in the fields rather than the young men as Boaz had suggested (2:22). It seems Naomi trusted the virtue of Boaz himself but not those in his employ.

Following the threshing floor scene, Naomi's role diminishes until after the birth of Obed. She seems content to step back and allow Boaz to negotiate Ruth's and her own future. Her evident pleasure at the arrival of Obed perhaps surpassed the usual grandmotherly affection by implying that the child replaced the two sons who had been prematurely lost to her.

Ruth. Ruth's appearance is never explicitly described, but she is referred to as a young woman and addressed as "my daughter" by both Naomi and Boaz. The beginning of episode 3 where she bathes, dresses, and anoints herself prior to going down to the threshing floor implies that she was an *attractive* young woman. In over half of the twelve times her name is used in the scroll, the appellation "the Moabite" is added, ensuring that her foreign status is continually referenced. There is no consensus on the meaning of her name. Robert Gordis suggests that "Ruth" means "willingness" or "desire" (1986, 299), appropriately descriptive of Ruth's character as it forms a contrast to Orpah who has turned her back on her mother-in-law. Robert Alter points to two Hebrew roots that may underlie the proper name: *r-w-h* suggesting "well-watered" or "fertile" or *ré'ut*, "friendship" (2019b, 625). Given the symbolic aspect of many of the other names in this scroll, I am inclined to accept the second of Alter's suggestions, with "friendship" appropriately pointing to her character.

Initially Ruth and Orpah are united in their action and speech, both accompanying Naomi as she sets out to return to Bethlehem, and both saying, "Surely with you we will return to your people" (1:10). But Ruth's insistence on remaining after Orpah turns back and her moving speech of commitment show her to be especially resolute and loyal in character. The poetic parallelism of her speech indicates a lifelong commitment, ending with death and burial, and perhaps is the reason this speech is often used for wedding vows. My literal translation of the Hebrew prepositions results in unusual but effective expression:

> Wherever you walk I will walk,
> and inever you lodge, I will lodge,
> your people my people
> and your gods my gods,
> inever you die, I die,
> and there I will be buried. (1:16-17a)

Ruth's ready adoption of Naomi's God is revealed by her swearing by YHWH in completion of this vow (1:17b).

The loyalty of Ruth is evident in her concern to provide food for Naomi and in her obedience to Naomi's instructions. Her subservient but well-mannered interactions with Boaz portray a woman of gracious character, aware of her low status in the social hierarchy but also willing to take risks to secure a good future for herself and her mother-in-law. Significantly, she is not portrayed as conversing with any character other than Naomi and Boaz. As already mentioned, Ruth is aware of Israelite law and prepared to act within its boundaries: gleaning in the fields as is the right of the widow and the sojourner, caring for the needy within her own family, and doing her part in ensuring that the family property and bloodline is redeemed.

Like Naomi, Ruth is a woman who is clever enough to subtly manipulate events to her advantage. When asking permission from Naomi to glean in the fields of Bethlehem (2:2), she is hoping to attract the attention of someone powerful enough to help them. It may be no "chance" that she "chanced" upon a field belonging to Boaz (2:3), since the beginning of episode 2 names Boaz as a near relative of Naomi. In their first encounter, Boaz pronounces a blessing on Ruth that she might find refuge under the "wings" of YHWH (2:12). When they meet again on the threshing floor, Ruth invites Boaz to spread out his wing over her (3:9), no doubt consciously echoing his earlier words and planting the idea that he could be the instrument of YHWH's blessing. When originally introduced to Boaz, she is referred to as a "young woman" (*na'arāh*), the feminine equivalent of the "young man" (*na'ar*) overseeing the reapers (2:6). But in the conversation on the threshing floor Boaz calls her a "woman of valor" (*'ēšet ḥayil*, 3:11), indicating that she has risen in his eyes to be equal to him, the one who is introduced in the scroll as a "man mighty of valor" (*'îš gibbor ḥayil*, 2:1). In episode 3 Ruth had done everything her mother-in-law had commanded her and was willing to do whatever Boaz told her to do, but the tables were turned when Boaz said to her, "everything that you say I will do for you" (3:11)! It seems he had picked up her subtle hints.

The threshing floor scene is where Ruth is treated as a woman of valor, an equal; but she returns to being referred to as "the Moabite" in episode 4 as Boaz negotiates her future, claims her, marries her, and impregnates her. At that point she all but disappears from the scroll. The indirect reference to Ruth by the Bethlehem townswomen as "your daughter-in-law who loves you" (4:15) is her final mention in the scroll as Naomi claims Ruth's son and the litany of male descendants from Perez unfolds. We will return to the disappearance of Ruth the Moabite again in the "Conundrums" section of this chapter.

Boaz. The introduction of Boaz as "a mighty man of valor from the clan of Elimelek" (2:1) tells us what to expect with this character, and we are not let down. The name likely comes from a combination of the preposition b^e and the adjective '*az* meaning "in him strength," a hypothesis that is supported by the fact that one of the two large columns constructed at the porch of the temple of Solomon was called Boaz (1 Kgs 7:21).

Boaz is a man of means and good standing in Bethlehem, evidence by his fields being reaped by multiple young men and women and an overseer who had charge of the other employees as well as his commanding presence at the gate of the town in episode 4. Although never hinted at in the story, his status and evident age suggest that Boaz was already a married man (or perhaps a widower himself). Contemplating this possibility removes some of the "romance" often attributed to the narrative but does not diminish his kindness or courtesy towards others. He addresses each interlocutor cordially, whether it be the servant, the reapers, the elders, or the stranger in their midst. The only deviation from this characteristic politeness is when he addresses *P'loni Almoni*, as discussed further below. His two long conversations with Ruth are especially considerate, ensuring that nothing is done to tarnish her reputation. While in the fields (2:8-14) he suggests that she cling to his young women and assures her he has let his young men know that they are not to touch her. When at the threshing floor (3:9-15) he ensures her safety through the night by inviting her to stay at his feet, then sends her on her way at dawn before she can be recognized. On both occasions, moreover, he is generous towards her, allowing her to eat and drink from his supplies such that she has surplus left over and to glean amongst the sheaves and not just in the areas normally reserved for the destitute. Before sending her home from the threshing floor he fills her mantle with barley, ensuring that she does not "return" to Naomi "empty" and thus signaling the reversal of fortunes for the widow who had "returned" to Bethlehem "empty."

By sending Ruth away from the threshing floor unnoticed, Boaz was able to retain the advantage in his conversation with *P'loni Almoni*. Unusually in Hebrew expression, the name Boaz comes at the beginning of episode 4 (usually the verb precedes the subject). At the end of episode 3 Naomi had commented that Boaz would not rest until he had settled the matter that day (3:18), and in fulfilment of this prediction he is immediately present and taking steps to bring about the redemption needed by the two widows (4:1).

Boaz is another character whose actions reveal planning, cunning, and resolution. He sits at the gate, the entry to the town where people would gather and decisions would be made. The arrival of *P'loni Almoni* ("behold the *go'el* was passing by of whom he had spoken," 4:1) is presented as another act of providence, but it was undoubtedly a calculated guess that he would pass by at such a frequented area. Using abrupt imperative verbs and the rude name *P'loni Almoni* (see below), Boaz calls the *go'el* over then ensures that there are witnesses for the legal transaction as he sets out the situation before him. At first he speaks only of the portion of the field belonging to Elimelek and sold by Naomi, offering first right of refusal to the more eligible *go'el* (4:3-4), and only after it is accepted does he add the detail of the Moabite widow who comes with the deal (4:5). *P'loni Almoni* hastily retracts his offer to redeem, leaving Boaz exactly where he had planned to be. He immediately affirms his right of redemption in front of the witnesses, stressing again that it is Ruth *the Moabite* he is willing to marry (4:9-10). This confident claim evokes from the elders a blessing on his house that likens this foreign wife to Rachel and Leah, the mothers of Israel (4:11-12).

P'loni Almoni. The name that Boaz uses to address the *go'el* is a phrase used in two other places in the Hebrew Bible, in contexts where it is obvious clarity is not necessary or desirable.[45] As a rhyming moniker, it functions as a nonsense term conveying that this is a person of little worth. The NRSV translation "friend" does not do justice to the original Hebrew, given that in Rabbinic literature it is claimed that this person does not deserve to be remembered by name due to his lack of piety in not accepting legal responsibility due to him. His initial eagerness to redeem the land followed by a quick withdrawal when he knew another wife was involved certainly portrays him as worthless. Kandy Queen-Sutherland suggests translating the phrase "phony baloney" in delightful replication of the Hebrew rhyme, commenting "P'loni Almoni is not a proper name but a rhyming, nonsense moniker that is at the least a slight and moves toward an insult" (2016, 148). The Hebrew in transliterated form has been retained in this script.

The rabbinic source *Midrash Ruth Rabba* suggests that the reticence of *P'loni Almoni* in taking on Ruth as a wife was out of fear rather than lack of piety (Alter 2019b, 636). The motif of a bad-luck wife whose husbands mysteriously die was not uncommon in ancient Israel, as evidenced by the parallel story of Judah and Tamar (Gen 38) and the postexilic novella of Tobit.

Orpah. The other Moabite daughter-in-law is rather unfairly called Orpah, a name similar to the Hebrew word for nape (*'oref*), because she turned her head back towards Moab and left Naomi on the road. As we noticed earlier, she and Ruth were in accord in their grief and initial resolution to remain with Naomi, but Orpah should be commended rather than condemned for obeying the exhortation of her mother-in-law.

Young Man. One of the few characters without a proper name, the young man who stands over the reapers nonetheless has more than a supporting role in the plot of episode 2. His lengthy speech in response to the question of Boaz about Ruth (2:6-7) shifts the point of view for the audience from Ruth (the outsider) to the Bethlehemites (insiders). Though he calls Ruth a "young woman"—the feminine counterpart to himself—he quickly adds "a Moabite" who returned from Moab with Naomi. He says nothing of her relationship to Naomi but describes her as gleaning *and gathering* and now resting.[46] It is possible that the young man is casting her in a negative light in his description of her (Grossman 2007). The subsequent singling out of her for special treatment by Boaz would only serve to heighten any such prejudice. Whether or not this can be assumed, the words of the young man do not dissuade Boaz from his kind treatment of Ruth but rather confirm the positive rumors that Boaz had already heard about her.

Townsfolk. The *women* of Bethlehem frame the story, suggesting that, at heart, this is a woman's tale. Together with the elders and others gathered at the gate, however, these extras in the miniseries are important as cues for the audience. They witness and respond to surprising events and draw parallels to other stories of their people. Their most significant role is to draw YHWH into the events, calling on YHWH to bless Boaz, Ruth, and Naomi as they come together to form a new household and to take their place in the history of the Israelite nation (4:11-12, 14-15).

Elimelek, Mahlon, Chilion. The husband and sons of Naomi are referenced but never appear in the miniseries. Elimelek (meaning "my God is king"), although not appearing elsewhere in the Hebrew Bible, is a name that could have been common in ancient Israel or Canaan.[47] The names of the sons, on the other hand, are "manifestly schematic names pointing to the fate of their bearers and would not have been used in reality" (Alter 2019b, 625). There is no narratorial condemnation of the Moabite wives Orpah and Ruth who were taken by Mahlon and Chilion while the family was residing in Moab. It is only in episode 4 that it becomes clear that Ruth was the wife of Mahlon.

The meaning of Mahlon is "sick," which is perhaps appropriate since it is his name that will not be cut off due to the levirate marriage of Ruth with Boaz, while Chilion is truly annihilated.

Voiceover Narrator. In discussing the narrator as a character, I am reminded of Ellen van Wolde's observation that the narrator plays a lesser role in this scroll than in other biblical narratives (1997, 16). Usually a biblical narrator is omniscient and matter-of-fact, as is the case here. Occasionally a narrator offers value judgments on the events being narrated, but no judgment is made in this scroll. There is one aside to the audience explaining a former practice of sandal exchange to seal an agreement. Otherwise the role of the voiceover narrator is to provide crucial information that is not conveyed in dialogue, such as the relationship between Boaz and Naomi and the connection between the child born to Ruth and David the king of the Israelites. The narrator has a critical role in episode 3 where there are no other witnesses to the events of the threshing floor. On three occasions the narrator uses the particle *hinneh* ("behold!") to draw special attention to events: when Boaz comes to the field where Ruth happens to be gleaning (2:4); when Boaz awakes on the threshing floor and finds a woman at his feet (3:8); and when the *goʾel* happens to pass by where Boaz is waiting (4:1). These particles indicate the narrator's interest and the desire for the audience to remain engaged in the series. They also implicitly point to the role of YHWH in the story, which is often the responsibility of a biblical narrator.

YHWH. As we have noted, YHWH has only a behind-the-scenes role in this miniseries. Naomi attributes her bad fortune, described in the backstory, to the hand of YHWH/*Shaddai*. There is ambiguity as to whether other events in the drama occur at the hand of YHWH, or by chance, or due to careful planning on the part of the main characters. A good miniseries will keep the audience guessing.

In the view of the other characters in this miniseries, YHWH is the bringer of both misfortune and blessing. As is typical in the portrayal of YHWH in biblical texts, blessing comes in the form of fertility, whether by growth of crops or childbirth. YHWH is also described as a restorer of life and provider of shalom. Unlike most other instances in the Hebrew Bible, in this scroll it is the human protagonists who offer *ḥesed* ("kindness") rather than, or perhaps on behalf of, YHWH.

Correlations

Explicit references and implicit literary motifs link the story of Ruth to other parts of the Hebrew Bible. The most obvious of these are the link made between Ruth and David and the parallels to the story of Tamar and Judah.

Ruth and David. The last word in the scroll of Ruth is "David," suggesting that the entire story is pointing towards his advent. I have commented elsewhere on the significance of the final word in a biblical script, leaving the audience with a lasting impression (2012, 157). The style of the genealogy of ten generations ending with David (4:18-22) is so different from the rest of the scroll that it may be a later appendage, perhaps in order to justify the inclusion of this "women's story" in the biblical canon. In my "miniseries" representation of the scroll of Ruth I leave these verses of genealogy to the closing credits, but I propose that a lasting visual image of the king to come remains with the viewer in parallel manner to the written script ending with the name of the great Israelite king. It is true that these verses include fathers and sons from Perez to David and do not mention the mothers. Any reader or viewer familiar with the stories of Israel, however, will be aware of the hint of scandal that lies behind the stories of Perez, Boaz, and David. It is fascinating that the New Testament opens with a genealogy extending from Abraham to Jesus that writes Tamar, Ruth, and "the wife of Uriah" (Bathsheba) back into the family tree while leaving out more significant matriarchs such as Sarah and Rachel (Matt 1:3; 1:5; 1:6).

Ruth and Tamar. The "hint of scandal" (Brenner 1993, 80) is not the only parallel linking the scroll of Ruth with the story of Tamar (Gen 38). Both are non-Israelite women married to men from the tribe of Judah. Both are widowed before they have children. Both seem to be aware of the obligation of male relatives of their dead husbands in relation to the Israelite law of levirate marriage. Both are instructed by their Israelite parent-in-law to return to their own family homes. Both take action to attract the attention of an older male relative by disguising themselves in different clothing. Both approach the man surreptitiously in public places (Tamar with a veil, Ruth under cover of darkness). Both are required to wait for the man to act on the situation. Both are ultimately commended by these men as women of good character.

The difference between the stories is the point at which the older relative recognizes the woman. Since Boaz is aware of her identity moments after he finds her at his feet at the threshing floor, he cooperates with her in keeping the meeting secret. In consequence, the blessing of the elders on the following day is highly ironic: "Let it be—your house—like the house of Perez whom she bore—Tamar—to Judah, from the seed that he will give—YHWH—to you from this young woman." It makes explicit the allusions to Tamar and Judah that have been present throughout the episodes.

Ruth and the Matriarchs. The blessing of the elders also mentioned Rachel and Leah: "And may he give—YHWH—the woman—the one coming to your house—like Rachel and like Leah who built, the two of them, the house of Israel." Rachel and Leah were the wives of Jacob who, along with their maidservants Bilhah and Zilpah, mothered the twelve sons of Jacob who would become the tribes of Israel (Gen 29:31–30:20; 35:16-18).

Sarah (wife of Abraham) and Rebekah (wife of Isaac) are not mentioned by name in the scroll of Ruth, but both can be inferred, nonetheless. As the beginning of the encounter between Boaz and Ruth in episode 2, Boaz offers an invitation to Ruth: "And when you get thirsty, and you can walk to the vessels and drink from them which they have drawn—the young men." The verb *ša'av*, translated here as "drawn," is only used for drawing water from a well. It is used in the story of Rebekah, who offers to draw water for the camels of Abraham's servant who has been sent to her family to secure a bride for Isaac (Gen 24:20). Rebekah's offer of hospitality at a well that partially prompts her betrothal to Isaac is thus consciously evoked and reversed in this scene, where Boaz offers water to Ruth that has been drawn by his young men. As the encounter continues in episode 2 Boaz says to Ruth, "you left your father (*'av*) and your mother, and the land of your birth (*'erets moladt*) and you walked (*lalekhet*) to a people who you did not know" (2:11). There is a noticeable echo of God's command to Abram, who is told to "walk (*lalekhet*) from the land of your birth (*'erets moladt*) and from the house of your father (*'av*) to the land I will show you" (Gen 12:1).[48] Abram was accompanied by Sarai his wife, who was also leaving the land of her birth and the house of her father. A correlation is thus made between Ruth and each of the Israelite matriarchs.

Ruth and the "Woman of Valor" (Prov 31:10-22). The significance of the correlation between Ruth and the *'ešet ḥayil* ("woman of valor") introduced in Prov 31:10 is more obvious in the Hebrew Bible than in the Septuagint and Christian Old Testament. This is because in the Hebrew Bible the scroll of Ruth follows directly after Proverbs. Proverbs ends with an acrostic poem celebrating a "woman of valor": a woman described as precious, trustworthy, a provider, a hard worker, diligent, strong, an independent businesswoman, generous, dignified, wise, one who practises *ḥesed* (kindness), and a fearer of YHWH. It is such a thorough description that it could be intended to be a description of the personification of Wisdom herself. When Boaz recognizes Ruth at the threshing floor in episode 3 he calls her a "woman of valor" (3:12). This word is used in 230 verses in the Hebrew Bible, but it is only in these two instances and one other verse in Proverbs where a woman is the subject of the adjective.[49] Even in the arrangement of biblical texts in the Christian Old Testament, then, a correlation is evident between Ruth and the ideal woman.

Ruth and Esther. In recent scholarship on the *Megillot* there has been an interest in intertextual connections or seams that give evidence for the history of growth of the collection (see Stone 2013). Kandy Queen-Sutherland (2016, 5–18) has set out many of the correlations between Ruth and Esther, which I will merely summarise here.

These are the only two books in the Hebrew Bible named for women. Despite the fact that both books end with short sections that ignore the female protagonists, their names are front and center for readers of the Hebrew Bible and Protestant Old Testament.[50] Both women are seen as "outsiders" in their context: the Moabite Ruth in the town of Bethlehem of Judah, and the Israelite Esther in the foreign nation of Persia. Each story has a worthless character standing in the way of the women's security: Haman in Esther and *P'loni Almoni* in Ruth. In both stories the women protagonists act with decisiveness and courage to secure their future. The usual role of women as child-bearers is usurped in these two stories. Children are ignored altogether in Esther and, while critical to the purpose of the story of Ruth, are only marginal to the portrayal of Ruth. She commits herself to Naomi initially, thus rejecting the possibility of motherhood, and when her child is born it is Naomi who is named as the one who will bring up the child. Finally, while there is a long line of biblical women who emerge as heroes in their stories, the singling out of Ruth and Esther as appellations for these two scrolls attests to the honor they enjoy in the Israelite traditions.

Ruth and the Postexilic Community. If, indeed, this scroll was written after the return from exile, there are clues in the story that make it particularly apposite for a postexilic audience. The book of Deuteronomy includes several chapters warning the Israelites of the perils of exile should they refuse to obey the commandments and keep the covenant. One of these threats is that they will find no "resting place" (Deut 28:65): "Among those nations you shall find no ease, no resting place (*manoaḥ*) for the sole of your foot." Twice Naomi uses this word to express her hope for her daughter-in-law (1:9; 3:1), and at the end of the story it is evident that this wish has been fulfilled. Another "exile" word in the Hebrew Bible is the verb *galah* with a basic meaning of "uncovering" or "removing" but that is often translated "to go into exile." When Naomi instructs Ruth to *galah* the feet of Boaz, another echo of the experience of exile would be conveyed to the audience.

Conundrums
What happened on the threshing floor? (Ruth 3:6-15). Once when delivering a sermon on the book of Ruth, I set out the situation as follows:

> Initially Naomi and Ruth survived on their gleanings, but since this arrangement would only last until the end of the harvest, they devised a scheme which brought the issue of levirate marriage to the attention of the owner of the fields—who also happened to be Naomi's kinsman. The details of this scheme are open to speculation: in fact, one commentary that I consulted warned against elaborating on the incident in a sermon, for fear of embarrassing the listeners. I've got you interested, now, haven't I? You might have to go home and read the rest of the book! However it happened, Ruth managed to draw attention to herself and secure the promise of Boaz's protection, and the way the story is told indicates that God's hand was in this union.

"However it happened," as it happens, has been a topic of much speculation in commentaries and essays on this book. The main question is whether sexual intercourse between Boaz and Ruth took place on the threshing floor. To some extent the possibility of sexual activity has already been raised by the use of the strong verbs *nagaʿ* ("molest"), *kalam* ("humiliate"), and *gaʿar* ("harass") in episode 2.

Some argue that when Ruth is instructed to "uncover the feet" of Boaz, it is well known that "feet" is a euphemism for a penis in Hebrew (van Wolde 1997, 22),[51] while others find the suggestion "highly dubious" (Alter 2019b, 632). Nonetheless, the verbs *bôʾ* ("enter"), *šākav* ("lie"), *gālah* ("uncover"), and *yādaʿ* ("know") *are* used frequently in connection to sexual activity.

Naomi tells Ruth that Boaz is a *zoreh* ("scatterer"). This is the Hebrew participle of the verb that means to sow seed. It seems significant that at the end of the episode Boaz sends Ruth home from the threshing floor with a garment full of grain. The innuendo behind this term becomes obvious in episode 4 when the word is used again as part of the blessing pronounced by the elders—this time explicitly referring to the production of offspring: "And let it be—your house—like the house of Perez whom she bore—Tamar—to Judah, from the seed (*zeraʿ*) that he will give—YHWH—to you from this young woman." Some difficulty has arisen from in the phrase "And she came in secret, and she uncovered from his feet and she lay down" (3:7). The lack of object marker that one would expect in the Hebrew means it is not clear what was uncovered—if it was the feet of Boaz that were uncovered, we would expect to see the direct object marker before the word for "feet." A parallel text in Ezekiel 16 raises the possibility that Ruth uncovered herself. My translation has retained some of the ambiguity that may have been intentional in the original story.

In the exchange between Ruth and Boaz, Ruth refers to herself as *ʾamātekā* ("maidservant"), using a different term to how she was described in episode 2—there she was a *naʿarāh* ("young woman") and *šipḥāh* ("slave-girl"). Her self-reference in this episode is suggestive of her being a different type of woman than the one he had met. At the same time, she invites him to "spread his wing" over her, undoubtedly reminding him of the blessing he had offered her earlier but perhaps also delicately suggesting that its metaphorical sense of marriage would be in order. In response, Boaz commends her for not going after *baḥûrîm* ("choice young men")—a word for young men based on the verb *bḥr* ("to choose").

Small details noticed when translating this section are also suggestive of activity that is only hinted at: unnecessary particles in the speech of Boaz in verse 12, here translated as verbal fillers, suggest that he could be directed to act as if put on the spot and was rapidly planning how to act:

> And now (er) truly (er) if a *goʾel* am I, and also there is a nearer relative than me. Lodge here tonight and it will be in the morning if he redeems you, good! Let him redeem, and if he does not delight to redeem you, I will redeem you—I—by the life of YHWH. Lie down until the morning.

Another lack of an expected particle in verse 14, this time a preposition, raises more double *entendre*, especially for a contemporary audience who is familiar with another use of the verb "come":

> And she lay down from his feet until morning and she arose before a man could notice his neighbor, and he could say to let it be known that she came—the woman—the threshing floor.

Although it is rarely seen in English translations, it seems significant that Boaz and Naomi both ask the same question of Ruth: "who are you?" (4:9,

16). Boaz's question is understandable, as he has been startled by a woman he does not recognize in the middle of the night. Naomi is likely asking "are you now Mrs. Boaz?" in a subtle reference to events that may have taken place. Rather than a verbal response, the voiceover narrator tells us that Ruth "told to her everything that he did to her—the man" (4:16).

One of the text-critical matters that Hebrew Bible exegetes must learn to interpret is called *ketib* ("written")-*qere* ("read") problems. These problems are identified with square brackets in the Hebrew text, indicating where the Masoretic scribes transmitted the tradition as they had received it (*ketib*) but included an alternative to be read out loud when the text was recited (*qere*). The third chapter of Ruth, episode 3 above, is replete with such *ketib-qere* issues, indicating the problematic nature of the material for text and expression as well as interpretation! For example, in the *ketib* version of Naomi's instructions to Ruth, the verbs are in first-person singular ("I will do . . .") but the *qere* version is second-person singular ("you should do . . ."). This confusion raises the question of who will be doing the seducing of Boaz at the threshing floor (Exum, 2012)!

At the very least, ambiguity exists in this episode that "teasingly hint[s] at an erotic experience" (Alter 2019b, 632) and "makes the sexual or erotic atmosphere of the threshing floor tangible" (van Wolde 1997, 22). The script of the scroll of Ruth retains this suggestiveness and leaves much of "what happened" to the imagination of the viewer. In an actual televised performance, dim lighting and soft focus would contribute to the ambiguity inherent in the original story portrayed in the scroll.

What happens with the laws? It is somewhat ironic that a book that is read during a festival celebrating the Law relies on the creative interpretation, manipulation, and improvisation of the Law to achieve its purpose. The levirate law, so central to this story, provides for a widow by stipulating that her brother-in-law take her as a wife and raise children in the name of her dead husband. Ruth had no brother-in-law to fulfil this duty, but creative reinterpretation of the law by Naomi and Ruth opened the possibility of having an older male relative in the family fulfil the role.[52] Such a possibility had evidently not occurred to Boaz himself, despite his obvious admiration for Ruth in episode 2. It was Ruth's invitation to Boaz to "spread your wing" that opened his eyes to the possibility.

Redemption of land by a *go'el*, another law referenced in this story, has also been improvised for the sake of the story. According to Leviticus 25, the right of redemption took place in the Jubilee year, but in the scroll of Ruth it was practised as soon as the male kinsmen were aware of the land that had been sold out of the family. Moreover, it seems to be Boaz who equates the redemption law with the levirate law, pointing out to *P'loni Almoni* that the two go hand in hand. Even if this were so, Ellen van Wolde (1997, 22) points out that since it is Elimelek's land that is being redeemed, the widow that *P'loni Almoni* would be obliged to marry would be Naomi! Thus, Boaz uses the law but transforms it slightly to achieve his own ends. He has been such a sympathetic character in the story, in contrast to the hapless *P'loni Almoni*, that the final result is pleasing to both the onstage audience (as evidenced by the blessings pronounced by the elders and the townswomen) and the contemporary audience.

A final improvisation of the Torah concerns the sandal. The Deuteronomic law states,

> When brothers reside together, and one of them dies and has no son, the wife of the deceased shall not be married outside the family to a stranger. Her husband's brother shall go in to her, taking her in marriage, and performing the duty of a husband's brother to her, and the firstborn whom she bears shall succeed to the name of the deceased brother, so that his name may not be blotted out of Israel. But if the man has no desire to marry his brother's widow, then his brother's widow shall go up to the elders at the gate and say, "My husband's brother refuses to perpetuate his brother's name in Israel; he will not perform the duty of a husband's brother to me." Then the elders of his town shall summon him and speak to him. If he persists, saying, "I have no desire to marry her," then his brother's wife shall go up to him in the presence of the elders, pull his sandal off his foot, spit in his face, and declare, "This is what is done to the man who does not build up his brother's house." Throughout Israel his family shall be known as "the house of him whose sandal was pulled off." (Deut 25:5-10)

Of the twenty-two occurrences of the word in the Hebrew Bible, most either refer to literal footwear or have the symbolic meaning of exclusion as in the Deuteronomy 25 passage. Several times, for example, the word is translated "shut out." The sandal symbolism in the scroll of Ruth is quite different since it is used in a positive transaction. When the narrator explains an ancient practice for which there is no other support in biblical traditions, it may be better understood as an "improvisation" of the Deuteronomic law.

What happens to Ruth? It seems odd that the character Ruth is absent from both the beginning and the end of the scroll of Ruth. Ellen van Wolde (1997, 9) concludes from this observation that the story is being told from the perspective of "the ongoing life of the Judahites." A "man from Judah, his wife and the two sons of his" leave Bethlehem at a time of famine and the remnant of the family returns to Judah and reestablishes life successfully. Such a perspective would be especially relevant to a postexilic audience. The tribe of Judah survives, even thrives, despite hardship and exile. The scroll ends with reference to David and, according to the biblical story, a descendant of David was there to take leadership in the restored community in the Persian era.[53]

It is true, however, that this man and his sons swiftly disappear also, and the story becomes focused on the women of Judah along with a Moabite. In many ways, this truly is a woman's story. As we have seen, Naomi is a major character and the Bethlehemite townswomen are present and vocal in episodes 1 and 4. At the end of episode 1 there is no acknowledgement of Ruth by the townswomen. Although the townswomen *do* refer to her as Naomi's daughter-in-law in episode 4, Ruth continues to be marginalized. It is the townswomen who name the child resulting from the union of Ruth and Boaz, and the name they choose (Obed, "worshipper") brings the focus squarely back to the issue of Israelite faith that underlies all of the books in the Hebrew Bible. While Ruth takes center stage in episodes 2 and 3, subtly manoeuvring events through the powerful male figure of the story, once she becomes part of Boaz's household in episode 4, she all but vanishes with attention returning to Naomi, of whom the townswomen announce, "born is a son to *Naomi*." Ruth is included in the blessings the townsfolk pronounce over Boaz and Naomi, but not by name. For the elders she is "the woman coming to your house . . . the young woman," and for the townswomen she is "your daughter-in-law." As van Wolde has suggested (1997, 28), it may be that it is the "foreigner" who disappears from the scroll, since once she is married to Boaz she is fully assimilated into the community of Israel.[54] As we noted at the outset, it is Ruth the proselyte who is lauded at Shavuot, the festival that is the focus for this scroll.

The way that Ruth the Moabite ultimately becomes marginalized in the scroll of Ruth raises the question of the treatment of the refugee and stranger, the focus of the final section in this chapter.

Connections with Ruth

When Ruth first speaks to Boaz, she asks, "Why have I found favor in your eyes to notice me for I am one that is noticed?" (2:10). The NRSV renders this question "why have I found favor in your sight, that you should take notice of me, when I am a foreigner?" but my translation reflects the common root *nkr* that underlies the key words. This literal translation highlights a very real issue, that foreigners are noticed because they are *noticeable*, they are different, they stand out. The scroll of Ruth accentuates this difference by referring to Ruth as "the Moabite" throughout the narrative until she marries Boaz and loses her individual identity. Jean-Pierre Ruiz points out, "the repeated emphasis on Ruth's Moabite heritage underscores an ambivalence toward immigrants that is by no means limited to the pages of the Bible" (2018, 17).

As Ruiz implies, the ancient story of Ruth has connections with our own world. Forced migration and the plight of refugees are amongst the most pressing issues of our time. Conflicts, poverty, and natural disasters due to changing climate patterns are all circumstances that result in individuals seeking refuge in other lands or opportunities for migration. In many places, however, such individuals are vilified and removed of their individual identity. Their plight becomes a political hot potato with governments scrambling to find "solutions" to the "immigration problem."[55] In my own Australian context, politicians have used rhetoric such as "illegal arrivals" and the three-word slogan "stop the boats" to their political advantage even whilst acknowledging that it is a fundamental human right to seek asylum. Most Australians would consider their country to be a place where justice and human rights are upheld, but the nation of Australia is now regularly denounced by the annual Amnesty International Country Report for a harsh offshore detention regime and indefinite detention policies for asylum seekers.[56] The COVID-19 crisis around the world has further exacerbated the predicament of displaced persons, since the first casualties of economic downturns are temporary or casual labor, often the only work options for non-citizens.

This quotation from the website of the United Nations Refugee Agency (UNHCR) on the plight of women highlights the relevance of a story of two widows seeking refuge:

> In some societies, women and girls face discrimination and violence every day . . . In times of displacement, this problem escalates. Women and girls make up about 50% of any refugee, internally displaced or stateless population, and those who are unaccompanied, pregnant, heads of households, disabled or elderly are especially vulnerable.[57]

Taking another look at the scroll of Ruth from the perspective of refugees and asylum seekers provides more connections with our own time and place. We noted above that observation of biblical laws is key for appreciation of the plot in the story. The Torah includes many passages referring to treatment of the poor, the orphan and widow, and the foreigner.[58] Exodus uses the same formulation as the Ten Commandments to prohibit wrong treatment of resident aliens, widows, and orphans: "*You shall not* wrong or oppress a resident alien (*ger*), for you were aliens (*gerim*) in the land of Egypt. You shall not abuse any widow or orphan" (Exod 22:21-22 [MT 22:20-21], NRSV). According to this Exodus tradition, Israel should treat the stranger kindly because they knew what it was like to be harshly treated in a foreign land.

Deuteronomic and Levitical legislation, with similar motivation, go even further by fleshing out what it is to welcome the outsider and the vulnerable. Such individuals should be included in the Israelite cult and its festivals, compensated for work, provided for in their need, allowed to glean during harvest, and accorded full justice in the community (Deut 16:11-22; 24:17-22; Lev 19:33-34).

Earlier in this chapter we considered the creative use of Israelite Law by characters in the scroll of Ruth. Boaz's treatment of Ruth and Naomi, for example, were actions of generosity that went beyond fulfilling the letter of the law. Boaz treated Ruth the Moabite as he treated his own workers and invited her to glean amongst the sheaves and the bundles, an invitation that went beyond the Deuteronomic commandment to leave that which had fallen for the poor: "When you reap your harvest in your field and forget a sheaf in the field, you shall not go back to get it; it shall be left for the alien, the orphan, and the widow, so that the LORD your God may bless you in all your undertakings" (Deut 24:19). Beyond that, Boaz provided food for Ruth and her mother-in-law and sought legal solutions to ensure their safety and ongoing care. On her part, Ruth did not act as a helpless victim. She committed herself to being Naomi's loyal companion, then acted within her limited power to achieve security for them both. It was her words to Boaz that he should "spread his wing" over her that suggested that the law of levirate marriage could extend beyond the immediate family to other kinsmen. When negotiating with the *go'el* who was the "nearer relative" than himself, Boaz combined the laws of redemption and levirate responsibility in order to make the purchase of Naomi's land less attractive to *P'loni Almoni*.

The scroll of Ruth demonstrates that when law is flexible, it can be used to provide life-giving opportunities for the needy. All too often, unfortunately, the laws of our lands are applied inflexibly to create barriers for those who are most in need in our communities. Yet that same legal system is open to challenge, as is evident in Australia where on more than one occasion legislation crafted by the Australian government relating to treatment of refugees has been challenged and found to be unlawful by the Australian High Court.[59]

Arguably, Boaz benefited economically from his generous treatment of the stranger in his midst, ending up with a new field of land as well as a new wife. This result is not condemned, however, either in the scroll of Ruth, in the rabbinic tradition, or in commentary by biblical scholars. Economic responsibility and advantage are positive goals for any society. Refugee advocacy groups in my context of Australia often point out that it is in Australia's economic interests to offer more humane treatment to asylum seekers. Offshore detention and mandatory in-country detention are far more costly solutions than community detention within Australia, and even the latter course of action costs around ten times more than allowing an asylum seeker to live in the community on a bridging visa while their claim is processed.[60]

The scroll of Ruth presents the story of one individual migrant and is a heartwarming account of her integration into the community of Israel such that her initial vow to Naomi (1:16) becomes a reality. She walks to Bethlehem and lodges there. The inhabitants of Bethlehem become her people, and YHWH becomes her God. We are often impacted when we personally meet or are exposed to the story of an immigrant or refugee because the "human side of immigration" is revealed (Melgar 2015, 269). In my experience, governments work hard at dehumanizing "problem" groups such as asylum seekers because they know that individual stories are powerful in changing attitudes.[61]

Ruth's "disappearance" at the end of the scroll, however, gives us pause. Do we accept immigrants and refugees only when they become fully integrated into our own societies and lose their "noticeability"? Ellen van Wolde speaks of Ruth "giv[ing] up her Moabite identity" (1997, 28), and Jean-Pierre Ruiz asks ". . . what she [Ruth] felt compelled to sacrifice in order to make it, what she may have compromised of her own Moabite heritage in order to survive as a foreigner" (2018, 20).

When able to live within the community and contribute their own distinctive traditions, refugees can enrich their new homelands in significant ways. We have an obligation, therefore, to welcome and care for the stranger without expecting them to lose their own valuable heritage.

Advocacy groups for migrants and refugees in many parts of the world consider that they have a responsibility to provide practical care and legal representation for those who have sought refuge in their country. As we consider the story of Ruth in the light of a current world refugee crisis, we must act within our own sphere of influence to ensure that the story of Ruth the Moabite finding a welcome and safe haven in Bethlehem, the house of bread, can become the story of all who seek refuge.

The Scroll of Lamentations

Introduction

I have long been drawn to a fundamental paradox in the scroll of Lamentations—that its raw, painful descriptions of the immediacy of suffering and devastation in the aftermath of warfare have been preserved in carefully crafted poetry that witnesses to excessive time and effort. As if it were stitched together like a dark-hued quilt, we are offered a pastiche of loosely connected images of a ruined city and its desolated inhabitants: keening women, starving children, rubble in the near-empty streets, mourning elders sitting in ash heaps, charred remains of the destruction of fire, dead bodies, people reduced to cannibalism. But when we take a step back from the *content* of the scroll, it is surprising to notice the *structure*: five chapters arranged with acrostic patterns in mind. This is no crazy quilt but a creatively planned artwork. In it the unthinkable has been presented as something worthy of deeper contemplation. Due to its *content*, undoubtedly, this is a little-known, rarely used part of Scripture, but its *arrangement* demands that it be given more attention and admiration!

From a historical point of view this scroll is valuable as a key witness to a seminal event in ancient Israel's history: the two-year siege of Jerusalem followed by the destruction of city and temple by the Babylonian army in 587 BCE, resulting in the exile of the majority of the population to refugee camps in Babylon. This was a crisis of immense proportions, and much of the content of the Hebrew Bible could be attributed to the wrestling of faith and revisiting of history in the light of this experience (Mathews 2019). Several psalms attest to a belief that as long as the God of the Israelites dwelt in the temple, the security of the nation would be maintained (e.g., Ps 46:5), a theological perspective shared with other ancient Near Eastern cultures about their temples and their deities. When the temple of Solomon and Judah's capital city were destroyed, it would have been reasonable to conclude that the national God had also been vanquished. Whilst later traditions would examine this theological crisis in a variety of ways, the scroll of Lamentations represents an early reaction to the disaster, describing devastation with little systematic theological reflection and few words of hope. The paramount interest of the scroll is the fate of the people. Painful experiences and emotions are not avoided or glossed over. This scroll represents the voices of those who are observing destruction and those who are suffering themselves, but there is no direct voice of God in either judgment or assurance. The scroll begins with a cry of pain and it ends in despair with the plea directed to YHWH: "If rejecting You have rejected us, will You be angry towards us forever?" (5:22. my translation). Although the crafting of the poetry suggests that the material has been reworked, its content remains focused on the actual moment of Jerusalem's destruction. There is no reference to the glorious past, no prophetic voice of judgment that is so closely associated with other descriptions of the punishment of Israel and Judah found in the Hebrew Bible, and no envisaging of a new future like we see in some of the forward-thinking prophets. Instead it sits in the present and waits. Corrine Carvalho speaks of the immediacy of the poetic images: "This is neither a chronological description of the siege of Jerusalem nor an epic poem about war . . . each poem lingers over distinct elements of the disaster from the perspective of those experiencing it" (2018, 67).

The nature and content of this scroll is well described in all versions of its name. "Lamentations" is an English translation of the Talmud's reference to the book as *qînōt*, a plural form of *qînāh* meaning "laments" or "elegies." The Greek title *Threnoi* and Latin equivalent *Threni* is sometimes translated into English as "dirges." All are references to songs or poems used in the context of funerals. The Hebrew title is taken from the first word of the scroll, *ʾēkāh*. This interjection that is a cry of pain or distress also is a fitting title for the scroll.

The Scroll and the Fast of *Tishah B'Av*

Like the other scrolls in the *Megillot*, Lamentations is set aside for special liturgical use. It is used in the Jewish observance of *Tishah B'Av* (the ninth day of the month of Av), the day that commemorates the destruction of both the First and Second temples built in Jerusalem (587 BCE and 70 CE respectively). Rabbinic tradition claims the temples were destroyed on the same day in the calendar—the ninth of Av. Later, commemoration for the defeat of Bar Kokhba was added, the last Jewish rebellion against the Roman Empire in 132 CE. In contemporary practice, all disasters of Jewish history including the Russian pogroms and the Holocaust are remembered. Commenting on the continued relevance of this poetry of lament, Robert Alter observes,

> One readily understands why it is that Jewish tradition fixed the recitation of these five laments as an annual ritual, not merely in commemoration of the destruction of the First Temple or the Second but also as a way of fathoming the ghastly recurrent violence that has darkened two millennia of history. (2019b, 645)

The day is marked by fasting and prayer that commences the previous sundown. It begins with a public reading of the book of Lamentations in the synagogue. Participants sit on low chairs or the floor as signs of mourning, a practice that is also observed when keeping *Shiva* to mourn the death of a loved one. Some begin preparing for this day three weeks prior by refraining from meat and alcohol and neither shaving nor cutting hair, signifying that it is inappropriate to be concerned about one's own comfort when remembering such loss (Brawer 2008, 235). According to Jewish tradition, the Messiah will be born on this day of mourning. This ensures that the fast day that commemorates destruction and loss includes within it hope for redemption. The Christian practice of including passages from Lamentations in lectionary readings of Holy Week similarly points towards redemption. The Sabbath that follows *Tishah B'Av* includes readings from Isaiah 40, which begins with the words "Comfort, comfort my people." Whether or not they are familiar with this practice, a number of scholars have proposed that the exilic prophet Second Isaiah was responding to that final unanswered question of Lamentations (O'Connor 2002, 139).[62]

As those who are fasting and mourning hear the scroll recited, they would hear echoes in several references to festivals within the scroll functioning as ready-mades: "the surrounding peoples [are] called to Jerusalem like festive pilgrims to destroy rather than to celebrate, to raise in the sacred precincts a fierce cry instead of the festive songs" (Alter 2019b, 644).

The Background of the Scroll

The compilers of the Greek Septuagint added a superscription to the scroll that attributed its authorship to Jeremiah and placed it after the book of Jeremiah amongst the prophets. Christian canons followed suit. Although the Targums and Rabbinic literature also understood Jeremiah to be the author, the Hebrew Bible tradition received by the Masoretic scribes has no attribution to Jeremiah within the scroll itself and has preserved the scroll amongst the *Megillot*. It is understandable that Jeremiah was linked to this tradition.

He prophesied doom over Jerusalem and was an eyewitness to its destruction, remaining in the city after other leaders had been exiled to Babylon (Jer 40:6). In 2 Chronicles 35:25 there is a reference to Jeremiah "lamenting" (*qyn*) over Josiah, king of Judah, who was killed in battle two decades before the downfall of Jerusalem. The verse in Chronicles also refers to a collection of laments (*qînōt*) sung by male and female singers. The poetry of Lamentations, however, is quite different from the style and content of Jeremiah's prophecies. His authorship of the scroll was first challenged in the eighteenth century CE, but only since the twentieth century CE has the book generally been interpreted by scholars without reference to Jeremiah as its author.

There is general consensus that the scroll initially came into being in the immediate aftermath of the destruction of Jerusalem and was written by eyewitnesses. If we rule out Jeremiah as a likely author, we can only speculate as to the identities of the original authors. We know from other verses in Scripture that lamenting was primarily the work of women (Jer 9:21 [MT 9:20]) and some of the poetry comes from a female perspective, but another section is identified as the words of a "strongman" (*geber*). As already intimated, it is probable that there was later recrafting of the poetry to create the tight alphabetic acrostic structure.

Whoever authored the work, it is striking that there is a vagueness and universality to some aspects of the poems. On the one hand, the descriptions of suffering are graphic and vivid: a "reality show" that holds nothing back (Queen-Sutherland 2013, 184). On the other hand, authors are not identified, when kings are mentioned they are left unnamed, and, most significant, Babylon is never acknowledged as the enemy. The deliberate lack of specificity means these poems are applicable to any context of oppression and suffering. The use of the poems to commemorate many disasters for the Jewish people, as pointed out above, is testimony to this.

It is also striking that only general terms are used to describe the failure of Israel that has led to punishment: transgression (*peša'*), sin (*ḥāṭā'*), and iniquity (*'āwon*). In the prophetic writings we see the community being chastised for specific moral and ethical failures such as exploitation of the poor and failure to judge fairly. The Deuteronomistic editors regularly pointed out that kings and their people were worshipping idols and neglecting the Torah. The poetry of Lamentations has no similar language and never spells out specific failures. The few references to disobedience that use the terms above (1:5, 8, 14, 22; 3:42; 4:6, 13, 22; 5:7, 16) and the lack of specificity about these failures witness to this scroll as one that will be used again and again as people of faith bring their failure and suffering before God, despite its historical foundations.

The scroll of Lamentations has similarities to Mesopotamian city laments from the second millennium BCE such as "Lamentation over the Destruction of Ur." These texts describe the abandonment of a city by its deity leading to its destruction (Dobbs-Allsopp 1993). Daniel Grossberg reminds us that no literary genre arises in a vacuum but points out that "Lamentations surpasses by far, both in its poetic sophistication and in its effect on readers, any of its forerunners" (2004, 1588).

Poetry in the Scroll

The scroll incorporates five distinct poems as evidenced by their acrostic and lineal structure. The first and second poems have twenty-two verses (corresponding to the twenty-two letters in the Hebrew alphabet). The first word of each verse begins with the appropriate alphabetic letter, and each verse has three lines. The third poem has sixty-six verses, with three single-line verses for each of the letters of the alphabet. The fourth poem returns to the pattern of the first two, except there are only two lines per verse. And the fifth poem is made up of twenty-two single-line verses but does not use an alphabetic acrostic. Poetic parallelism is most evident in the fifth poem, with the verses divided by the disjunctive *zaqef qaton* accent. The Hebrew pause markers *setumah* (ס) and *petuchah* (פ) are used in a similar way in the first four poems: a *setumah* comes at the end of each verse in the first, second, and fourth poems and at the transition to a new letter of the alphabet in the third poem. Each of the first four poems ends with a *petuchah*. In the fifth poem, by contrast, there are no *setumah* markers and only one *petuchah*, which comes at the end of verse 18. This seems to mark a transition from the community's desperate description of their plight that they have laid before YHWH, introduced by a demand that YHWH remember, take note, and see (5:1), to a more conventionally worded prayer of praise and petition.

The reason for the differing forms of these five poems, naturally, is debated amongst scholars. Some see it as evidence of different authors, of a gifted individual poet who played with different forms, or perhaps even of an editor who compiled the first four poems and then tried his hand at a fifth, though not as elegantly (Alter 2019, 643)! The question of why acrostics have been used is also debated. I am not the only reader of the scroll who is intrigued by the disparity between content and form. Acrostic poetry is used elsewhere in the Hebrew Bible (Pss 9–10, 25, 34, 37, 111, 112, 119, 145; Prov 31:10-31; Nah 1:2-8), but it is particularly striking in its use with variations in Lamentations. Psalm 119, with an acrostic made up of eight lines for each letter of the alphabet (176 verses in total), is another impressive literary feat, but according to Robert Alter it is far more formulaic and conventional in content than the poetry of Lamentations (2019b, 644).

The simplest explanations that have been proposed focus on mnemonics and aesthetics. As would be familiar to any who have used alphabetic mnemonics to recall information, this is a common technique used in education. It is assumed that, especially in the predominantly orally based ancient world, memorization for recitation would have been aided by such devices. Indeed, one of the earliest references to the structure of Lamentations found in *Midrash Lamentations Rabbah* claimed that Lamentations was written with an alphabetic acrostic "so that it will be learnt by the chanters" (quoted in Assis 2007, 712). An explanation that focuses primarily on the aesthetics of the poetry is implied in Wesley Fuerst's comment: "Many oracles and poems in the Old Testament probably originated with oral expression, but measured, careful literary power and artifice are very evident here" (1975, 208).

Others have sought more symbolic explanations with psychological and social roots. A prominent theory for the use of the acrostic form is its metaphorical force of totality and completeness. The same rabbinic midrash mentioned above includes this reason for the acrostic: "Why is the book of Lamentations composed as an alphabetic acrostic . . . Because it is written (Dan. 9) 'Yea, all Israel have transgressed' . . . which is written from Aleph to Taw" (Assis 2007, 713).

This idea was picked up by Norman Gottwald, whose work on Lamentations has been influential since the mid-twentieth century. He argued, "Those who entertain this idea of completeness, therefore, instinctively feel that in naming the whole alphabet one comes as close as man may to a total development of any theme or the complete expression of any emotion or belief" (1954, 29). For Gottwald, the function of the acrostic was "to encourage completeness in the expression of grief, the confession of sin and the instilling of hope" (1954, 28). Others have emphasized a different aspect of totality by suggesting that all that befell Jerusalem was comprehensively covered in the poetry.[63]

Another line of analysis suggests the use of the acrostic was a technique that deliberately brought order to a chaotic situation, seeking to contain an incomprehensible reality. As Kathleen O'Connor proposes,

> Lamentations' alphabetic devices are deeply symbolic. They expose the depth and breadth of suffering in conflicting ways. The alphabet gives both order and shape to suffering that is otherwise inherently chaotic, formless, and out of control . . . it tries to force unspeakable pain into a container

that is familiar and recognizable even as suffering eludes containment. (2002, 13)

These explanations that focus on order and totality fall short when we observe that the acrostics and lineal structure are imperfect in the scroll. In three of the poems the letters *ayin* and *pe* are out of order and the final poem only connects with the acrostic pattern by having the same number of verses as letters in the alphabet. Some verses have a greater or lesser number of lines than expected by the normal pattern (1:7, 19; 2:4, 19; 4:14). Perhaps this lack of perfection signifies that finding order and fully containing grief is impossible. We will return to this aspect of the poetry in the commentary section of this chapter.

Contemporary discussion of biblical poetry places less emphasis on meter than in the past, but it is often noted that some of the poetry in Lamentations has a characteristic unevenly balanced meter found in other poetry that could be classified as lament. It is described as a *qinah* meter, based on the Hebrew word for "lament" as discussed above. This is not the pattern for all verses in the scroll, however, and the fifth poem has a more regular pattern throughout.

Another significant feature of the poetry of the scroll is its differing perspectives, briefly mentioned above. Changes in verbs and pronouns and shifts from third-person to first-person voice indicate different speakers, not in an alternating dialogue as was seen in the Song of Songs scroll but in a series of different voices taking turns in drawing the attention of God to their particular experience. Corinne Carvalho speaks of this "dialogical" reading of the scroll: "each poem has distinct speakers or voices, resulting in a kind of ancient 'Vantage Point,' where the story of the fall of the city is told over and over from different perspectives" (2018, 66).[64] Although the scroll uses some of the imagery of the prophetic tradition, such as a personified Daughter Zion who is ravished by her gloating enemies and the use of famine as a means of punishment, it lacks the voice of YHWH that is so prominent in the prophets who claim to bring the word of the Lord to their audiences, whether in judgment or comfort.

The Purpose of the Scroll
"Every life, and every land and people, has reasons for lament and complaint" (Bier and Bulkeley 2013, xv). As if in response to this claim, the scroll of Lamentations bears vital witness as canonical Scripture that is relevant to life. It may not offer satisfying *answers* to the problem of suffering, but it reminds

anyone who is suffering that they are not alone. Arguably, the best-known verses in the scroll express optimism and hope:

> The steadfast love of the LORD never ceases,
> His mercies never come to an end;
> They are new every morning;
> Great is Your faithfulness. (3:22-23, NRSV)

It is significant that these verses come approximately in the center of the scroll. As we have seen in the scrolls of Song of Songs and Ruth, there is often a deliberate focus on the center in Hebrew composition. Yet these verses are a mere drop in the bucket of a much greater outpouring of pain, and so the weight of that greater witness is given a valid place in expressions of faith. Continued use of this material in liturgical and community settings allows for solidarity between people of faith and all who mourn or suffer.

Commenting on the relevance of the scroll's poetry across generations, John Collins claims that Lamentations "fills its role in the canon by testifying to the depth of human suffering and expressing the basic human emotion of grief" (2004, 350). The emphasis that Collins places on *human* suffering and *human* emotion is significant. Israel's god YHWH never speaks but is fully present, nonetheless. The laments are addressed to YHWH with several direct appeals that YHWH should see the suffering one (1:9, 11, 20; 2:20-21; 3:58-60; 5:1). The speakers also accuse YHWH of being responsible for the suffering (1:12-15, 17, 21; 2:1-9, 17; 3:3-16, 43, 45-47; 4:11, 16) and unwilling to hear their prayers (3:44, 56). They expect YHWH to deliver retribution to their enemies (3:64-66; 4:21-22) but seem uncertain if YHWH will again return to be their God (5:19-22). I was fascinated to discover that when this scroll is recited in Jewish liturgy the cantor returns to the second-last verse in the scroll and repeats it several times as the conclusion of the recitation. Rather than ending with the possibility of eternal rejection, the plea "Restore us, renew us" is repeated instead.

By refusing to name a human enemy, the human lamenters in Lamentations are left with YHWH as the enemy on whose mercy they must throw themselves. Like other lament literature in Scripture, anger and hurt is expressed in strong speech that reflects honest, undiluted passion. The underlying relationship between the petitioner and YHWH, expressed through the phrase "my Lord" used regularly in the poems, implies that YHWH does not need to be protected from such language, and humanity need not cower in the presence of their creator. The language of the scroll sends another message also. Corinne Carvalho points out that, in the context of colonization by stronger powers, naming YHWH as enemy rather than the Babylonians is, in fact, a defiant act of faith:

> For those whose daily existence was framed by a message of their insignificance, the assertion of a God in control of the colonizer's meta-narrative served a subversive social function. The replacement of Babylon with God rhetorically removes any power or agency from Babylon and resituates it in God. (2018, 77)

As we consider a broader theological purpose of the scroll of Lamentations, we need to do more than appreciate its aesthetic qualities or focus on the central note of hope. It invites us to lean into the experience of suffering, witness the depth of pain, and allow it to motivate empathy and action. As Carvalho puts it, "The poems of Lamentations . . . demand a response from their audience, even if audiences, including scholarly audiences, have found ways to resist" (2018, 65). For those who are hearing this scroll from a place of suffering, it will give words to grief. For others, it will be a reminder that, even if transmitted through images and metaphorical language, the poems attest to events that occurred in real, lived space. As such it can be understood as "Trauma Literature" (Kaplan 2005). If we are not survivors of trauma ourselves, by immersing ourselves in this material we become witnesses and agents for social change. Words of poets who experienced the destruction of Jerusalem and its temple as an epoch-changing crisis can inspire reflection on crisis in our own time and across our world. The experiences of Holocaust, the Balkan conflict, and 9-11 are just a few contemporary crises that have been brought into conversation with the poetry of Lamentations.[65] The fact that this poetry has inspired so many connections supports Erhard Gerstenberger's comment that "we rightly should marvel at the enduring dynamics of this age-old poetry" (2013, 127).

Creativity in Lamentations—Performance Poetry

A number of commentators have highlighted the performative nature of the scroll of Lamentations. Kathleen O'Connor, for example, focuses on the dialogic nature of the composition when she proposes,

> I imagine the book as a public performance of speakers in which survivors stand up, each in turn, to tell of their particular pain and to demand God's attention. Together the voices possess only the raw harmony of common wounds, even as they offer competing and irreconcilable opinions of the disaster. (O'Connor 2008, 28)[66]

The carefully crafted acrostic arrangement of the poetry, however, suggests a written foundation rather than an oral one. For this reason, I am envisaging the work as a type of performance poetry. A non-oral basis is implied, yet the impact is strongest when the poetry is orally delivered.[67] Such a conceptualization may not be too far from the original use of the scroll of Lamentations. David Rhoads, a founding scholar of Biblical Performance Criticism, argues that all Scripture was "performance literature—either as transcriptions of prior oral compositions or as written compositions designed for oral performance" (2006, 119).

As an art form, poetry has long had a performative element. Sagas and epics existed in oral form before writing, being passed on through generations and across communities. Written records of this literature attest to their oral preservation over long periods in varied contexts. The aesthetic and rhetorical features of poetic composition distinguish it from forms of writing that primarily impart information. Repetition, rhythm, rhyme, and wordplay are all employed as devices in poetry to express and evoke emotion. The human voice and accompanying gestures powerfully add to both feeling and meaning. Arguably, poetry readings have been part of most cultures for most of history.

In the United States, "beat poetry" of the 1940s was a post-war movement in which writers such as Allen Ginsberg and Jack Kerouac focused on the vocal and performed aspects of their work that questioned mainstream politics and culture. In recent decades, interest in performance poetry has been revitalized by "slam poetry"—spoken poems enacted at public gatherings, often in a competition format. Poets are given a limited time to perform and are judged by audience members. Like performance art, the medium breaks down the barrier between performer and audience.[68] Following on from beat poetry of an earlier generation, contemporary slam poetry often focuses on controversial issues such as the environment, politics, education, gender equality, and racism. Poets use a variety of techniques to engage their audiences. The influence of rap music is evidenced in the preeminent device of rhythm used in most forms of slam poetry. Some performers incorporate humorous wordplay (for example, alliteration and tongue twisters). For others, the phenomena of "slam voice" is used to convey anger or distress. Serious and controversial issues can be addressed in performance poetry in entertaining or attention-grabbing formats, giving greater exposure to those issues. While there may appear to be a primary focus on individual performances, poetry reading events can include a series of poems on a similar theme and poems performed by more than one poet.[69] Emotion and passion are integral to the poetry, intended to make an audience feel what the performer feels and to inspire and empower others.[70]

Perhaps the editors who recrafted the poetry of Lamentations by enhancing its aesthetics were convinced that the content of the poems should not be lost. The pain of those suffering the loss of city and temple should not go unnoticed. The acrostic structure is effective in drawing attention to the poetry, creating a compelling performance that would be enhanced by vocal tone and gesture. A series of poems from different voices gives opportunity to explore the events from different angles. I envisage one voice taking over from another when emotion runs too high. I hear the anguished cry of a keening woman beginning three of the poems, after which a more dispassionate observer describes her situation until she can raise her voice again. I hear a male voice—a keening strongman—expressing pain either from personal experience or vicariously, rising to a point of conviction of steadfast faith and stepping in again to take up the poem when the community voice falters. I hear shared voices (the keening community) taking care to express their common experience with unified expression. Each of these keeners uses powerful words and emotional themes to help the audience feel and even see what they have experienced. The final poem, however, turns from keening to conventional confession and petition, demonstrating that the real audience these poets have in mind is YHWH—the God who caused their suffering and the God who has the power to change their future.

I have translated these poems from the Hebrew with an English-language acrostic but have by necessity covered A to V in the alphabet rather than A to Z, corresponding with the twenty-two letters of the Hebrew alphabet. I have followed the imperfection of the original by reversing my Ps and Qs in three of the poems (where *ayin* and *pe* are reversed in Hebrew). I have also taken an occasional liberty in rearranging verses to enable effective use of the acrostic (2:10; 3:4, 31, 33, 53, 63; 4:20). Diacritics are added for assistance in performance. I have noted above where the *setumah* (ס) and *petuchah* (פ) pauses are used in each poem. I have also indicated where verses are broken by the disjunctive *athnach* (double slash) or the lesser disjunctive *zaqef qaton* (single slash).

For each of the five poems, I have provided my initial quite literal translation and followed it with the poem envisaged as a performance piece in which rhythm is highlighted. I have, by necessity, removed and altered occasional words in the rhythmic version, but have maintained the acrostic structure. Further discussion of my creative reworking of the Lamentations scroll follows below.

LAMENTATIONS
POEM 1

[א]¹ Arghhh! She sat alone—the city—great of people,
She became like a widow//Great among the nations,
A princess among the provinces, she became for slavery. ס

[ב]² Bewailing she wails in the night and her tears are on her cheeks,
Not any for her are comforters from all her lovers//
All her friends betrayed her, they have become for her foes. ס

[ג]³ Collected into exile is Judah after suffering and after much servitude,
She lived among the nations, she did not find rest//
All her pursuers overtook her in the narrow places. ס

[ד]⁴ Devastated are roads of Zion without those coming for a festival,
All her gates are desolate, her priests are sighing//
Her maidens are grieved, and she is bitter to herself. ס

[ה]⁵ Enemies of her are at her head—her foes took ease,
Because YHWH made her suffer over the greatness of her transgressions//
Her children have gone to captivity before the faces of the enemy. ס

[ו]⁶ From Daughter Zion has departed all her majesty//
Her princes are like stags who have not found pasture,
And they go without strength before the faces of the pursuer. ס

[ז]⁷ Gone to memory is Jerusalem, the days of her suffering and her wandering,
All her precious things that were from the days of old//
In the falling of her people into a hand of an enemy, and not any helper for her.
They saw—her enemies—and they mocked over her destruction. ס

[ח]⁸ Heinous sin she sinned—Jerusalem—thus unclean she was//
All those honoring her made her worthless, because they saw her nakedness,
Even she sighed and turned away. ס

[ט]⁹ **I**mpurity in her hems, no memory of her future,
And she came down astonishingly, not any as comforter for her//
See, YHWH, my suffering. Because he became great—my foe. ס

[י]¹⁰ **J**ust his hand stretched out—an enemy—over all her precious things//
Because she saw that nations came into her sanctuary, of whom You commanded,
'They shall not come into congregation with you'. ס

[כ]¹¹ **K**eening—all her people, seeking bread,
They gave their precious things for food to return to their very being//
See, YHWH, and look! Because I was worthless. ס

[ל]¹² **L**ittle or nothing to you all passers-by on the road,
Look and see if there is pain like my pain; which was dealt to me//
Which he inflicted—YHWH—on the day of his burning anger. ס

[מ]¹³ **M**ighty are the heights from which he sent fire into my bones to rule her//
He spread out a net for my feet, he made me come back,
He made me desolate all the days of my sickness. ס

[נ]¹⁴ **N**obbled to a yoke—my transgressions—by his hand,
They knotted themselves [into] his yoke over my neck . . . he made my strength fail//
He gave me—my Lord—into the hands of [those] I cannot stand. ס

[ס]¹⁵ **O**verthrew all my warriors—my Lord—in my midst,
He called over me a festival to break my chosen//
A wine press he trod—my Lord—for the young woman, Daughter Judah. ס

[ע]¹⁶ **P**residing over these things I am weeping, my eyes, my eyes pour out water,
Far from me is a comforter to revive my very being//
They will be—my sons—desolate, because strong is [the] foe. ס

[פ]¹⁷ **Q**uietly she reaches out—Zion—with her hands . . . not any comforter for her,

[צ]¹⁸ He commanded—YHWH—for Jacob: Surrounding him are his enemies//
She will be—Jerusalem—a filthy thing among them. ס

Righteous is he—YHWH—because his mouth I rebelled against//
Hear—now—all peoples, and see my pain,
My young women and my young men have gone into captivity. ס

[ק]¹⁹ **S**ending calls to my lovers—they deceived me
My priests and my elders in the city perished//
Because they were seeking food for themselves and restoring their lives. ס

[ר]²⁰ **T**ake note YHWH, because trouble is mine, my belly is churning,
Overturned is my heart in my midst, because rebelling I have rebelled.//
From the street a sword bereaves; in the house is like death. ס

[ש]²¹ **U**ncaring they hear because sighing am I. Not any will comfort me.
All my foes who heard my wickedness laughed! Because You have acted.//
Bring on a day You called and let them be like me. ס

[ת]²² **V**ie with all their wickedness, let it come before Your face and deal with them,
Like You dealt with me over all my transgressions//
Because great is my sighing, and my heart is sick.

פ

PERFORMANCE POEM 1

The Keening Woman
Arghhh!
The Observer
>She sat alone—
>the city—great of people,
>became like a widow//
>Great among the nations,

>   a princess in the provinces,
>   she became a slave. ס
>
> **B**ewailing in the night
>   her tears are on her cheeks,
>   Not for her is comfort
>   from any of her lovers//
>   All her friends betrayed her,
>   and have become her foes. ס
>
> **C**ollected into exile
>   after suffering and service,
>   She lived among the nations,
>   But never found her rest//
>   Her pursuers overtook her
>   in the narrow places. ס
>
> **D**epeopled roads of Zion
>   None coming for feast,
>   All her gates are desolate,
>   all her priests are sighing//
>   Her maidens are aggrieved,
>   she is bitter to herself. ס
>
> **E**nemies at her head—
>   her foes have taken ease,
>   YHWH made her suffer
>   over her transgressions//
>   Her children going captive
>   before the enemy. ס
>
> **F**rom daughter Zion gone
>   all her majesty//
>   Her princes are like stags
>   who haven't yet found grass,
>   And going without strength
>   before the pursuer. ס

Gone to memory is 'Salem,
    suffering and wandering,
All her precious things
    that were from days of old//
her people in enemy hands,
    and no helper left for her.
They saw—her enemies,
    her downfall they have mocked. ס

Heinous sin she sinned
    thus unclean she was//
Once honored, now she's worthless,
    because they saw her naked,
Even then she sighed
    and turned herself away. ס

Impure in her hems,
    no memory of her future,
her fall is quite amazing,
    Not for her is comfort//
The Keening Woman
    See me, YHWH, suffering!
        Great has become my foe. ס

The Observer
Just enemy hands stretched out
        over all her precious things//
    She saw nations in her sanctuary,
        The ones You had commanded,
    'Do not let them come
        and congregate with you'. ס

Keening—all her people,
    Always seeking bread,
they gave their precious things
    for food to clutch their flesh//
The Keening Woman
    See me, YHWH, look!
        See that I am worthless. ס

Little are to you
>   Those passing on the road,
>   Is there pain like my pain;
>   which has been dealt to me//
>   Which YHWH has inflicted
>   his day of burning rage. ס

Mighty from the heights
>   he sent fire to my bones//
>   He spread out for my feet,
>   A net to bring me back,
>   Desolate he made me
>   all my bloody days. ס

Nobbled to a yoke
>   —my transgressions—by his hand,
>   Knotted to *his* yoke
>   on my neck my strength has failed//
>   He gave me—my own Lord—
>   into hands I cannot stand. ס

Overthrew my warriors—
>   my Lord did in my midst,
>   He called for me a festival
>   to break my chosen ones//
>   A wine press trod my Lord
>   for the woman, Daughter Judah. ס

Presiding now I weep,
>   my eyes, my eyes pour water,
>   Not for me is comfort
>   No revival for my flesh//
>   My sons will now be desolate,
>   For too strong is our foe. ס

The Observer
Questing Zion's hands . . .
>   not for her is comfort,
>   Commanded—YHWH—for Jacob:

"Surround him with his foes"//
Jerusalem will be
   a filthy thing for them. ס

The Keening Woman
Righteous now is YHWH—
   his mouth I disobeyed //
Hear—now—all you peoples,
   Come and see my pain,
My maidens and my youths
   Gone to captivity. ס

Sending, calling lovers,
   they have forgotten me.
My priests and elders perished//
   Seeking food for themselves,
   Shoring up their lives. ס

Take note YHWH, of my trouble,
   Hear my belly churn,
My heart is overturned,
   I rebel and disobey.//
From the street a sword bereaves
   In the house is death. ס

Uncaring are they, sighing am I.
   Not for me is comfort.
All my foes are laughing!
   But it was You who did it.//
Bring on a day You called,
   and let them be like me. ס

Vie with all their evil,
   Come and deal with them,
Like You dealt with me
   over my transgressions//
Do You see my sighing?
   Do You see my heart is sick?

פ

LAMENTATIONS POEM 2

[א]¹ **A**rghhh! He snorts with his anger—my Lord—over Daughter Zion,
He threw down from the heavens [to] earth the splendor of Israel//
He has not remembered the footstool of his feet in the day of his anger. ס

[ב]² **B**ecause he consumed—my Lord—and did not spare all the dwellings of Jacob,
He destroyed in his wrath the fortresses of Daughter Judah, he struck down to the earth//
He profaned a kingdom and her princes. ס

[ג]³ **C**utting down with a burning anger, the whole horn of Israel,
He took back his right hand from the face of the foe//
And he blazed in Jacob like a fire flaming, eating all around. ס

[ד]⁴ **D**rawing his bow like a foe, standing his right hand like an enemy,
And he slew all desires of eyes//
In a tent of Daughter Zion, he poured out like fire his fury. ס

[ה]⁵ **E**rstwhile my Lord like a foe who consumed Israel,
He consumed all her citadels, he destroyed his strongholds//
And he multiplied in Daughter Judah mourning and more mourning. ס

[ו]⁶ **F**or he violated like the garden his booth, he destroyed his festival//
He forgot—YHWH—in Zion festival and Sabbath,
And he spurned with the indignation of his anger king and priest. ס

[ז]⁷ **G**ave away—my Lord—his altar, spurned his sanctuary,
Delivered into a hand of a foe the walls of her citadels//
A sound they gave in the house of YHWH like a day of a festival. ס

[ח]⁸ **H**e decided—YHWH—to ruin the wall of Daughter Zion,
He stretched out a line, he did not restrain his hand from the consuming//

              And he caused lament for rampart and wall, together they languished. ס

[ט]⁹   **I**nto the earth they sank—her gates—He destroyed and he broke her bars//
              Her king and her princes in the nations, there is not any Torah,
              Even her prophets cannot find a vision from YHWH. ס

[י]¹⁰   **J**erusalem's young women bow down to the earth their heads//
              They sit on the earth and are silent—the elders of Daughter Zion.
              They threw dust on their heads, they girded on sack-cloths. ס

[כ]¹¹   **K**ept from weeping are my eyes, churning is my belly,
              Poured out on the earth is my bile over the destruction of the Daughter of my people//
              In the fainting of little ones and suckling ones, in the streets of the town. ס

[ל]¹²   **L**et us hear them say to their mothers, where is grain and wine?//
              In their fainting they are like the slain in the streets of the city,
              In the pouring out of their lives on the lap of their mothers. ס

[מ]¹³   **M**ay I ask how I can bear witness for you? What will I compare to you, Daughter of Jerusalem
              What can I liken you to, and let me comfort you young woman, Daughter Zion//
              Because great like the sea is your brokenness, who can heal you? ס

[נ]¹⁴   **N**o truth in your prophets—they have seen for you emptiness and deception,
              They have not uncovered your iniquity to restore your restorations//
              But have seen for you burdens of emptiness and folly. ס

[ס]¹⁵   **O**ver you they strike their fists—all passers-by on the road,
              They scoff and shake their heads over Daughter Jerusalem//
              'What! Is this the city they called perfection of beauty? Joy to all the earth?' ס

[פ]¹⁶   **Q**uickly they open their mouths against you—all your foes,
              They scoff and they gnash teeth, they say 'we consumed!//

'Only this is the day that we waited for! We found, we saw!'
ס

[ע]17 **P**lanned it and did it—YHWH—he carried out his utterance which he commanded
from days of old,
He destroyed and did not spare//
And he rejoiced over you—a foe, and exalted the horn of your enemies. ס

[צ]18 **R**aised a cry—their hearts—to my Lord//
O wall of Daughter Zion, make it flow like a torrent—weeping—day and night,
Let there be no rest for you, no silence, Daughter of your eyes. ס

[ק]19 **S**tand up, shout out in the night at the head of the watches,
Pour out like water your heart, before the face of my Lord.//
Lift up to Him your fists over the very being of your little ones,
The ones fainting for hunger at the head of every laneway. ס

[ר]20 **T**ake note YHWH, and consider, to whom have You dealt thus?//
Should they eat—women—their fruit, little ones, newborn children?
Should they be slain in the sanctuary of my Lord—priest and prophet? ס

[ש]21 **U**pon the earth they lie down, laneways—youth and elder,
My young women and my young men have fallen by the sword.//
You slew in the day of Your anger. You slaughtered, You did not spare. ס

[ת]22 **V**oicing out like on a day of a festival my terrors from all around,
And there was not on the day of the anger of YHWH escaper or survivor//
The ones whom I bore and made great, my foe has brought an end to them.

פ

PERFORMANCE POEM 2

The Keening Woman
Arghhh!
The Observer
    He snorts his anger—
        My Lord at Daughter Zion,
He threw from heaven down
    the splendor of Israel//
No more footstool at his feet
    in the day of my Lord's anger. ס

But he consumed—my Lord—
    Did not spare all Jacob's dwellings,
His wrath destroyed his Daughter,
    She was struck down to the earth//
Then He profaned a kingdom,
    and her princes too. ס

Cut down with burning anger,
    the horn of Israel,
He took back his right hand
    from the face of the foe//
He blazed a fire in Jacob,
    eating all around. ס

Draws his bow like a foe,
    His right hand like an enemy,
He slew all desires of his eyes//
    In the tent of Daughter Zion,
Poured out like fire his fury.ס

Erstwhile my Lord a foe
    Consuming Israel fully,
Consuming all her citadels,
    Destroying all his strongholds//
Heaping up for Daughter Judah
    mourning and more woe. ס

For sullied his garden booth,
    his festival he destroyed//
He forgot—YHWH—in Zion
    Both festival and Sabbath,
He spurned with his fierce anger
    Together king and priest. ס

The Keening Woman
Gave away—my Lord—his altar,
    spurned his sanctuary,
delivered over to a foe
    the walls of citadels//
the sound in the house of YHWH
    like a day of a festival. ס

The Observer
He decided—YHWH—to ruin
    the wall of Daughter Zion,
He stretched out a line to consume,
    he did not restrain his hand//
lament for rampart and wall,
    together they fell away. ס

Into the earth sank her gates,
    He destroyed and broke her bars//
Her king and her princes are scattered,
    No more to hear the Torah,
Her prophets even are lost,
    No vision for them from YHWH. ס

Jerusalem's women bow down
    Their heads upon the earth//
They sit on the earth and are silent—
    the elders of Daughter Zion.
dust falling on their heads,
    girding on their sacks. ס

The Keening Woman
Kept from weeping are my eyes,

churning is my belly,
    Poured out on the earth is my bile
        For the death of my Daughter my people//
Fainting are sucklings and babes,
    in the streets of the town. ס

The Observer
Let us hear them say to their mothers,
    where is our grain and our wine?//
As they faint like the slain
    in the streets of the city,
As their lives pour out
    on the laps of their mothers. ס

May I ask if I can bear witness?
    What compares to you, Daughter Salem?
What woman can liken to you,
    Let me comfort you, Daughter Zion//
For great like the sea you are broken,
    who is left to heal you? ס

No truth in your prophets—
    who saw nothing for you,
  ignored your iniquity
    with no restoration//
but have seen only burdens
    of emptiness and folly. ס

Over you they strike fists
    passers-by on the road,
They scoff, their heads shake
    over Daughter Salem//
'Where's the city of beauty?
    The joy of the earth?' ס

Quickly mouths open,
    Your foes against you,
They scoff and gnash teeth,
    They say, 'we consumed!'//

They say, 'On this day
    We found, and we saw!' ס

Planned it and did it,
    YHWH kept out his word
which he charged from days of old,
    He destroyed and did not spare//
A foe rejoiced over you,
    and exalted the horn of your foes. ס

Raised a cry from their hearts to my Lord//
    O wall of Daughter Zion,
make it flow like a torrent and weep
    day and night don't let it cease,
Let there be no rest for you,
    no silence from your eyes. ס

Stand up, shout out in the night
    at the beginning of the watches,
Pour out like water your heart,
    before the face of my Lord.//
Lift up to Him your fists
    over the life of your babes,
the ones who faint near death
    at the head of every lane. ס

The Keening Woman
Take note YHWH, and think,
    to whom have You dealt this way?//
    Should they eat—the women—their fruit,
        Their little ones, their newborn babes?
Is the sanctuary of my Lord
    For slaying prophet and priest? ס

Upon earth they lie themselves down,
    Youth and elders in the lanes,
    My women and my men
        Have fallen by the sword.//

You slew in the day of your anger.
>> You slaughtered, You did not spare. ס

Voicing out on a festival day
>> My terrors are all around,
> On the day of the anger of YHWH
>> None escape, none survive//
> The ones whom I bore and made great,
>> my foe has brought to the ground.

פ

LAMENTATIONS POEM 3

[א]¹ **A**m I the strongman who has seen suffering/by the rod of his wrath,
[א]² **A**m I driven and made to walk (in) darkness and no light?
[א]³ **A**gainst me only He turns and overturns his hand all the day. ס

[ב]⁴ **B**roke my bones/wasted away my flesh and my skin,
[ב]⁵ **B**esieged upon me and encircled me—poison and hardship,
[ב]⁶ **B**uried in dark places He made me sit like dead ones of long ago. ס

[ג]⁷ **C**losed in around me and I cannot escape, He made heavy my chains,
[ג]⁸ **C**rying out I am, and calling for help/He shut out my prayer,
[ג]⁹ **C**losed my road with cut stone/my paths He twists. ס

[ד]¹⁰ **D**oes a bear ambush like He to me?/A lion in secret places?
[ד]¹¹ **D**irecting me off my road and tearing me in pieces, He places me in desolation.
[ד]¹² **D**irected his bow and made me stand/like a target to the arrow. ס

[ה]¹³ **E**ntering into my innards/the sons of his quiver.
[ה]¹⁴ **E**ver I became laughingstock to all my people/their taunting song all the day.

The Scroll of Lamentations

[ה]¹⁵   **E**ven filled me with bitterness, sated me with wormwood. ס

[ו]¹⁶   **F**urther, He made me grind with gravel my teeth/He made me cower in the ashes.

[ו]¹⁷   **F**ar from shalom is my very being . . . I have forgotten goodness,

[ו]¹⁸   **F**or I say 'gone is my dignity/ and my hope from YHWH.' ס

[ו]¹⁹   **G**ive a thought to my suffering and my wandering, to the wormwood and the poison.

[ו]²⁰   **G**iving thought, she remembers/and despairs over me—my very being.

[ו]²¹   **G**athers this to my heart, therefore I make myself hope: ס

[ח]²²   **H**is loving kindness—YHWH's—because it will not end/ because it will not finish—his compassion.

[ח]²³   **H**appening new every morning/great is your faithfulness.

[ח]²⁴   **H**e is my portion—YHWH—says my very being/thus I make myself hope in Him. ס

[ט]²⁵   **I**s good—YHWH—to those who await Him/to the very being who seeks Him,

[ט]²⁶   **I**s good—waiting and silence/for the salvation of YHWH,

[ט]²⁷   **I**s good for the strongman/because he carries a yoke in his youth. ס

[י]²⁸   **J**ust let him sit alone and let him be silent/because *He* lays it on him,

[י]²⁹   **J**ust let him give to the dust his mouth/perhaps there will be hope,

[י]³⁰   **J**ust let him give to his smiter a cheek and let him be filled with reproach. ס

[כ]³¹   **K**eep on rejecting forever? My Lord will not.

[כ]³²   **K**eep on inflicting grief?/He will have compassion like his great loving kindness.

[כ]³³   **K**eep on afflicting from his heart?/He will not aggrieve the sons of men. ס

| [ל]34 | Let him crush under his feet/all prisoners of the earth,
| [ל]35 | Let the judgement of the strongman/stretch out in front of the face of Most High,
| [ל]36 | Let a man twist his lawsuit!/My Lord will not see. ס

| [מ]37 | May someone say this: 'let it be!'/If my Lord has not commanded.
| [מ]38 | Moreover, from the mouth of Most High shall not go out/the evil and the good?
| [מ]39 | Must he complain—a living man/a strongman over his sin? ס

| [נ]40 | Now let us examine our ways and let us search/and let us return to YHWH.
| [נ]41 | Next, let us lift up our hearts on our fists/to God in the heavens.
| [נ]42 | Naturally, since we transgressed and rebelled/You did not forgive. ס

| [ס]43 | Overshadowed with anger You have pursued us/You slew, You did not spare,
| [ס]44 | Overshadowed with a cloud are you/stopping the passing of a prayer.
| [ס]45 | Offal and garbage You made us in the midst of the peoples. ס

| [פ]46 | Quite wide all our foes open their mouths against us,
| [פ]47 | Quivering and quavering overcome us, disaster and destruction.
| [פ]48 | Quickly water come down from my eye/over the brokenness of the Daughter of my people. ס

| [ע]49 | Poured out from my eye and not ceasing, without any respite,
| [ע]50 | Perhaps He will look down and see/YHWH—from the heavens.
| [ע]51 | Piercing my very being is my eye/over all the Daughters of my city. ס

| [צ]52 | Reaching out to trap me like a bird—my foes for nothing.
| [צ]53 | Raining down stones on me/they threw my life into the pit.
| [צ]54 | Round my head flowed waters. I said 'I am cut off.' ס

[ק]⁵⁵ **S**o I called out Your name, YHWH/from the pit's depths.
[ק]⁵⁶ **S**ay You will hear my voice/do not close your ear to my need, to my cry,
[ק]⁵⁷ **S**tep close on the day I call You/You said 'do not be afraid.' ס

[ר]⁵⁸ **T**ake up, my Lord, the lawsuit of my very being, redeem my life.
[ר]⁵⁹ **T**ake note, YHWH, of my wrong/judge my judgement.
[ר]⁶⁰ **T**ake note of all their vengeance/all their schemes for me. ס

[ש]⁶¹ **U**p to now You heard their reproach, YHWH/all their schemes against me,
[ש]⁶² **U**tterings of the ones standing against me and their muttering/ against me all the day,
[ש]⁶³ **U**p they get and down they sit—look!/I am their taunt song. ס

[ת]⁶⁴ **V**isit on them payback, YHWH, like the work of their hands.
[ת]⁶⁵ **V**olunteer for them anguish of heart/Your curse be on them!
[ת]⁶⁶ **V**anquish with anger and destroy them/from under the heavens of YHWH.

פ

PERFORMANCE POEM 3

The Keening Strongman
Am I the strongman
who has seen the rod of his wrath
Am I the driven one
walking in dark with no light?
Against me and only me
his hand turns all the day. ס

Broken my bones/
Wasted my flesh and my skin,
Besieging me, circling me
—poison and hardship,
Buried in dark, made me to sit
with the dead from long ago. ס

Closed in around me, I cannot escape,
heavy He made my chains,
Crying out loud, and calling for help/
He has shut out my prayer,
Closed in my road with well-cut stone/
my paths He likes to twist. ס

Does a bear ambush like He to me?/
A lion in secret places?
Directing me off my road, tearing me up,
He puts me in desolate places.
Directed his bow, He made me stand/
like a target to the shaft. ס

Entering my innards/
the sons of his quiver.
Ever am I laughed at by all my people/
their taunting song all of the day.
Even with bitterness filled me,
with wormwood sated me. ס

Further, with gravel my teeth He ground/
He made me cower in ashes.
Far from shalom is my flesh . . .
I have forgotten Your goodness,
For what should I say? 'gone is my hope/
my dignity fled from YHWH.' ס

Give a thought to my suffering,
the wormwood and poison,
Giving thought, I recall/
and my being despairs,
Gathers this to my heart,
therefore I have hope: ס

His kindness will not end/
his compassion not yet done,
Happens new each morning/
great is Your faithfulness.

He—YHWH—is my portion—says my very being/
thus will I hope in Him. ס

Is good—YHWH—to those who wait/
to the ones who seek Him out,
Is good—waiting and silence/
for YHWH's saving hand.
Is good for the strongman/
who carries a yoke in his youth. ס

Just let him sit and let him be silent/
for *He* has laid it on him,
Just let him give his mouth to the dust/
perhaps there will be hope,
Just let him give a cheek to his smiter
and let him be filled with reproach. ס

Keep on rejecting?
Not forever, My Lord.
Keep on inflicting?/
Compassion will come like his kindness.
Keep on afflicting?/
He no longer wants to aggrieve. ס

Let Him crush underfoot/
all the prisoners of earth,
Let the case of the strongman/
come before the Most High,
Let a man twist his lawsuit!/
My Lord will not see. ס

May someone say this: 'let it be!'/
If my Lord has not commanded.
Mandated from the Most High's mouth/
the evil and the good!
Might he complain—a living man/
a strongman for his sin? ס

The Keening Community
Now let us search and try our ways/
to YHWH let us turn.
Next, let us lift our hearts on fists/
toward our heavenly God.
No, we transgressed and disobeyed/
so You will not forgive. ס

Overshadowed with ire You pursued us/
You slaughtered us, You did not spare,
Overshadowed with cloud You ignored us/
stopping the passing of prayer.
Offal and garbage You made us
in the midst of the peoples around us. ס

Quite wide are the mouths of our foes,
open and gaping around us.
Quivering and quavering they see us,
disaster and destruction. ס

The Keening Strongman
Quick water comes down from my eye/
broken is my people's Daughter. ס

Poured out from my eye and not ceasing,
never with any respite,
Perhaps He will look down and see/
YHWH looking from heaven.
Piercing my being my eye/
over all my city's Daughters. ס

Reaching out like a trap for a bird—
for no reason they are my foes.
Raining down stones over me/
they threw down my life to the pit.
Round my head the waters flowed.
I said 'I am cut off.' ס

So I called out YHWH/
from the depths of the pit.
Say You will hear me/
hear my need, hear my cry,
Step close on the day that I call You/
keep saying 'do not be afraid.' ס

Take up, my Lord, the case of my being,
redeem for me my life.
Take note, YHWH, of all my wrong/
judge me with my judgement.
Take note of all their vengeance/
all their schemes for me. ס

Up to now You heard their reproach,
YHWH/all their schemes on me,
Utterings and mutterings of those opposed/
against me all the day,
Up they get and down they sit—
look!/I am their taunt song. ס

Visit on them payback, YHWH,
like the work of their hands.
Vouch for them an anguished heart/
let Your curse be on them!
Vanquish and destroy them now/
from under the heavens of YHWH.

פ

LAMENTATIONS POEM 4

[א]¹   **A**rghhh! It is blackened—gilt—it changed—the good gold//
Poured out are the holy stones at the head of all the streets.

[ב]²   **B**egotten of Zion, the precious ones, worth their weight in fine gold//
Arghhh! Now regarded as pots of clay, the work of the hand of the potter. ס

[ג]³ **C**ommon jackals even draw out the breast to nurse their young//
The Daughter of my people is now cruel like ostriches in the wilderness. ס

[ד]⁴ **D**oes it cling—the tongue of the suckling one—to his palate for thirst?//
The little ones beg for bread, not any offer it to them. ס

[ה]⁵ **E**aters of delicacies are desolate in the streets//
The ones brought up in crimson embrace ash-heaps. ס

[ו]⁶ **F**or it was greater—the iniquity of the Daughter of my people—than the sin of Sodom//
That was overturned in a moment, and no hands were laid on her. ס

[ז]⁷ **G**ood and pure were her Nazirites like snow, whiter than milk//
Redder were bones than rubies, like sapphire their form, ס

[ח]⁸ **H**ere now to be darker than soot in their appearance, not noticed in the streets//
Shrunk their skin on their bones, withered to be like wood. ס

[ט]⁹ **I**nfinitely better are they slain by a sword than slain by hunger//
Than they who pine away from lack of produce of the field. ס

[י]¹⁰ **J**ust see how hands of women of compassion boil their lads//
They become food for them. Broken is the Daughter of my people. ס

[כ]¹¹ **K**ept for last—YHWH—his fury, poured out his burning anger//
And He started a fire in Zion which consumed her foundations. ס

| [ל]¹² | **L**ittle did they believe—the kings of the earth and all the inhabitants of the world//
That enemy and foe would enter the gates of Jerusalem. ס |
|---|---|
| [מ]¹³ | **M**aybe from the sins of her prophets and the iniquities of her priests//
The ones pouring out in her midst blood of righteous ones. ס |
| [נ]¹⁴ | **N**ow they wander blind in the streets, defiled with the blood//
With none able to touch their garments. ס |
| [ס]¹⁵ | '**O**ut, Unclean' they call to them. 'Out, out, do not touch!'
Because they are fugitives and even wanderers//
They say amongst the nations, 'they are not again to sojourn.' ס |
| [פ]¹⁶ | **Q**uid pro quo YHWH destroyed them, never again to regard them//
The faces of the priests were not lifted up, the elders were not shown favor. ס |
| [ע]¹⁷ | **P**ining still are our eyes for help—useless!//
In our watching we watched for a nation that could not save. ס |
| [צ]¹⁸ | **R**outing our routes from going in our streets//
Came near our end, numbered our days, because it came—our end. ס |
| [ק]¹⁹ | **S**wifter are our pursuers than the eagles of the heavens//
Over the mountains they chased us, in the wilderness they waited for us. ס |
| [ר]²⁰ | **T**aken in their traps, breath of our noses, anointed of YHWH//
Of whom we said 'in his shade we will live among the nations.' ס |
| [ש]²¹ | **U**lulate and rejoice, Daughter Edom, those sitting in the land of Uz// |

Even over you the cup will pass—you will drink and be exposed. ס

[ת]²² **V**anquished is your iniquity, Daughter Zion, not again will you be exiled//
He will punish *your* iniquity, Daughter Edom, He will uncover *your* sins.

פ

PERFORMANCE POEM 4

The Keening Woman
Arghhh!
The Observer
    Blackened is the gilt—
        Changed the treasured gold//
Poured out are holy stones
    at the head of all the streets. ס

Begotten of Zion, precious ones,
    Worth their weight in gold//
The Keening Woman
    Arghhh! Now only pots of clay,
        Work of the potter's hand. ס

The Observer
Common jackals offer breast
    to suckle their own young//
Cruel is my people's Daughter
    An ostrich in the wild. ס

Does it cling—the tongue of the suckling
    to his palate for his thirst?//
Do little ones beg for bread,
    While no-one gives to them? ס

Eaters of delights
    desolate in the streets//

The ones brought up in crimson
>> Embracing ashen-heaps ○

For the iniquity of my people's Daughter
>> Is worse than Sodom's sin//
> Turned over in a moment,
>> and no hands laid on her. ○

Good and pure are those set aside,
>> like snow, as white as milk//
> Redder their bones than rubies,
>> like sapphire jewels their form, ○

Here now they are darker than soot,
>> Strangers in the streets//
> Shrunken their skin on their bones,
>> Withered away like wood. ○

It's better they're slain by a sword
>> than slain by wasting away//
> By pining away from starvation,
>> Nothing coming from the field. ○

Just see how compassionate hands
>> of women are boiling their lads//
> Food for the desperate they are.
>> My people's Daughter is broken. ○

Kept his fury—YHWH—for last,
>> poured out his burning rage//
> And He started a fire in Zion,
>> her foundations it consumed. ○

Little did they believe—
>> Dwellers and kings of the earth//
> That enemy and foe would come
>> And enter the gates of Salem. ○

Maybe the sins of her prophets,
>> iniquities of her priests//

The ones pouring out in her midst
> blood of the righteous ones. ס

Now wandering blind in the streets,
> They find themselves tainted with blood//
None able to touch their garments. ס

'**O**ut, Unclean' they call.
> 'Out, out, do not touch!'
Now fugitives and wanderers//
> In the nations they dwell no more. ס

Quid pro quo He destroyed them,
> Never to show them regard//
The faces of priests are lowered,
> Favor from elders was stayed. ס

The Keening Community
Pining still are our eyes
> for useless help//
In our watching we watched,
> No nation could save. ס

Routing our routes,
> We can't go in our streets//
We numbered our days,
> it is coming—our end. ס

Swift our pursuers,
> Like eagles of the heavens//
Over mountains they chase us,
> in the deserts they wait. ס

Taken in their traps,
> anointed of YHWH//
Of whom we had said
> 'in his shade we will live.' ס

Ululate and rejoice,
> Daughter Edom in Uz//

> For to you comes the cup,
> Drink and be bare. ס

Vindicated are you, Daughter Zion,
> Your exile is no more//
> Punished are *you*, Daughter Edom,
> For He will uncover *your* sins.

פ

LAMENTATIONS POEM 5

1. Remember, YHWH, what it was to us/take note and see our reproach.
2. Our inheritance was turned over to strangers/our houses to those who are noticed.
3. Orphans we have become with no father/our mothers are like widows.
4. Our water with silver we have drunk/our wood with a price comes.
5. Up to our necks we were pursued/we were weary—there was no rest for us.
6. To Egypt we gave a hand/to Assyria to satisfy bread.
7. Our fathers sinned and they are no longer/we their iniquities have borne.
8. Slaves rule over us/not any deliverer from their hand.
9. With our very being we will purchase our bread/from the face of the sword in the wilderness.
10. Our skin is like an oven made black/from the face of raging hunger.
11. Women in Zion they raped/young women in the cities of Judah.
12. Princes by their hands are hung up/faces of elders are not respected.
13. Young men to grinding mills they lift up/and boys under the wood stagger.
14. Elders from the gate have gone/young men from plucking their stringed instruments.

15	Gone is the joy of our hearts/overturned to lament is our dancing.
16	Fallen is the crown of our heads/woe to us because we have sinned.
17	Over this we were sick to our hearts/over these were darkened our eyes.
18	Over Mount Zion which is desolate/jackals walk on it.

פ

19	You, YHWH, forever sit/Your throne to generation and generation.
20	Why to eternity will You forget us?/Will You forsake us for a length of days?
21	Make us return to You, YHWH, and let us return!/Renew our days like old!
22	Because if rejecting You have rejected us/will You be angry towards us forever?

PERFORMANCE POEM 5

The Keening Community

1	Remember, YHWH, what it was to us/ take note and see our reproach.
2	Our inheritance to strangers is overturned/ our houses to those who are noticed.
3	Orphans are we with no father/ our mothers like widows will be.
4	Our water with silver we drank/ our wood with a price always comes.
5	Pursuing us up to our necks/ Weary and no rest for us.
6	To Egypt we gave them our hand/ to Assyria to give us our bread.
7	Our fathers sinned and have gone/ their evils we now bear.
8	Slaves are ruling over us/ Who will save us from their hand?
9	With our flesh we purchase our bread/

	because of the wilderness sword.
10	Our skin like an oven black/
	from the face of raging hunger.
11	Our women in Zion they raped/
	young women in cities of Judah.
12	Princes by hands are hung up/
	elders no longer respected.
13	Young men to mills lifted up/
	and boys under heavy wood stagger.
14	Elders from the gate have gone/
	young men from plucking their strings.
15	Gone is the joy of our hearts/
	overturned to lament is our dancing.
16	Fallen the crown of our heads/
	woe to us for we have sinned.
17	Now we are sick to our hearts/
	Now we have darkened our eyes.
18	We grieve over desolate Zion/
	jackals walk on it.

פ

19	You, YHWH, will forever sit/
	Your throne for generations.
20	Will You forget us evermore?/
	Will You forsake us all our days?
21	Make us return, YHWH, let us return!/
	Renew us in days like old!
22	In rejecting have You have rejected us?/
	Will You be angry forever?

Commentary on Lamentations

It seems especially appropriate to comment on the scroll of Lamentations through a performance lens. Elements that imply public performance of the scroll include its acrostic structure, aiding it in being learned by chanters as referenced in *Midrash Lamentations Rabbah*. Even if originating as an immediate reaction to the destruction of Jerusalem and its temple, it is probable that within a generation the poems were edited for regular commemoration of the destruction of the temple in community settings. Inner-biblical evidence points to a practice of fasting and mourning in the fifth month (*Av*) that commenced soon after the temple's destruction (Zech 7:3). Contemporary practice of reading aloud from the scroll on the fast of *Tisha B'Av* continues this tradition. Commenting on the effect of the acrostic structure, Corinne Carvalho notes that, "While the alphabetic acrostic functions in part on a visual level, this structure also has an oral effect on an audience. If the alphabetic structure served the audience more than the singer, this would suggest that the poems presume a public performance" (2018, 70). The different voices in dialogue, both individual and communal, also point to performance. The poets and poems respond to each other.

The discussion in this section will begin with some comments on the *crafting* of the scroll mirrored in my own translation. It will then take a deeper look at the scroll's *constraining* use of acrostic through the performance concept of "framing" as a way of containing emotion. Third, we will attend to the different *keening* voices in the scroll.

Crafting

I have already commented on the spectrum of translation methods ranging from formal (word-for-word) to functional (dynamic equivalence). I have also noted that in my translations, which fall at the formal end of the spectrum, I aim to stay close to the original Hebrew's use of vocabulary and word order, replicating the same Hebrew words and roots with the same English words and mirroring sentence structure, even at the risk of falling into "Yoda-speak."[71] The characteristic sentence pattern in Hebrew is verb-subject-object, while in English the pattern is subject-verb-object. We should note, however, that in Hebrew poetry the normal syntactic pattern is not as rigidly followed. Hebrew poetry with an acrostic structure has an additional unusual effect, as explained by Robert Alter: "This form [the alphabetic acrostic] leads to even more syntactic inversions than is common in biblical Hebrew, with the object of the verb 'fronted' at the beginning of many lines, but the poet exploits this pattern for expressive emphasis" (2019b, 657).

I am committed to a highly iconic translation because I am translating for *performance*. I want to hear as closely as possible what an original audience may have heard in an oral presentation of Scripture. If we can hear the repetition of words and sounds, notice which words come at the beginning of clauses signifying greater emphasis (fronting), be attentive to when verbs change from singular to plural or masculine to feminine, and have our attention drawn to when techniques such as chiastic structures or wordplay are being employed, we may have a better idea of what was intended for an audience to hear.

In translating Lamentations, it seemed important to replicate the acrostic pattern in my English translation. Not only does it highlight the intricacy of the original artistry of the scroll, but the patterns are also obvious whether read silently or spoken aloud. This creates an expectancy for the audience that encourages a heightened attention to the material. In an article on the use of the acrostic in Lamentations, Elie Assis notes that many have commented on the acrostic pattern and others discuss the theological impact of the scroll, but few have brought these concepts together. In the view of Assis, the acrostic form was employed *in order to* draw attention to the internal tension between form and content:

> The acrostic form was adopted so that the book would interact with the reader not only on an emotional level but on a rational one as well. The atmosphere of contemplation expressed through acrostics is meant to lead the reader to uncover a message and meaning beyond the deep expression of pain. The strict acrostic is designed so that the reader, deeply moved by the dreadful situations described in the book, will return to it for a second reading, but this time in order to reflect on it. (2007, 718)

For a modern audience, it seems to me, there should be a similar response to the scroll. We should be aware of both the painful content *and* the care with which it has been conveyed to us and ask ourselves how these aspects are related. My discussion below under the subheading "Constraining" will offer some reflections in this regard.

Others have attempted acrostic English translations of Lamentations, including recognized Bible translations. The translation of Ronald Knox (1955) is described by Delbert Hillers as a *tour de force*, but Hillers then adds, "though it must be said that Knox strains the English language more than the author of Lamentations did the Hebrew" (1972, xxiv). I have some sympathy for this critique made by Hillers. I turned to the Knox translation several times when stuck for inspiration but was rarely comfortable to replicate his version as it seemed to have departed too far from the Hebrew text. Hillers himself comments that, "for obvious reasons," he made no attempt to reproduce the acrostic feature in his own translation. He and many others, however, include the Hebrew letter at the beginning of verses in order to "call the reader's attention to this phenomenon in the original" (1972, xxiv). Bible versions that do this include the *Tanakh Translation* (Jewish Publication Society, 1985), the *Douay-Rheims* 1899 American Edition, the *Jubilee Bible* (Russell M. Stendal, 2000),[72] *The New English Translation* (*NET Bible*, 2006), and Robert Alter's translation (2019b).

Along with the *Knox Bible Translation*, I am aware of two newer translations that replicate the alphabetic acrostic: *The Voice Bible* (2012) and a translation made available online by its author, David Lee (2020). *The Voice Bible* is the result of collaboration among scholars, pastors, writers, musicians, poets, and other artists and was commissioned and published by Thomas Nelson and the Ecclesia Bible Society. David Lee offers a "beat-driven, rhythmical version" and also retains "Z" in his acrostic translation, insisting that "aleph to tav" must surely be conveyed in its totality by translating from "A to Z" and omitting other more dispensable letters![73]

It is worth comparing these listed translations against my own in order to demonstrate the principles that guided my translation. I have selected three verses from Poem 3 because the triple acrostic is readily apparent, and two of the three verses begin with the same Hebrew word. It will be clear when comparing the translations below that, along with myself, only the *Tanakh* and Robert Alter have translated the same Hebrew words consistently.

Tanakh Translation

7	ג	He has walled me in and I cannot break out; He has weighed me down with chains.
8		And when I cry and plead, He shuts out my prayer;
9		He has walled in my ways with hewn blocks, He has made my path a maze.

Douay-Rheims

| 7 Ghimel | He hath built against me round about, that I may not get out: he hath made my fetters heavy. |
| 8 Ghimel | Yea, and when I cry, and entreat, he hath shut out my prayer. He shuts out my prayer; |

⁹ Ghimel   He hath shut up my ways with square stones, he hath turned my paths upside down.

Jubilee Bible
Gimel
7   He has hedged me about that I cannot get out; he has made my chain heavy.
Gimel
8   Even when I cried and shouted, he shut out my prayer.
Gimel
9   He has enclosed my ways with hewn stone; he has made my paths crooked.

NET Bible
ג (**Gimel**)
7   He has walled me in so that I cannot get out;
         he has weighted me down with heavy prison chains.
8   Also, when I cry out desperately for help,
         he has shut out my prayer.
9   He has blocked every road I take with a wall of hewn stones;
         he has made every path impassable.

Robert Alter
7   He walled me in, I could not go out;   ג
         piled heavy bronze fetters upon me.
8   Even though I cried out and shouted,
         He blocked my prayer;
9   He walled in my way with hewn stone,
         He twisted my paths.

Knox
7   Closely he fences me in, beyond hope of rescue; loads me with fetters.
8   Cry out for mercy as I will, prayer of mine wins no audience;
9   Climb these smooth walls I may not; every way of escape he has undone.

The Voice
⁷ Cut off from every avenue of escape, God has fenced me in

    and tied me up with heavy chains.
⁸ Crying and carrying on do me no good;
    God shuts out my prayer.
⁹ Closed in and blocked by walls of cut stone,
    what paths I have left, He has twisted and confused my steps.

Lee
Confined, inescapably walled,
    he chained me and weighted me;
Cry though I into the void,
    he blanks out my prayer;
Confounding my walkway with boulders,
    he twisted my paths.

Mathews

[ː]⁷	Closed in around me and I cannot escape, he made heavy my chains,
[ː]⁸	Crying out I am, and calling for help/he shut out my prayer,
[ː]⁹	Closed my road with cut stone/my paths he twists.

    Word choice in translation is of particular interest to me. It is possible that translators who choose to translate the same Hebrew word with different English words do so in order to improve the aesthetic of the translated material. Repetition of words in English prose is deemed lazy and is drummed out in primary school—even as I write this book I am constantly reaching for the thesaurus to expand my lexical options! Biblical Hebrew has a smaller vocabulary than English, but Hebrew composition style is also different from English composition. In *The Art of Biblical Translation*, Robert Alter addresses principal aspects of biblical style including word choice: "The biblical writers . . . are so sparing in their use of language that the choice of single words is constantly telling, and if the translator gets one word wrong, it may throw an episode off-balance or even altogether misrepresent it" (2019a, 46).

    The vocabulary in biblical poetry is more expansive than in biblical narrative, but that only enhances the concern that if a poet chooses to repeat a word, shouldn't we respect and trust their choice? In the example I have used for comparison above, the repetition of "closed" (*gādar*) in the first and third verses of the triad effectively creates a chiasm that draws attention to the middle verse where the sufferer is crying out precisely because he feels closed in on either side! This effect is not as striking when different words are used to translate the Hebrew verb *gādar*.

I have not found any other translators who have followed the reversal of *ayin* and *pe* in the second, third, and fourth poems. It seems to me to be significant to replicate this imperfection in a performance of the poetry. For an audience following the acrostic this reversal will be surprising and elicit reflection on the intention of the original author. The correspondence with letters from the English alphabet enables a quip about whether the author was minding their Ps and Qs or, more likely, *not* minding their Ps and Qs. There may have been an intention to throw the audience off-kilter, reminding them that even with the tight structure of the acrostic, the world of the poet is still in turmoil.[74]

Commitment to literal replication of Hebrew in translation means paying less attention to meter. My "performance poem" versions of each poem aim to create audible poetic rhythm, a device privileged by performance poets, but some of the detail of the original is lost. I recommend a comparison with the translations of Robert Alter and David Lee. Alter wants to capture the "terrific compactness" of the poetry but has not attempted an acrostic translation (2019a, 93). Lee's translation both incorporates the alphabetic acrostic and replicates the *qinah* three-two stress pattern that has been recognized in some of the poetry of Lamentations.[75] In my own translations I have laid out the lines in shorter versets and included diacritics so that the performative nature of the poetry becomes more obvious.

Of the translations surveyed here, only *The Voice* translators have joined me in ascribing voices to the various poems, with *The Voice* attributing individual verses to the following personalities: Lady Jerusalem (1:9b, 11b, 18-22; 2:18b), Little Children (2:12), Passers-by (2:15b), Enemies (2:16b), Eternal One (4:7). *The Voice* translation also begins three of the poems with the anguished cry "Aaghh" (but fails to translate *ěkāh* this way in 4:2b). Surprisingly, no voice is identified for Poem 3, and the translation ignores the self-identification in 3:1 (*ănî hageber*, "I am the strongman") by translating the verse "Afflicted, I have seen and know what it's like to feel the rod of God's anger." Others have postulated identities behind the poems. Nancy Lee (2008, 39–42) identifies four voices: a prophetic voice that could have been Jeremiah, "Jerusalem's poet" (a female voice), and two other minor poets or singers who add laments. Erhard Gerstenberger suggests five alternating voices: a neutral speaker, the desecrated "dame" Zion/Jerusalem, God in person, an individual supplicant, and a community or congregation (2013, 123). Other than *The Voice* translation, as noted above, few would recognize one of the voices as belonging to God, with Kathleen O'Connor specifically claiming that God's is the "missing voice" (2002, 15). The voice of God is quoted twice (1:10, 3:57) and as such the poems provide part of that missing perspective even if not in God's own voice.

The dynamic nature of performance allows for, and even encourages, different renditions of the same script. My allocation of voices to the different poems, therefore, is just one amongst many possible interpretations.

Constraining

I understand the use of acrostics in Lamentations as a framing technique. We know of frames from the visual arts, where a painting or artwork is set in a frame or on a pedestal to allow the work to be viewed. Being the supporting or defining structure, it is often ignored in favor of the artwork itself. Frames are historical and cultural artifacts that have become boundaries for artworks. Even the simplest children's drawings usually take place on paper—an artificial rectangular field. Graffiti is acceptable in communities when public spaces are made available for such expression, thereby sanctioning and controlling it. Slam poetry that expresses anger or distress takes place in designated venues and times and is absorbed by expectant and appreciative audiences. In all these ways the frame has a *constraining* effect for the artwork.

Though taken for granted, even ignored, the frame is paradoxically the very thing that creates space for the artwork to be viewed and interpreted. As Louis Marin comments, "Through the frame, the picture is never simply one thing to be seen among many, it becomes the object of contemplation" (1996, 82). By separating the artwork from its surrounding environment, the frame draws our attention to the work. Richard Shusterman makes the same point when referring to events or stories that are "set apart from the ordinary stream of life" by being dramatized as theatrical performances (2001, 367). He speaks of dramatization as the staging or framing of scenes. The French term *mise-en-scène* is often used as a synonym for framing. By drawing attention to or setting apart the artwork, the frame has a *heightening* function.

A third function of the frame is its *clarifying* role. A frame shapes the way an artwork is perceived. Nudity, for example, could be framed either as art or pornography depending on its form of presentation and location of reception. This clarifying function is also apparent when we apply the concept of framing to other forms of communication. When we begin a story with "once upon a time" our audience immediately knows that we are not expecting them to believe our story as if it were recounting historical events. A poem and a news report could have the same subject matter but be perceived differently by an audience. Harry Baker, a British Slam Poetry champion, speaks of the potential for poetry to create a world where experiences, dreams, and beliefs can be communicated.[76] Both the composer of a poem and the audience member has a role in recognizing and interpreting the frame. The performer chooses the frame for presentation of the work and is constrained by the parameters of the form selected, but through this frame they can manipulate the audience's experience (for example, by pausing after witty wordplay to enable a reaction from the audience and to ensure that laughter does not obscure the next few words of the poem). An audience's appreciation and interpretation of the work will be enhanced by recognition of its frame.

Shusterman's essay "Art as Dramatization" alludes to all three of the frame's functions that have been identified: its constraining function is seen in that it demarcates what is framed from the rest of life; its heightening function is seen in the way it highlights and intensifies reality; and its clarifying function is seen in the context it gives for viewing the work or experience. Commenting on Aristotle's theory of catharsis, and preempting my turn to the acrostic structure of Lamentations, Shusterman notes,

> Art's frame permits us to feel even life's most disturbing passions more intensely, because we do so within a protected framework where the disruptive dangers of those passions can be contained and purged, so that neither the individual nor society will suffer serious damage. (2001, 370)

A framing structure has been identified for biblical lament literature, with typical laments including an address to YHWH, a complaint, words that reassure the speaker, motivational clauses for YHWH to act, a petition for justice or vengeance, and a vow of praise anticipating YHWH's intervention (Westermann 1981, 64). Though including deep anguish, sorrow, loss, anger, pain, and death, the laments nonetheless have a structure that points towards trust and hope for a new future.

The poems of Lamentations make use of this lament frame but adapt it by minimizing positive features and expanding complaints. The vow of praise is absent altogether. There are words of hope and reassurance in the third poem, but they are followed by more words of despair and doubt. That the poems are addressed to YHWH, however, attests to the confidence of expressing negative emotions within a preexisting relationship. The preservation of these poems as Scripture assures us that cries of pain and suffering are honored within faith rather than being ignored or denied.

The acrostic structure imposed on the poems of Lamentations has an even greater constraining effect than that imposed by the general lament frame. It creates order out of chaotic circumstances, compelling the poet to consider each word that is used to paint the picture of destruction, to express the pain of loss, and to search for a valid way of addressing YHWH within those experiences. It keeps a check on unbridled emotion by reining in thoughts and feelings and structuring them to fit within a predetermined order.

Like the scrolls of Songs and Ruth, this scroll has a special focus on the center of the composition. We can distinguish a broadly chiastic framing structure in the scroll of Lamentations with pairing between the first and fifth poems and between the second and fourth poems, leaving the third poem standing on its own. Poems 1 and 5 focus on the aftermath of the destruction of Jerusalem and Poems 2 and 4 describe the destruction as it happens. Poem 1 has no words of hope, and the words addressed to YHWH are merely asking that YHWH see the plight of the sufferer. Poem 2 is similar in its perspective and the nature of its address to YHWH. By contrast, Poems 4 and 5 both include expressions of hope for a new future. Though there are no words addressed to YHWH in Poem 4, at the end there is an assertion that punishment will pass from Judah to Edom, one of Judah's enemies.[77] Poem 5 concludes with a prayer addressed to YHWH, pleading for return and renewal. Poem 3 has the greatest level of theological reflection on the disaster, with a declaration of faith in YHWH's goodness and dependability approximately halfway through the poem (3:22-33). As Assis has argued (2007, 721–24), the acrostic structure draws attention primarily to this central poem and it is no accident that the verses of 3:22-24 are the best-known and treasured section of the scroll. The final triad of this hopeful section of Poem 3 (vv. 31-33) uses chiastic repetition to drive home the dependability of YHWH. The middle verse that begins *kî ʾim-hôgāh* ("for if he makes suffer . . .") is surrounded by emphatic negatives *kî loʾ yiznaḥ* ("for he will not reject") and *kî loʾ ʾinnāh* ("for he will not afflict").

The overall chiastic structure of the scroll and the specific acrostic arrangement in four of the poems attest to an intentional framing that constrains the set of poems, pointing the attention of the audience to the central faithful claims. The lack of an alphabetic acrostic in Poem 5 is the exception that proves the rule. Such a heavily imposed constraint is not needed due to the poem's more conventional lament frame: address to YHWH (5:1), complaint (5:1-18), motivational clauses for YHWH to act (5:19-20), a petition for justice (5:21). Though the poem has no words that reassure the speaker, these were heard in Poem 3. The other missing element in the lament structure is a vow of praise anticipating YHWH's intervention. Instead, the poem ends with an open-ended question: "Because if rejecting You have rejected us/will You be angry towards us forever?" (5:22). This, too, is theologically significant. Like the middle verse of the triad 3:31-33, the verse begins *kî ʾim* ("for if . . .") and this time the verb is *māʾas* ("to reject"), but there is no reassuring *kî loʾ* to precede or follow the question. The final sentiment of doubt is a reminder that, for some, pain does not come to an end. All we can do is hold on to assurances and promises and knowledge of the character of God (full of mercy and loving-kindness) and follow the practice of returning to the previous prayer, "Make us return to You, YHWH, and let us return!/ Renew our days like old!"

The constraining aspect of framing is not the only feature of acrostics that helps us appreciate the poetry of Lamentations. Its heightening role draws attention to the poetry and lets us hear the expressions of pain. By drawing attention to the words, the poet clarifies the experience of those suffering. We notice that this is wartime poetry. Like other experiences of war, it includes starvation, rape, torture, death in the streets, destruction of homes and livelihoods. Poetry gives words to experience. This poetry becomes a resource for others who also suffer and grieve. Daniel Smith-Christopher likens the poetry of Lamentations to that of blues music. There is also a set format for composition of blues music,

> But the artistry is in the creative and artistic uses of the recognizable form to discuss hard times, suffering, and personal desire and grief in a myriad of ways. Despite the negative themes, blues music has a discernibly healing impact, as listeners identify with the complaints and protests of hard times and mistreatment. (2015, 108)

Performance poets also speak of the value of slam events that enable the voices of those outside the dominant sphere to be heard and enable expression of experiences that otherwise remain buried. Emthithal Mahmoud, a refugee from Dafur, was interviewed by *The Guardian* after winning a World Poetry Slam Championship in 2015. She stated, "The poems I shared during this competition helped me grapple with personal experiences that left me speechless and only able to move forward through poetry."[78]

In contemporary situations of crisis and pain the scroll of Lamentations continues to be a resource for those who are powerless to express their pain, ensuring that their plight is neither ignored nor minimized. At the annual Jewish observation of *Tisha B'Av*, the scroll of Lamentations is recited in order to draw together many historical experiences of suffering. Contemporary biblical scholars have likewise made links between the biblical tradition and experiences of war and suffering in our own time (Lee and Mandolfo 2008).

By framing experiences of suffering within poetry that draws our attention, such experiences are given new voice and fresh visions for a different future.

Keening

I have identified four separate voices in my translation of the scroll of Lamentations. Despite the tradition linking the scroll to Jeremiah, there is no direct evidence to identify historical characters as authors of the poems.[79] As discussed earlier, generalities seem to be deliberately employed such that this material is available to be used universally. The archetypal Israelite leaders of king, priest, and prophet are all mentioned within the scroll but only as background figures. The voices themselves seem to be representative of ordinary members of the community who identify themselves strongly with their destroyed city in which they have lived and worshipped.

The keening woman represents the city of Jerusalem/Zion. In referring to "my warriors, my chosen ones, my sons, my maidens and my youths, my priests and elders" (Poem 1), "my daughter my people, my women my men" (Poem 2), her voice is that of a desperate mother, responsible for all in her care but unable to stem the tide of destruction. Other voices refer to her as Daughter Judah, Daughter Zion, and Daughter Jerusalem ("Daughter Salem" in performance poems), which function as ready-mades for the prophetic use of this term to represent the community. Unlike the daughter in the prophets, however, here she voices her protest and demands that YHWH look on her suffering (Mandolfo 2007). Even while admitting her failure, she protests that her punishment is too harsh.

The observer, though standing back and describing what is seen as if from a distance in third-person speech, is nonetheless neither unsympathetic nor judgmental about the experiences described. As has often been noted, the observer's stance changes partway through Poem 2 from spectator to advocate, directing speech to the keening woman, encouraging her to continue protesting, finally exhorting:

> Stand up, shout out in the night at the head of the watches,
> Pour out like water your heart, before the face of my Lord.//
> Lift up to Him your fists over the very being of your little ones,
> the ones fainting for hunger at the head of every laneway. (2:19)

The self-identified "strongman" of Poem 3 may best be understood as a representative sufferer. The language at times is similar to that of the suffering servant of Isaiah's scroll. Unlike the other voices, there is no admission of sin or guilt from the strongman. His voice, as already noted, has the strongest note of hope and trust that God's characteristics of loving-kindness, compassion, faithfulness, and salvation will again be known. He advocates acceptance, waiting, and silence.

Finally, the keening community is identified by plural first-person speech. As if standing on the sidelines, they respond to the other speakers. The first time they speak as one voice is in the psalm-like response to the strongman: "Now let us examine our ways and let us search / and let us return to YHWH." (3:40) The next few lines indicate a lack of confidence that this will be effective, and they break off partway through the acrostic with the wonderfully alliterated but devastating assertion "Quivering and quaking overcome us, disaster and destruction" (3:48). The strongman must take up the next line to maintain the acrostic and see the poem to its end. In Poem 4 the observer reaches the unhappy conclusion that YHWH would "never again regard them" (4:16), and the communal voice strikes up again. They describe the communal experience of invasion and the capture of their king ("anointed of YHWH") and conclude that poem with a sarcastic taunt of their neighbour, Daughter Edom, expressing the desire that the cup of punishment will pass on to others who are just as culpable. The community voice continues in Poem 5. In a series of short, sharp couplets they describe their plight again: dispossession, death of the population, prohibitive costs of survival, starvation, rape, slavery, an end to life as it had been. Finally, there is an admission of sin (5:16), but the reference to jackals on Zion is a pointed reminder to YHWH that the temple has also gone. The *petuchah* after verse 18 indicates a long silence, an effective device in performance. It marks a dramatic change of tone from complaint and lament to petition and prayer. Perhaps there has been a meaningful glance from the strongman; perhaps they have seen the woman bowed to the floor, spent in anguish. There is an appeal to the everlasting nature of YHWH, stressed in the vocabulary ("forever," "for generations," "to eternity," "a length of days," and "days of old"). They throw themselves onto the uncertain grace of the eternal one.

A number of ready-mades link the scroll to the broader expressions of cult and community. References to festivals heighten the experience of mourning by reminding listeners of happier times (1:4; 2:6, 7, 22). The use of "yoke" (1:14; 3:27) is a metonym for servitude and suffering (Gen 27:40; Lev 26:13; Deut 28:48; 1 Kgs 12:4; Isa 10:27; Jer 28:14). The verb *špk* ("to pour out") is used frequently in the poems (2:4, 11, 12, 19; 4:1, 11, 13). It is also used in the Hebrew Bible to refer to the blood poured out in sacrifice on the altar. This common use of the verb would evoke a sense of the lives of those suffering being sacrificed before YHWH. References to blood (4:13, 14), dead bodies (2:12, 20; 3:6; 4:9), and sickness (1:13, 22; 5:17)[80] function as ready-mades that recall cleanliness laws and stand as a reminder of the distance between the suffering community and their cultic faith. While the majority of these ready-mades have a negative effect, the phrase "Do not be afraid" (3:57), quoted from YHWH, is a ready-made from prophetic literature where it functions as a salvation oracle. It assures the listener that YHWH has taken note of their circumstances and increases the possibility of YHWH's intervention. Found in Poem 3, it is a significant ready-made for the speaker of the poem and his audience. Despite this, the last poem ends on a note of fearful uncertainty: "Will You be angry forever?" (5:22).

Connections with Lamentations

At the heart of the scroll of Lamentations is a keening over loss of home. For the survivors of the siege and attack on Jerusalem, life as they knew it was forever changed. With the temple destroyed and the exile of a significant proportion of the surviving population, major sources of livelihood had disappeared. The poorest were left amongst the ruins, and all the known structures undergirding society were stripped away.

Perhaps the most significant connection we can make with our own times is with the reality of climate change attributed to increased levels of atmospheric carbon dioxide from the mid-twentieth century onwards. The world as we know it is rapidly changing and we are in danger of losing our home, this planet. Even if the privileged are able to remove themselves from some of the worst effects and the poorest of our planet experience the greatest levels of devastation, climate change is affecting us all and is testing our faith in our communities, our leaders, and our God.

The United Nation's Intergovernmental Panel on Climate Change (IPCC) handed down its first report in 1990 and regularly updates predictions and statistics that rise alarmingly with each new report.[81] Key conclusions the panel has reached, supported by 97 percent of the world's climate experts, are that human influence on the climate system is undeniable; continued emission of greenhouse gases will have severe and irreversible impacts; adaptation and mitigation strategies are urgently needed; there is no single solution, but policies and cooperation is needed at all levels; and global emissions must reach zero by 2050 at the latest.[82] At the end of the first decade of this millennium, climate scientists were calling for action, warning that there was less than a decade to act before we reached irreversible tipping points. We are now in the third decade of this millennium and the situation continues to worsen. The most recent report predicts a global rise of average temperatures of 1.5 percent by 2030, ten years earlier than predicted in reports from a decade ago, evidencing the lack of effective action in the intervening period.

In response to this report, UN Secretary General Antonio Guterres warned that it is a "Code Red for Humanity."

The effects of climate change have been seen across the world. There has been a rise in extreme weather events including droughts, floods, wildfires, and king tides. Effects on the oceans include marine heatwaves and increased ocean acidity leading to loss of coral reefs. In the plant and animal kingdoms extinction of species is rife, and an increasing number of species are considered critically endangered. Rising average temperatures mean that polar ice sheets are melting and subsequently sea levels are rising. Encroaching seas threaten communities and entire nations with literal loss of their homes, creating climate refugees. Medical organizations have named the climate crisis an urgent public health crisis affecting access to clean air, safe drinking water, sufficient food, and secure shelter.[83] Climate change is truly a global phenomenon, crossing national, racial, and credal boundaries.

Like in the scroll of Lamentations, we are lamenting for our damaged home. For some, especially those members of our world community who have contributed least to global warming but are most affected by it, the cry may be "why is God punishing *us*?" (Rossing 2010, 119). This is one of the voices heard in the scroll of Lamentations, and it continues to ring out as a "kairos moment" in our own time, as noted by Barbara Rossing: "Deep spiritual questions about God's disfavour and punishment are a common response to the experience of calamitous disruptions in normal weather patterns that people are experiencing" (2010, 120). For many of us, however, there will be a communal recognition of our own sin, and the sin of our forebears, that has led to the situation. These voices we also hear in the scroll.

The opening lines of Gerald Manley Hopkins's poem "God's Grandeur" are often cited in praise of the beauty of creation:

> The world is charged with the grandeur of God.
> It will flame out, like shining from shook foil;
> It gathers to greatness, like the ooze of oil
> Crushed. Why do men then now not reck his rod?

As we read on in the poem, we see that the question of the fourth line is followed by a lament on how humankind has spoiled that wondrous creation:

> Generations have trod, have trod, have trod;
> And all is seared with trade; bleared, smeared with toil;
> And wears man's smudge and shares man's smell: the soil
> Is bare now, nor can foot feel, being shod.

This nineteenth century poet sounds surprisingly contemporary as we contemplate the effects humanity has wrought on the created world and the ongoing disregard for the earth that can no longer be felt under shodden feet. Perhaps already in the poet's time, but definitely in our own time, it is a call to lament.

Biblical scholarship in recent years, much of it inspired by the work of Walter Brueggemann, has given renewed attention to the value of lament in contemporary practice and worship. Lament is prominent within the biblical tradition, comprising around a third of the Psalter alongside the scroll of Lamentations. Laments are preserved that complain, rage, seek vengeance, and demand attention from God. As Brueggemann has claimed, the Hebrew Bible "regularly assumes that this is a proper, legitimate form of prayer and that Israel (and by extension, the faith community today) has a right and an obligation to ask of God in insistent ways" (2002, 118). Lament is a theological response that values the present moment and encourages us to sit with pain without being tempted too quickly to reflect on the past or envisage a new future. Lament gives words to the unspeakable, naming suffering with tears and emotion rather than explanation. As such it acknowledges and honors grief. By preserving and transmitting the scroll of Lamentations despite traditions of restoration and hope that followed in their history, Israel's grief was not written out of their story.

When focusing on climate change, the practice of lament is vital but not limited to faith communities. Events in public spaces such as protest marches, music concerts, and performance poetry are giving words to communal grief over the state of our planet and drawing attention to it as an issue worth our time and energy. The National Centre for Atmospheric Science at the University of Reading in the UK has developed a series of "warming stripes" graphics—visual representations of the change in average temperature per year as measured over more than a century (1901–2020).[84] Graphics exist for the globe and for many individual nations, and the common trend in each graphic is that the stripes turn from mainly blue at the start of the twentieth century to mainly red in more recent years, illustrating the rise in average temperatures. A coalition of Christian churches in Australia undertook a project of knitting scarves that correspond to the Australian warming stripes graphic. These scarves were presented to each of the Commonwealth government's members of parliament in the leadup to the 2021 Climate Change Conference held in Glasgow.[85] Such a simple visual representation of the plight of the planet is intended to start conversations and spur action.

The second stanza of Gerald Manley Hopkins's poem expresses confidence in the resilience of the natural world:

> And for all this, nature is never spent;
> There lives the dearest freshness deep down things;
> And though the last lights off the black West went
> Oh, morning, at the brown brink eastward, springs—
> Because the Holy Ghost over the bent
> World broods with warm breast and with ah! bright wings.

Such confidence in the durability of nature and the intervening power of God characterizes the majority of lament traditions in the Hebrew Bible with their framing structure that concludes in trust and hope for a new future. As has been seen, hope is also a feature in the scroll of Lamentations, although it is found in the middle of the scroll rather than the end. Writing on the presence of Psalm 23 in contemporary film and song, Karl Jacobson speaks of the characteristic "interplay of lament and trust, the exhortation to confident faith and the argument of present reality" (2009). This observation applies also to the scroll of Lamentations, albeit "lament" and "description of the present reality" outweigh "trust" and "confident faith." Unless there is that element of faith, however, despair will leave no room for action. Martin Luther King Jr. spoke of the "fierce urgency of now" in the context of the civil rights movement of the 1960s. This phrase is equally relevant in our time (Rossing 2010, 126). Depending on where we stand as we hear the poems of Lamentations spoken afresh into our context of climate change, they will give words to our suffering, will prompt our self-examination and admission of culpability, and/or will inspire us to become witnesses acting towards social change.

Unlike in the prophetic tradition, in the scroll of Lamentations there is no vision of a new Jerusalem. The voices in the scroll, speaking from the perspective of ordinary citizens bearing the brunt of disaster, cannot see past their crumbling present circumstances. But the voicing of their pain demands response. As we make connections between the scroll of Lamentations and the suffering of our planet, we must respond. At the very least it is an invitation for recognition of wrongdoing and repentance. Could it also serve as a wake-up call, a code red, to inspire action? Communities of faith should join in cries to the God of creation to see, to hear, to act, to renew. Knowing how close our world is to a critical tipping point, however, may mean the only option we have is to cry out in fearful uncertainty.

The Scroll of Ecclesiastes

Introduction

Eric Christianson begins his commentary on Ecclesiastes (also known as Qohelet) with a series of "testimonia" on the characteristics and value of the scroll. I am tempted to begin this introduction in similar fashion but will just list a few phrases from my own sources: "something of an enigma" (Strawn 2020); "the most peculiar book of the Hebrew Bible" (Alter 2019b); "one of the Bible's most challenging books" (Brettler 2005); "unlike the rest of the Old Testament" (Fuerst 1975); "the strangest book in the Bible" (Scott 1965). The first quotation Christianson uses comes from Gregory of Nyssa (c. 380 CE), who asserts that one must prepare to read Ecclesiastes by first reading Proverbs, because training is needed for the soul to receive such material in the same way that athletes train in the gymnasium (2012, 1)!

The fact that Gregory links Ecclesiastes and Proverbs alerts us to the nature of the scroll as one of the books classified as "wisdom literature," along with Proverbs and Job (and, in Catholic and Orthodox canons, Wisdom of Solomon and Ben Sirach). This literary term has been created by biblical scholars based on similar characteristics between books, but it is not without its challenges.[86] The wisdom tradition has little focus on the traditional Israelite concepts of covenant, cult, Torah, salvation history, and prophetic revelation. Instead, its primary source of inspiration is observation. To be "wise" is to reflect on one's observations of patterns in human action and the natural world and to generalize about the human condition and the world on the basis of observation and experience. Conventional wisdom traditions both accept wisdom as God's gift (Prov 2:6) and emphasize teaching and learning from others (Prov 13:20; 12:15; 19:20; 21:11; Job 8:8). The writer of Ecclesiastes seems to be skeptical about conclusions drawn by others, especially by those who compiled the book of Proverbs. He adopts the method of observation, using the verb *rʾh* ("I saw") eighteen times in the scroll, but rejects the conclusion that this leads to wisdom:

> And I have seen all of the work of God, for he is not able—the man—to find the work that is done under the sun, which although he toils—the man—to seek it, he will not find it. / And although he says he wants to know it—the wise man—he is not able to find it. (8:17)

The protagonist examines creation, society, wealth, work, justice, relationships, and death, concluding that all things are like *hevel*, traditionally translated "vanity," but the Hebrew word represents the transitory qualities of expelled breath (see below for further discussion of this term). As Bandstra comments, contrasting the book of Ecclesiastes with other wisdom literature, "The wisdom enterprise up until now had prided itself in discovering and articulating the order of nature, but that has turned into something quite different, a reason for despair" (1995, 457).

In contrast to the scrolls of Songs and Esther, there are many references to God in Ecclesiastes. Yet God (always Elohim, never YHWH) is distant, unable to be fathomed. The definite article is nearly always used with God's name. According to the scroll of Ecclesiastes, God is creator and provider but allows good gifts to be taken away (6:2). God gives work and toil for humankind to busy themselves with, but that toil is ultimately pointless, like chasing the wind (1:13-14). God judges, but the same fate of death comes to all whether they lived righteously or not (9:2). No prayers, complaints, or laments are addressed to God. As Scott notes in his commentary,

> In Ecclesiastes, God is not only unknown to man through revelation; he is unknowable through reason . . . the mysterious, inscrutable Being whose existence must be presupposed as that which determines the life and fate of man, in a world man cannot change, and where all his effort and values are rendered meaningless. (1965, 191)

Surprisingly, then, joy in life is also a theme found in this scroll. Four times the scroll claims there is nothing better than to eat, drink, and enjoy work (2:24; 3:12; 3:22; 8:15). And it is possibly these exhortations to be glad in toil and refreshment that link this scroll to the Feast of *Sukkot* (Booths).

The Scroll and the Festival of *Sukkot*

The scroll of Ecclesiastes is read during the Festival of *Sukkot*, the third of the pilgrimage festivals along with Passover and Shavuot. It celebrates the fall harvest and the blessing of four species of plant that grow in Israel. It is named for the temporary booths (*sukkot*) built outside homes prior to the festival and used for accommodation or meals during the week-long celebration (see Lev 23:34-42). There is a focus on hospitality as the booths give opportunity for meeting with others and, symbolically, for meeting with the divine presence. The practice of building booths probably derived from temporary field dwellings used by laborers during harvest time in the biblical period. The *sukkot* are built to give shelter from the elements, but according to rabbinic tradition the roof must be constructed of natural materials to allow a view of the stars. As such, Andrea Lieber claims it is a powerful symbol of Judaism: "Like the *sukkah*, Jewish tradition provides us with a framework of protection and shelter. But at the same time, this structure doesn't blind us to the larger world" (2012, 168). The festival's historical remembrance is of the forty years of wandering in the wilderness following the exodus from Egypt. It "remembers the fragility of existence during those long years of wandering, but at the same time, celebrates with great joy the protection God provided during that turbulent period" (Lieber 2012, 166).

During the celebrations four species of plants are gathered (Lev 23:40): citron (*etrog*), date palm (*lulav*), myrtle (*hadass*), and willow (*aravah*). The three leafy species are bundled to form a *lulav* that is held together with the citron fruit and waved in all four directions to attest to God's mastery over all of creation. In Kabbalist tradition the palm represents the spine, the myrtle the eyes, the willow the lips, and the citron the heart. The week's rituals include prayer for adequate rainfall over all the earth's vegetation in the coming year, suggesting its origins in an ancient agricultural fertility festival.

Along with the historical memory of the wilderness wanderings, this festival marks the completion of the yearly cycle of reading the Torah (*Simchat Torah*), which is celebrated in synagogues by dancing with the scrolls. Sometime between the eighth and tenth centuries CE in post-Talmudic Jewish tradition, Ecclesiastes was classified as one of the five *Megillot* to be read during a religious festival. Peter Machinist suggests that celebration of work completed, expressed both as joy and as a mood of reflection on memory and time past, resonated with themes in the scroll of Ecclesiastes (2004, 1605). Joel Kaminsky and Joel Lohr have an even more nuanced view of the connection between the scroll and the festival:

This is an unusual liturgical pairing in that Succot is a harvest festival that is defined by the Hebrew words *zeman simchateinu*, "the time of our joy," but the book of Qoheleth seems rather fatalistic and pessimistic. Clearly, the ancient Jewish sages who made this pairing noted Qoheleth's recurring advice to enjoy food and drink and enjoy life while in the world (5:18 [MT 5:17]; 8:15; 9:7). But they likely had an additional insight: true joy in life comes not from deluding oneself about the fact that our lives are fleeting and often trouble filled, but rather in finding ways to embrace the limited and sometimes difficult lives we live. (2015, 245)

The Background of the Scroll
The presence of parts of Ecclesiastes amongst the Dead Sea Scrolls indicates that it was already included in the canon of the Hebrew Bible before the Christian era, yet there was rabbinic debate in the second century CE and even later over whether it "defiled the hands" (see discussion in Songs chapter). As we have noted above, many thoughts expressed in the scroll did not correspond easily with the rest of the canon. Ultimately, however, the ancients made room for this "deeply critical and even strident voice that did not sing in tune with the others" (Murphy 1990, 55).

Scholars debate whether the "voice" in Ecclesiastes represents one or more authors. Ancient tradition ascribes authorship to King Solomon. The composition is introduced as "The words of Qohelet, son of David, King in Jerusalem" (1:1), a claim that is repeated almost verbatim in 1:12. At face value, such an epithet could refer to Solomon, who was the son of David and was king in Jerusalem. The book is a search for wisdom, and Solomon was connected to the tradition of wisdom (1:18). Most of the scroll is written in first-person speech and the second chapter sounds autobiographical with reference to building houses, planting gardens, amassing wealth and luxury including many slaves and concubines. The jaded assessment of these achievements (2:10-11) led to the suggestion that it was the aged King Solomon, looking back and regretting his failures, who authored the scroll.

The name Qohelet, however, gives pause, as it is not known elsewhere in connection with Solomon. Although often translated "teacher" or "preacher," *qohelet* is a noun with a plural feminine ending from the root *qhl* meaning "to assemble." This influenced the Greek Septuagint's title "*Ekklesia*" ("public assembly"), a term that became associated with the early church and continues in the English word "ecclesial" or "ecclesiastical." It has been debated whether Qohelet "assembled" wisdom (Rashi) or conflicting opinions (Metzudat Zion) or people to whom he could speak wisdom (Septuagint), but no consensus has been established (Machinist 2004, 1606). Robert Alter has pointed out, however, that the other times the root *qhl* is used in the Hebrew

Bible, it always refers to the assembling of people (2019b, 673). A description of Qohelet that forms an epilogue in the final chapter of the scroll claims,

> And more than being an assembler of wisdom/ again he taught the people knowledge, and he weighed up and searched and ordered many proverbs. // And he sought—Qohelet—to find words of beauty / and he was writing upright words of truth. // The words of the wise are like goads and like nails driven in, mastered in collections / given by one shepherd. (12:9-11)

This describes Qohelet as a sage whose characteristic teaching was by means of carefully crafted wise sayings that could nonetheless be provocative and disturbing, like the prods used by shepherds. These verses are almost universally attributed to a different author, however, and may have been corralling the unwieldy material of the scroll into the familiar category of wisdom speech to lend some legitimacy to the scroll. The introduction (1:1) and final few verses (12:9-14) are written in third person and were probably added to the composition at a later date. Within the main part of the book, the language, themes, and Aramaic influence on vocabulary and grammar suggest a postexilic date. There are two Persian loanwords but no Greek words, suggesting a date of composition in the Persian era.

So who was Qohelet? The style and content suggest an elderly, wealthy man of leisure, free to pursue intellectual activity, living in a bureaucratic setting with access to international trade. Several references to Jerusalem (1:12, 16; 2:7, 9; 8:10) may indicate the scroll's origin there. Despite the references to royalty, the scroll gives a generally negative view of royal life. Writing appreciatively of the literary style of the scroll, Alter suggests, "It is best to think of Qoheleth as the literary *persona* of a radical philosopher articulating, in an evocative rhythmic prose that occasionally scans as poetry, a powerful dissent from the mainline Wisdom outlook that is the background of his thought" (2019b, 673).

The Literary Character of the Scroll
Translation of the scroll of Ecclesiastes is not an easy exercise. The Hebrew itself is not especially obscure, but the ideas and language are complex. The topics are not clearly structured. Words, thoughts, and ideas are frequently repeated, and contradictory claims are made. We are admonished to take satisfaction from toil even though it is vexatious; to pursue knowledge though it brings sorrow and goading; to embrace youth and recognize that everyone

grows old; to eat and drink and enjoy ourselves while at the same time contemplating the fate of death for all humanity. Alter speaks of the movement of Qohelet's thought as "freewheeling and associative" (2019, 677). In this scroll, as in the scroll of Lamentations, there is a deliberate connection between content and structure. The looseness of form drives home the point that nothing under discussion is solid and able to be pinned down because there is always a contrasting thought.

A key metaphor that frames the scroll and is repeated throughout it is found in the Hebrew word *hevel*. The influential translation of the KJV, based on Jerome's Latin Vulgate translation of *vanitas*, is "vanity of vanities, all is vanity." This phrase opens and closes the original composition (1:2; 12:8), and the word *hevel* is found at the midpoint of the scroll (6:9), which breaks the scroll into two halves of 111 verses each. The numerical value of the Hebrew word *hevel* is 37, and when the word is repeated three times in the opening thematic statement the total value is 111. Clearly an author has spent time carefully structuring this composition with numerical principles in mind (Murphy 1990, 52; Peters 1919, 21).

The translation of *hevel* is much debated. Russell L. Meek (2016) helpfully summarizes the history of interpretation of the word since ancient times. Early Jewish interpreters understood it primarily in the literal sense of breath and the associated metaphorical sense of temporality or brevity. The similarity to the name Abel (*hāvel*) underscores the transitory meaning because the son of Adam and Eve in Genesis 4, murdered by his brother Cain, "doesn't even get a speaking part" (Strawn 2020, 146). The Septuagint consistently translated *hevel* with the Greek *mataiotēs* that had the same literal and metaphorical sense. Other similar words are vapor, steam, ephemerality, insubstantiality.

With Jerome's Latin translation of *vanitas*, influenced by dualistic thinking that contrasted spiritual and temporal worlds, the term was interpreted as a value judgment with words like emptiness, falseness, and futility becoming common translations. Jerome's interpretation of the book of Ecclesiastes is characterized as *contempus mundi*, which holds that the entire earthly realm lacks value. Whilst Reformers rejected this notion as devaluing God's good creation, they held on to the identification of "vanity" with human sinfulness.

In modern interpretation there is a large range of translations for *hevel*. Meek groups them as words relating to mystery (incomprehensible, unknowable, enigmatic); absurdity; emptiness (zero, nothing, void); breath (vapor, transience, ephemeral). Eugene Peterson translated *hevel* as "smoke" in *The Message*, giving a slightly negative connotation to the idea of tainted "breath."

Meek notes also that "vanity" persists in many translations. Finally, some translators use multiple referents for the same Hebrew word according to its context in the scroll.

Robert Alter (2019b, 675) insists that *hevel* is a metaphor rather than an abstraction, which, for him, renders "vanity" inaccurate as a translation. The metaphor has a broad scope, including futility, absurdity, insubstantiality, ephemerality, elusiveness, and the waste vapor exhaled when breathing out on cold day that is the opposite of the inspired *ruaḥ* (breath, spirit) that animates life. Alter uses the translation "mere breath" and the superlative form "merest breath" in his own translation of Ecclesiastes. Some contemporary authors simply retain the transliterated *hevel* to allow readers to choose their own interpretation (for example, Wolfe 2020, lii). I have elected to translate *hevel* with the word "dross." The majority of times it is used in the scroll it is signifying that, in the view of the Qohelet *persona*, the topic of discussion is worthless. The lingering sibilant sound at the end of the word "dross" contributes to its ephemeral connotation.

Whichever way *hevel* is translated, it is applied to most of the topics that are broached in Ecclesiastes, whether positive or negative. Wisdom, foolishness, work, pleasure, knowledge, skill, laziness, righteousness, wickedness, wealth, poverty, vows, discernment, love, hatred, youth, age, death—all are *hevel* to Qohelet. Willie Van Heerden (2001, 164) summarizes some of the ways in which interpreters have tried to resolve the differences within Ecclesiastes. Some have sought to harmonize the discords and others to subtract sections of the scroll as later additions. Some view contradictory material as quotations by the author who then goes on to refute them. More recent commentaries have invited us to hear a dialogue or a dialectic style, and some have even diagnosed psychological disturbance in the author of Ecclesiastes! Van Heerden believes that the author is unable to resolve the tensions he articulates, stating,

> He does not resolve these antinomies, but only describes them, bemoans them, and suggests how to live in such a refractory world. The contradictions do not make the book incoherent. On the contrary, Qohelet's persistent observation of contradictions is a powerful cohesive force, and an awareness of it brings into focus the book's central concern: the problem of meaning in life. (2001, 164)

In coming to the scroll via Biblical Performance Criticism, the concept of multiple voices in conversation on the meaning of life is one that has potential for performance. I have been especially influenced by the view of David Penchansky (2012), who speaks of three Qohelets: Pessimistic Qohelet, Fear God Qohelet, and Enjoy Life Qohelet. The idea of Qohelet as a literary *persona* can easily be expanded to conceptualize several literary *personas* sharing the same stage. The "creativity" section below will pursue this idea.

The Purpose of the Scroll
That the scroll of Ecclesiastes was preserved in Scripture may be due to its connection to Solomon or perhaps due to the editorial hand that aligned it with a more conventional perspective by concluding with these words: "All has been heard / The God you must fear, and his commandments you must keep. For this is for all humankind. // For every deed The God will bring into judgment along with every hidden thing / whether good or evil" (12:13-14). Nonetheless, the canon of Hebrew Scripture is not uniform in doctrine, genre, or approach to the questions of life. Robert Alter argues that the questioning and pessimistic style of this scroll may, in fact, have ensured its preservation as Scripture because it shows a writer ". . . who unblinkingly saw all human enterprise as herding the wind, who envisaged the same grim fate for rich and poor, for the righteous and the wicked, and who was led to question whether wisdom itself in the end had any advantage over foolishness" (2019b, 678).

Barry Bandstra offers similar a perspective, adding thoughts on how Ecclesiastes would have functioned for a postexilic community. In his view the scroll dates to the Greek era, but his comments would be equally apt if the original audience were under Persian colonial rule:

> There was truth in what Qoheleth said, at least at some level. It probably rang true especially to Judeans who were looking to survive in a world dominated by Greek rule, where they felt at the mercy of higher political powers. They were unable to see God's larger purpose and felt unable to affect it significantly. The Jewish community struggled with Ecclesiastes. Because of its somewhat troubling observations, they perceived the need to retrieve the book from heresy and give it an orthodox patina. The editorial history of the book gives evidence of their efforts . . . The concluding editorial is really quite remarkable. It attests to the vitality of the faith of the postexilic community. It obviously accepted, even perhaps encouraged, the creative kinds of thinking that took Torah to the edge in their efforts to apply Torah to their current circumstances. It took great effort—and the integration and synthesis were certainly not complete—yet room was made for theological thinking that stood on the verge of being unorthodox (Bandstra 1995, 458–59)

The editorial hand, so clearly at odds with the originality of thought and honest setting out of observation in the rest of the scroll, is perhaps deliberately creating distance between the *persona* whose views are not those of everyone. The value of the scroll of Ecclesiastes is that it is intentionally provoking thought and dialogue rather than commanding assent (Weeks 2010, 84).

Creativity in Ecclesiastes—A Television Talk Show

Dialogue seems to be at the heart of the scroll of Ecclesiastes. At the very least, an editorial hand is evidenced by third-person speech standing out from the first-person address that dominates the scroll. In 1:1 the scroll is introduced as "the words of Qohelet," and in 12:9-10 the composition steps away again to describe the character Qohelet, using terminology that is familiar to the wisdom tradition of the Hebrew Bible, including *ḥokmāh* (wisdom), *daʿat* (knowledge), *ḥiqqēr* (searching), and *mešālîm* (proverbs). An editor has therefore taken the words of Qohelet and inserted them between an introductory and explanatory frame, situating the author amongst the Israelite sages.

Even if we were to assume a single orator in the *persona* of Qohelet, he is having a dialogue with himself. As already noted, he circles around similar themes and presents contradictory views on the same topic:

> We hear Qoheleth admonish us to enjoy youth *for* we grow old; to enjoy toil *yet* it is a sorry business; to enjoy the *woman* whom we love *but* there is not one good woman in a thousand (!); to eat, drink, and wear festive garments *yet* sorrow, fasting, and mourning are better; to pursue knowledge *but* it only increases sorrow; to embrace life, *yet* like the sword of Damocles the ancient sentence, "you must die," hangs over us. (Crenshaw, quoted in Penchansky 2012, 58, italics original)

In particular, there is a disconnection between the assertion that God will judge fairly (3:17; 11:9; 12:14) and the concern that it matters not whether one has lived a righteous or sinful life; both lifestyles will result in the same fate (3:16; 7:15; 8:14; 9:2).

On this basis, many people see a further editorial note in the final two verses of the scroll, which begin "End of words. All has been heard" (12:13a). This seems an emphatic conclusion to the scroll, but there is still more—direct speech using imperative verbs "Fear God" and "keep his commandments" (the first reference to commandments in the scroll). These notions are frequently found in the Torah and Deuteronomistic history (Gen 22:12; Exod 9:30; Deut 7:9; 8:2, 11; 26:18; Josh 4:24; 22:5; 1 Sam 12:14,

24; 1 Kgs 8:58) and therefore represent more conventional theology than much of the discussion in the rest of the scroll. These last verses also reintroduce the concept of judgment with the assurance that God's judgment *will* be just. These last two verses, therefore, pick up and emphasize the idea scattered throughout the scroll that God who will judge humankind must be feared (2:26; 3:17; 5:7 [MT 5:6]; 7:18; 8:6, 12; 11:9). If so, there are at least two differing perspectives aside from the editorial voice.

A third dominant view focuses on the good things in life as gifts from God (2:24; 3:12-13; 5:18-19 [MT 5:17-18]; 8:15; 9:7, 9; 11:7). This perspective opposes the assertion that *everything* is *hevel*.

In addition, there are poetic sections that stand out with their heightened parallelism and use of metaphor. Two poems about time (3:1-8; 9:11) and one on aging and death (12:2-7) are especially evident as compositions that may have existed independently from the scroll in its earliest form.

While it is possible to slice the pie of Ecclesiastes in many different ways, I have chosen to present it as a conversation between three different *personas*, moderated by a host. The format of a television talk show is familiar. Such shows range in content from light to serious and are often broken up by musical items (and advertisements if on commercial television channels). After breaks, the dialogue resumes, often with some repetition of ideas. The conversation is free-flowing, and a good host maintains interest by astutely drawing out the views of guests and guiding the discussion, reiterating their points, and keeping material up his or her sleeve if needed to give the audience variety. Importantly, guests are tolerated even if they have different views, and value judgments are rarely made by the host of the show.

While it is possible to discern different voices in the scroll, one voice dominates. The catchphrase "all is dross" is scattered throughout the scroll (1:2, 14; 2:1, 11, 15, 17, 19; 2:21, 23, 26; 3:19; 4:4, 7, 8, 16; 5:10 [MT 5:9]; 6:2, 4, 9, 11; 7:6; 8:10, 14; 9:1; 11:8, 10; 12:8) and a pessimistic outlook on life represents the leading perspective. For this reason, the talk show is styled as one with a host, a keynote speaker, and two panelists offering different perspectives on the topics under discussion. The host ties the conversation together, inserting leading questions of his own along the way. The entire script is lifted directly from my translation of the scroll of Ecclesiastes. Lack of identified speakers as we see in narrative ("then he/she said . . .") and lack of punctuation in the original Hebrew gives freedom to break the dialogue into questions and responses, imagining the flow of the conversation.

Informed by Lisa Michele Wolfe's commentary on Ecclesiastes (2020) and undoubtedly influenced by The Byrds' beautiful rendition "Turn, Turn, Turn," I have envisaged the two "time" poems (3:1-8; 9:11) as musical interludes sung by a female voice.[87] Wolfe acknowledges that the scroll of Ecclesiastes has a predominantly masculine perspective but notes that the verbs and themes in the time poem are activities relating to women in other parts of the Hebrew Bible. It begins with two verbs specifically relating to activities in which women had particular roles: giving birth[88] and dying (see Jer 9:20 [MT 9:19]). Stories of Esther, Ruth, the Woman of the Song of Songs, Daughter Zion, Tamar, Deborah and Jael, Rahab, Judith, and the woman of Proverbs 31 amongst others show that women plant, pluck up, heal, kill, break down, build up, grieve, laugh, weep, dance, embrace, seek, keep and release, tear and sew, keep silent, speak, love, hate, take part in war, and long for peace. As Wolfe comments,

> [A] study of the key words in the poem of 3:1-8 shows that, for the most part, it would not have excluded women's experiences. Indeed, biblical women have significant connections to many of the stichs in this poem. This analysis does not preclude the association of the poem with an M [masculine] voice . . . What it does show is that women readers, then and now, might have found a place for themselves in this classic philosophical reflection. (2020, 43)

I have also interpreted the "aging" poem of 12:2-7 as a preexisting piece outside of the conversation that takes place in the talk show. Each of these poems focuses on themes that are discussed elsewhere in the scroll but have an independent style that invite this characterization. There is only one *petuchah* in this scroll and three *setumah* markers that surround the time poem of 3:1-8, and the third precedes the second short time poem. These are envisaged as opportunities for commercial breaks.

TELEVISION PANEL DISCUSSION
ECCLESIASTES

THE WORDS—a weekly panel discussion
Special Guest: Qohelet

[narrow angle shot, showing just the host and Qohelet]

Host, *addressing Qohelet*:
1:1-3a [Your] words, Qohelet, son of David, king in Jerusalem: "Dross of dross, dross of dross. All is dross." What gain for the human being in all his toil?

Qohelet:
1:3b-7 The one who toils under the sun? A generation goes and a generation comes, and the earth forever stands. And it rises—the sun, and it sets—the sun, and back to its place it hurries, it is rising there. It goes to the south, and round to the north. Around and around it goes—the wind, and over and around him comes the wind. All the rivers are going to the sea, and the sea is not full. To the place where the rivers are going, there they return to go again.

Host:
1:8 All those words are wearisome!

Qohelet:
1:8b-9 A man is not able to speak, not satisfied is the eye, not filled is the ear with hearing.
What is, that is what will be. What is done, that is what will be done. And not any of all of it is new under the sun.

Host:
1:10 There IS a word of which it is said, see! This is new! This!

Qohelet:
1:10b-1:11a Already it was forever, from before us. There is no remembrance of the first things.

Host:
1:11b And also of the last things that will be?

Qohelet:
1:11c There will be no remembrance of them from those who are last.

פ

[after the commercial break]

Caption at the bottom of the screen:

1:12 Qohelet—was king over Israel in Jerusalem.

Qohelet:
1:13a I gave my heart to seek and explore in wisdom over all that is done under the heavens.

Host:
1:13b It is an evil task God gave to the sons of humanity to be tasked with.

Qohelet:
1:14 I saw all the doings that were done under the sun. And look, all is dross and herding wind.

Host:
1:15 The crooked is not able to be straight! The deficient is not able to be numbered!

Qohelet:
1:16-17 I spoke, I did, on my heart, saying, I . . . Look. I was made great. I added wisdom over all who were before me in Jerusalem. And my heart saw MUCH wisdom and knowledge! And I gave my heart to the KNOWING of wisdom and to the knowing of silliness and folly, and I knew also that this is herding wind.

Host:
1:18 Because in much wisdom is much vexation? And those who add knowledge are those who add pain?

Qohelet:
2:1-3a [Well] I said, I did, in my heart, go now. Let me test pleasure and let me see good. But look. Also this is dross. For laughter I said "madness!" And for pleasure, "what is this doing?" I explored in my heart, to stimulate with wine my flesh. And my heart is guided with wisdom and yet holding onto folly until I see.

Host:
2:3b What it is then good for the sons of humanity to do under the heavens for the number of the days of their lives?

Qohelet:
2:4-7a [Well], I made great my works. I built for myself houses and I planted for myself vineyards. I made for myself gardens and paradises and I planted in them trees of all fruits. I made for myself blessing of waters, To make drink from them a forest of sprouting trees. I purchased slaves and maidservants, and the sons of the house were for me. Also purchases of cattle and sheep—many there were for me,

Host:
2:7b More than all who were before in Jerusalem!

Qohelet:
2:8-10a I gathered for myself also silver and gold, and treasure of kings and provinces. I made for myself tenors and sopranos, and delightful things for the sons of humanity, even concubines. And I was great, and yes, I added more than all who were before me in Jerusalem. Indeed, my wisdom stood before me. And all which they asked of me—my eyes that is—I did not keep from them, I did not withhold my heart from any pleasure, for my heart was pleased from all my toil,

Host:
2:10b This was the reward!

Qohelet:
2:10c-11a From all my toil I turned and faced myself—all my doings that my hands had done, and all the toil which I had toiled to do, And look, all is dross and herding wind.

Host:
2:11b And not ANYTHING is advantage under the sun?

Qohelet:
2:12-16a I turned and faced myself to see wisdom and silliness and folly. For what is the human being who comes after the king? He can only do what he has already done. And I saw—I myself—that there is advantage in wisdom over folly, like the advantage of the light over the dark. The wise have eyes in their heads, and the fools in darkness are walking. And yet I know, also I, that one fate is fated for them all! And I said—I myself—in my heart—the fate of the fool—also I—it will be my fate. And why am I wise—I myself—even more? And I spoke in my heart, that also this is dross. For there is not any remembrance for the wise—as with the fool.

Host:
2:16b Forever?

Qohelet:
2:16c-18a Already in the coming days all is forgotten. And how will he die? The wise together with the fool. And I hated life! For evil over me was the doing that was being done under the sun. For all is dross and herding wind. And I hated all the toil which I toiled under the sun.

Host:
2:18b What will be left for the human being who is after me?

Qohelet:
2:19-21a Who knows? Wise will he be or a fool? And who will have control over all *my* toil which I toiled and my wisdom under the sun? Also this is dross. And I turned around—I myself—to despair in my heart, over all the toil which I toiled under the sun. For there is a human being whose toil in wisdom and in knowledge and in skill

and for a human being who did not toil in it, he gave him his portion. Also this is dross.

Host:
2:21b And a great evil.

[Wider angle shot, now showing the three guests]

Qohelet:
2:22-23 For what becomes of the human being in all his toil and in the striving of his heart
Which he toiled under the sun? For all his days are vain, and vexatious is his task. Also in the night his heart will not lie down. Yes, this is dross to him.

[One of the other guests is shifting in his seat impatiently with his hand raised, and the host motions for him to speak]

The Optimist
2:24 Nothing but GOOD for the human being who relishes and drinks, and lets his body see good in his toil. I've seen this—I myself—that from the hand of the God is this!

Host:
2:25 Who can relish and who can enjoy more than HIM?

The Pietist *(interjecting)*:
2:26a For to a human being who is good before him, he will give wisdom and knowledge and pleasure, and for the sinner he gave a task to gather and to collect, to give to the one who is good before the God.

Qohelet:
2:26b This is dross and herding wind.

Host, perceiving it is time for a break, introduces a song by the folk singer 'Season':

Host:
3:1   For all, 'Season,' and her new hit,
      'A time for all matters under the heavens.'

ס

Season:
3:2-8   A time for birthing and a time for dying;
A time for planting and a time for uprooting the planted;
A time for killing and a time for healing;
A time for breaking through and a time for building;
A time for grieving and a time for laughing;
A time for weeping and a time for leaping;
A time for casting away stones and a time for gathering stones;
A time for embracing and a time to be far from embracing;
A time for seeking and a time for ceasing;
A time for keeping and a time for releasing;
A time for tearing and a time for sewing;
A time for silence and a time for speech;
A time for loving and a time for loathing;
A time of war and a time of peace.

ס

Host [after the commercial break and to the panel as a whole]:
3:9 What advantage is there for the worker in what he toils?

The Optimist:
3:10-11a I have seen the task which God gave to the sons of humanity to be tasked with. Everything he made beautiful in its time.

Qohelet:
3:11b Indeed! Eternity he has put in their heart, without which the human being cannot find the work which he worked—the God that is—from beginning until end.

The Optimist:
3:12-13 I know that there is not any good in them but to enjoy and to work for good in his life. And indeed every human being who relishes and drinks and sees good in all his toil, a gift of God this is!

The Pietist:
3:14-15 I know that all HE works—the God that is—will be forever, over this not any can add and from it not any can take. And the God has worked so let them fear before him. That which was already is, and the thing that is to be already will be. And the God seeks out the pursued.

Qohelet *(frustrated)*:
3:16 But again, I have seen under the sun in the place of justice—there is wickedness, and in the place of righteousness—there is wickedness.

The Pietist:
3:17 I have said, I in my heart, the righteous one AND the wicked one the God will judge. For a time for all matters and over all the work is there.

Qohelet:
3:18-19a I have said, I in MY heart, over the things of the sons of humanity the God is testing them, to see that they are a beast, they themselves. For the fate of the sons of humanity
and the fate of the beast is a single fate. As one dies, so the other, and the life-breath of the one is for both.

Host:
3:19b And the advantage of the human being over the beast is nothing?

Qohelet:
3:19c-20 All is dross. All are going to a single place. All will be from the dust, and all return to the dust.

The Optimist:
3:21-22 But who knows? The life-breath of the sons of humanity is going upwards, and the life-breath of the beast is going downwards, to beneath the earth. And I have seen that there is not anything better but that the human being should enjoy his work, for that is his lot. For who can bring him to see what will be after him?

Qohelet:
4:1-5 I went back—I myself—and saw all the oppression that is done under the sun, and look! The tears of the oppressed and not any for them comfort, and from the hand of their powerful oppressors not any for them comfort. And I thought, I myself, of the dead who have already died, Better than the living who are living still. And better than both of them are those who have not even been, who have not seen the evil doings that are done under the sun. And I have seen, I myself, all toil and all skill, deeds that are the envy of a man for his neighbor, Also this is dross and herding wind. The fool hugs his hands and relishes his own flesh.

The Optimist *(interjecting)*:
4:6 Better is a full fist that is quiet than two handfuls of toil and herding wind.

Qohelet *(continuing)*:
4:7-8a And I went back—I myself—and saw dross under the sun. When there is one without a pair, no son or brother for him, and no end for all his toil, also his eyes are not satisfied with wealth.

Host:
4:8b Why am I toiling? And depriving my body of goodness?

Qohelet *(continuing)*:
4:8c This *is* dross and an evil task it is!

The Optimist *(consoling tone)*:
4:9-12 Better are the two than the one, for there is for them good wages for their toil. For if they fall, the one makes his friend stand up and alas for him who falls and has not any to make him stand. Also if they lie down—two of them—and it will be warm for them, but for

one, how to be warm? And if one should overpower him, the two will stand against him.
And the three-fold thread is not quickly broken.

The Pietist:
4:13-14 Better a lad poor and wise than a king old and foolish who does not know how to be wary still. For from the prison house he came out to reign for also in his kingdom he was born poor.

Qohelet:
4:15-16 I saw all living things that are moving under the sun alongside the SECOND lad who will stand in his place. There is not any end to all the people, all who were before him and all who will come later, and none enjoy him. For also this is dross and herding wind.

The Pietist:
4:15-16 I saw all living things that are moving under the sun alongside the SECOND lad who will stand in his place. There is not any end to all the people, all who were before him and all who will come later, and none enjoy him. For also this is dross and herding wind.

Host:
5:5 Yes, better to not vow than to vow and not complete it!

The Pietist:
5:6 Do not let your mouth cause your flesh to sin,
and do not say before the God that it was a mistake.
Why should he be angry—the God that is—over your sound
and dismiss of the work of your hands.

Qohelet:
5:7a There are many dreams, and much dross, and many words.

The Pietist:
5:7b The God you should fear!

Qohelet (changing the topic):
5:8-10 If oppression of poor and violation of justice and righteousness you see in the province, do not be astounded over the matter for a

high one over another high one is watching, and higher ones still over them! And there is advantage in the earth in all this. A king belongs to a serviced field. One who loves silver is not satisfied with silver, and one who loves abundance has no gain. Also this is dross.

The Optimist:
5:11a As good things multiply, those who relish them multiply.

Qohelet:
5:11b-12 And what benefit for its master except what his eyes see? Sweet is the sleep of the slave, whether little or much he relishes. But for those abundant in wealth no rest for him when he sleeps.

Host:
5:13 [Yes], there is an evil illness I have seen under the sun, wealth being kept by its master for his own evil.

Qohelet:
5:14-16a And that wealth is destroyed in the evil task, and he sires a son with not anything in his hand—nothing! Like as he came out of his mother's womb, naked he shall return just like he came, and nothing will he carry from his toil that he brought in his hand. Yes, this is an evil illness: how he came, thus he goes,

Host:
5:16b And what advantage for HIM when he toils into the wind?

Qohelet:
5:17 All his days in darkness he relishes, and vexation—much of it—and illness and hostility.

The Optimist *(interjecting, frustrated)*:
5:18-20 Look, what I have seen—I myself—is good. It is beautiful to relish and drink and to see good things in all his toil which he toils under the sun, from the book of the number of days of his life which he gave to him—the God that is—for this is his lot. Also each of the human beings who he gave—the God that is—wealth and possessions and his power to relish it and to carry his lot and to enjoy his toil, this is a gift of God it is. For he will not much remember the

days of his life. For the God will make him answer with the joy of his heart.

Qohelet:
6:1-5 There IS an evil which I have seen under the sun, and much of it over the human being: a man to whom the God gives wealth and possessions and glory and nothing lacking for his body and for all which he desires for himself, but the God will not empower him to relish it, instead, a different man will relish it. This is dross and an evil illness! If a man sires a hundred and lives many years, and many are the days of his life, yet his body is not satisfied with goodness and also a burial wasn't for him, I say better than him is one who was miscarried! For in the dross he comes and in the darkness he goes, and in darkness his name is covered. Also sun he has not seen and not known, more rest for this one than him.

Host:
6:6a Although he lives a thousand years twice over, goodness he will not see?

Qohelet:
6:6a-8 Is not to one place all are going? All the toil for the human being is for his mouth. And even so the flesh is not filled. For what more for the wise than the fool? What good is it for the poor to know how to walk among the living?

The Optimist *(interjecting)*:
6:9a Better an eye that discerns than a body that wanders!

Qohelet:
6:9b-11a Also this is dross and chasing wind. What has been was already called its name, and what is known is he—a human being. And he is not able to dispute with one stronger than him. For where there are many words—much dross.

Host:
6:11b What more for the human being?

The Optimist:
6:12-7:1a Who knows what is good for the human being in life? The few days of life of his dross pass like the shadow. Indeed who can declare for the human what will be after him under the sun? *Tov shem mishemem tov!* A good name is better than good oil.

Qohelet:
7:1b The day of death is better than the day of one's birth.

The Pietist *(taking the opportunity)*:
7:2-4 It is good to go to the house of drooping, better than going to the house of drinking. This is the end for each human being. And the living should take this to heart. Good is vexation, better than laughter, for facing evil is good for the heart. A heart of wisdom is in a house of drooping, but a heart of foolishness is in a house of joy.

Qohelet:
7:5-6 Good to hear a rebuke of wisdom! Better than a man hearing a song of fools. For like the crackle of the nettle under the kettle—this is the laughter of the fool. And also this is dross.

The Pietist:
7:7-8 For oppression is madness for the wise. And a bribe corrupts the heart. Good is the end of something—better than its beginning. Better to be long-winded than high-spirited.

The Optimist:
7:9-12 Do not be quick in your spirit to be angry, for anger in the bosom of fools lodges. Do not say what they were like—the former days, that they were better than these. For it is not in wisdom you are asking about this. Good is wisdom if it is inherited, and an advantage to anyone who sees the sun. For the shadow of wisdom is like the shadow of silver. And the advantage of understanding is that the wisdom will give life to its master.

The Pietist:
7:13 See the work of the God. For who is able to straighten what he has made crooked?

The Optimist:
7:14a On a good day enjoy good!

Qohelet:
7:14b And on an evil day watch out!

The Pietist:
7:14c HE has made one alongside the other—the God that is—for what reason the human being cannot find out.

Qohelet:
7:15 The whole I have seen in the days of my life of dross: There are righteous destroyed in their righteousness and there are wicked prolonging in their evil.

The Optimist:
7:16-17 Do not practise much righteousness and do not gain much wisdom. Why devastate yourself? Do not practise much wickedness and do not be a fool. Why die if not your time?

The Pietist:
7:18-20 It is good that you hold this, and from another as well do not rest your hand, for he who is a God-fearer will go out from all of them. Wisdom strengthens the wise more than ten rulers who are in the city. For there is no human being righteous on the earth who does good and does not sin.

Qohelet:
7:21-23 Also to all the words they speak do not give your heart, then you will not hear your servant cursing you. For also many times your heart knows that also you have cursed others. All this I have tested with wisdom. I have said, "let me be wise" yet she is far away from me.

Host:
7:24a Far away? What is that?

Qohelet:
7:24b And deep, deep.

Host:
7:24c Who can find it?

Qohelet:
7:25-26a I turned around, I myself, and my heart, to know and to explore and to seek out wisdom and reckoning, and to know wickedness is folly, and foolishness is silliness. And I found, I myself, more bitter than death is the woman, she who snares and her heart traps and her hands fetter.

The Pietist *(interjecting)*:
7:26b Good is the one before the God, he will escape from her but the sinner will be captured by her.

Qohelet:
7:27a See this I have found . . .

Host:
7:27b [Let's hear what] Qohelet says!

Qohelet:
7:27c-28a One by one to find a reckoning. This is what my body was seeking.

Host:
7:28b But did not find?

Qohelet *(slowly and precisely)*:
7:28c One human being in a thousand I have found, but a woman in all these I have not found.

The Optimist:
7:29a Except, see, I found this. That the God made the human being upright.

Qohelet *(interjecting)*:
7:29b And they sought out many reckonings.

Host *quiets everyone and reads an old quote from Qohelet:*
8:1   Who is like the wise man?
           And who is knowing the interpretation of a word?
       Wisdom in a human being makes his face shine,
           And the grim look of his face is transformed.

Qohelet *(grinning)*:
8:2a The utterance of a king—obey it!

The Optimist:
8:2b-3a In view of the word of the oath of God. Do not be afraid of him, just walk away, do not stand on an evil word.

Qohelet:
8:3b-4 All which he pleases he does. In the word of a king is authority and who says to HIM "what are you doing?"

The Pietist:
8:5-6 The one obeying a command will know no evil word, and time and judgment he will know—the wise heart. For all matters there IS a time and judgment, for the evil of the human being is great on him.

Qohelet:
8:7-11 Not anyone knows what will be, for what will be, who can tell of it? Not any human being has authority over the wind to hold back the wind. And not any has authority over the day of his death, and not any has discharge from the war, and wickedness does not deliver its master. And I have seen and given my heart to all doings that are done under the sun, a time when a human being has authority to do harm to another human being. And I have seen the evil ones buried—they would come and go from the holy place, and they were praised in the city when they did thus, also this dross! When not anything is done to sentence the evil work quickly, thus filled up the heart of the sons of humanity for doing evil.

The Pietist:
8:12-13 Although a sinner does evil a hundred times and lengthens their days, I know it will be well for the God-fearers who fear before his face. And good it will NOT be for the evil, and they will not be

made long—their days—like a shadow—those ones who are not fearing before the face of God.

Qohelet *(agitated)*:
8:14 There IS dross which is done on the earth: there ARE righteous ones and what happens to them is like the work of the wicked, and there *are* wicked ones and what happens to them is like the work of the righteous. I say also THIS is dross.

The Optimist *(awkwardly trying to change the topic)*:
8:15 I myself laud enjoyment, for there is nothing better for the human being under the sun than to relish and to drink and to rejoice and this will accompany him in his toil all the days of his life which the God has given to him under the sun.

Qohelet:
8:16-17a Well, I gave my heart to know wisdom, and to see the task that is done on the earth.
Also in the day and in the night not any sleep was seen in my eyes. And I HAVE seen all the works of the God, that the human being is not able to find the work that is done under the sun, which though the human being toils to seek it, he will not find it.

Host:
8:17b Although he says he wants to know it—the wise man—he is not able to find it!

Qohelet:
9:1-2a I have given my heart to examine all this: that the righteous and the wise and their works are in the hands of the gods. Also love, also hatred, not any can know—any human being—all this is dross before them. There is to all the one fate: to the righteous and to the evil, to the good and to the clean and to the unclean and to the sacrificers and to those who give no sacrifice. Like the good, like the sinner, like the one swearing, like the one who refrains from swearing.

Host:
9:2b This is an evil in all that is done under the sun—that there is one fate for all.

Qohelet:
9:3 So the hearts of the sons of humanity are full of evil, and silliness is in their hearts, in their lives, and after it to their death.

The Optimist:
9:4 For the one who is joined to all living there is a confidence: *A living dog is better than a dead lion!*

Qohelet:
9:5-6 But the living—they know that they will die. And the dead—they are not knowing anything! There is not again any reward for them. Forgotten is their memory! Also their love, also their hatred, also their jealousy is already destroyed, and they no longer have any portion forever in all that is done under the sun.

The Optimist *(exhorting the audience)*:
9:7-10 Go, relish with enjoyment your bread, and drink with a good heart your wine. For he has already accepted your works—the God that is! At all times let your clothes be white and put oil on your head—let there be no lack. See through life with a woman you love, all the days of your life of dross, which were given to you under the sun, all your days of dross, for this is your portion in life and in your toil which you are toiling under the sun. All that your hand finds to do, in your strength do it! For there is not any doing and reckoning and knowledge and wisdom in Sheol, which is where you are going.

ס

Host *[after the commercial break]* introduces another song by *Season*:

Season:
9:11 I went back and I saw under the sun
    Not to the swift is the race
        Not to the mighty is the war
    Not to the wise is bread
        Not to the intelligent wealth
    Not to the knowledgeable favor,
For time and chance befall all.

Host:
9:12 He doesn't know—the human being—that his time is like the fish that are taken in the evil net and like the birds caught in the trap? Like this they are snared—the sons of humanity—for the evil time that will fall on them suddenly?

The Optimist:
9:14-15a I have seen this wisdom under the sun and great it is to me. A city—a small one—and men in it few and there came to it a king—a great one—and surrounded it and built over it siegeworks—great ones! And there was found in it a man, poor, wise, and he delivered the city with his wisdom.

Qohelet:
9:15b-16 And no human being remembers that man—that poor one! I said, I myself, better is wisdom than might, yet the wisdom of the poor is despised, and his words—not any of them are heard!

The Pietist:
9:17-18a Words of wisdom, quiet ones ARE heard, more than the shouting of a ruler among fools. Better is wisdom than instruments of battle.

Qohelet:
9:18b But one sinner destroys much good.

The Pietist:
10:1-3 A dead fly makes odious the flowing oil of the perfumer. Heavier than weighty wisdom is a little foolishness. A heart of wisdom goes to his right, and a heart of a fool to his left. And also in the road when the fool is walking, his heart is absent. And he says to all, a fool is he!

The Optimist:
10:4 If the wind of the ruler gets up over you, do not let your place be put to rest, for calmness will put to rest great sins.

Qohelet:
^{10:5} There is evil I have seen under the sun like the mistake that goes out before the face of power.

The Optimist:
^{10:6-7} He was set—the fool—over many heights and the rich in lowly places sit. I have seen slaves upon horses and princes walking like slaves on the earth.

The Pietist:
^{10:8} He who is digging a pit will fall into it. And the one breaking a wall—a snake will bite him.

Host:
^{10:9} He who quarries stones will be hurt by them. The one splitting trees will be endangered by them.

The Optimist:
^{10:10a} If the iron is blunt and has not had its edges whetted, it will need mighty strength.

The Pietist:
^{10:10b} And the advantage of success is wisdom.

Host:
^{10:11} If the snake bites before it has been charmed, there is no advantage to the master charmer!

The Optimist:
^{10:12} Words in the mouth of a wise one brings favor but lips of a foolish one swallow him.

The Pietist:
^{10:13} The words of his mouth are the beginning of foolishness, and the end of his mouth is evil silliness.

Qohelet (*interrupting*):
^{10:14-18} FOOLS make many words! He does not know—the human being—what will be from after him. Who can tell it? The toil of fools

makes them weary—he does not know how to walk to a city. Alas for you, earth, when your king is a lad and your princes in the morning relish their food. Happy are you, earth, when your king is a son of nobles and your princes in the proper time relish food, in strength, not in a drunken stupor. The rafter sags through double laziness and the house leaks due to the idleness of their two hands.

The Optimist:
10:19 For laughter is the making of bread, and wine gives joy to life! And silver answers them all.

Qohelet:
10:20 Also in your thoughts do not curse a king, and in your bedroom do not curse the rich, for a bird of the heavens will make that sound walk, and a master of wings will tell the word.

The Optimist:
11:1-3 Send your bread on the face of the waters. For in many days you will find it. Give a portion to seven or even to eight for you will not know whether there will be evil on the earth. If the clouds are full, rain on the earth will pour down. And if a tree falls in the south or in the north, the place where it falls—there it will be.

Host:
11:4 And the one observing the wind will not sow! And the one looking on clouds will not reap!

The Pietist:
11:5 Just as you know nothing of the way the life-breath enters the bones in the womb.
So you do not know the work of the God who made everything.

Qohelet:
11:6 In the morning sow your seed, in the evening do not let your hand be put to rest. For you know nothing of what will succeed—this or this? Or whether both will be good.

The Optimist:
11:7-8a And sweet is the light, good for the eyes to see the sun. For if many years he lives—the human being—in all of them let him rejoice.

Qohelet:
11:8b And let him remember the days of darkness for many there will be. All that comes is dross.

The Optimist *(appealing to the audience)*:
11:9a Rejoice, young man, in your laddishness, and let your heart be good to you in the days of your youth, and walk in the ways of your heart and in the desires of your eyes.

The Pietist *(also to the audience)*:
11:9b-11a And know that over all these the God will bring you into judgment. And remove anger from your heart, and pass over evil from your flesh.

Qohelet *(stage whisper)*:
11:11b Lad time and the prime of life are dross.

Qohelet moves to the lectern for his poetry reading

The Pietist *(taking the opportunity)*:
12:1 Remember your creator in the days of your youth until the days of evil come and the years come near when you say "not any to me matter".

[narrow angle shot, showing just Qohelet]

Qohelet *(from the lectern)*:
12:2   Until it turns dark—the sun and the light and the moon and the stars,
         And they return—the clouds—after the rain.
         Until the days when they trembled—the keepers of the house,
         And twisted are men of valor.
         And they cease—the grinding women—for they are few,

> And darkened are the ones seeing at the windows.
> And closed are the doors of the souk.
> > Low is the sound of the grinding,
> And he rises for the sound of the bird,
> > But bowed down are all the daughters of song.
> From the heights he is afraid and terrors in the road.
> > It blooms—the almond—and it drags—the grasshopper,
> And it breaks—the desire.
> For going is the human being to his eternal house,
> > And they will turn in the souk—the mourners.
> Until it is demolished—the cord of silver,
> > And crushed is the bowl of gold,
> And shattered is the pitcher on the well,
> > And crushed is the wheel on the bore.
> And it returns—the dust—to the earth like it was,
> > And the life-breath returns to the God who gave it.

Applause

Qohelet *(shrugs)*:
12:8 Dross of dross, all is dross.

[Wider angle shot, showing the full panel again]

Host:
12:9-10 Not only wise, Qohelet; not only one who gathers wisdom, also he teaches knowledge to many people, and weighs up and searches and orders many proverbs. And he has sought out—Qohelet—to find words that mattered, and has been writing upright words of truth.

Qohelet *(smiling)*:
12:11-12 The words of the wise are like goads and like nails driven in, mastered in collections, given by one shepherd. And further than these, my son, be warned. In the making of books there is not any end, and much study is a weariness of the flesh!

Host:
12:13a End of words. All has been heard.

The Pietist *(urgently standing and raising his voice)*:
12:13b-14 The God you must fear, and his commandments you must keep. For this is for every human being. For every deed the God will bring into judgment along with every hidden thing, whether good or evil.

[Over these last words a reprise of one of Season's songs begins to swell and the camera pans back to see the panel shaking hands and exiting]

Commentary on Ecclesiastes

I have read Ecclesiastes as a certain type of performance—a conversation in the context of a talk show. While this is clearly not the only way one can interpret this scroll, it highlights the differing perspectives offered in a free-flowing discussion about the pursuit of wisdom. I will initially examine each of the *panelists* to draw out the differences between the three perspectives, asking if any or all of them offer themselves as models for reenactment for lives of faith. Second, I will draw out the *performative* aspects that are highlighted when the scroll is read this way. Finally, when reading or hearing this scroll, we notice the contemporary nature of much of the discussion. I will draw out the *prevailing wisdom* inherent in the scroll.

Panelists

Qohelet. Qohelet is the key *persona* in the text. Unlike the book of Proverbs, which presents wisdom as a series of self-evident truths, the scroll of Ecclesiastes identifies the individual who carries the debate and uses his own observations and experience as the basis for assertions that are made. In this it is similar to the book of Job. As noted above, all wisdom literature prioritizes experience, but Job and Ecclesiastes offer protagonists who articulate their own personal quest for understanding their experience. It is important to recognize that a persona functions as a literary device to offer or test ideas and is not necessarily reflecting the actual life of the original writer. As with any great literary character, however, we are invited to analyze the character's perspective and find resonances and challenges for our own thinking.

The catchphrases of Qohelet, "all is dross" and "herding wind," unite the scroll by framing and being scattered throughout the discussion. Any idea that is explored ultimately circles back to the assertion "all is dross (*hevel*)." Of the many possible meanings of *hevel* discussed above, I have interpreted it as a blend of worthlessness and ephemerality. Its frequent combination with "evil" (1:13-14; 2:17, 21; 4:3-4, 8; 6:2; 8:10) ensures that the connotation is more negative than positive. The word *hevel* is frequently paired with "herding wind" (*reʿût rûaḥ*), a phrase that implies a pointless exercise. The verb *reʿût* has the same root as "tending a flock," so the translation "herding the wind" (Alter 2019b) is arguably more representative of the Hebrew than "chasing after wind" (NRSV).[89] Nonetheless, each translation implies a futile activity. When these phrases are combined with the observation that there is ultimately no difference between a wise man and a fool or even between a human being and a beast, since all end up with the same fate of death, they offer a predominantly pessimistic outlook. Qohelet at times may be quoting traditional wise sayings (2:13-14; 4:5; 7:6; 8:1), but he seems to do so in order to point out problems with the conventional wisdom they contain.

Notably, it is Qohelet whose speech is marked by the greatest use of first-person pronouns. Independent pronouns are not always necessary in Hebrew because verbs incorporate the pronoun, so when they occur, they stand out. Of the twenty-eight occurrences of "I" (*anî*) in the scroll, all but five are spoken by Qohelet. This is an indication of his self-absorption and bias for his own observation over received wisdom and fits with my characterization of Qohelet as a "celebrity" guest in a talk show. He is not without a sense of self-irony, however. Though claiming "I was great" in comparison to others in Jerusalem (1:16; 2:9), he accepts that even if a king has inherent authority, he cannot control key aspects of life (8:7-8).

Qohelet's poem on death (12:2-7) and his rhythmic style (9:2a, 5-6) demonstrate accomplished oratory skills. Though "preacher" is not the best translation of "Qohelet," it is easy to see how such an appellation became popular.

The Optimist. Clearly there is an optimistic voice in the scroll of Ecclesiastes, even if it is not the dominant voice. It commends enjoyment of life and claims that good things come as a gift from God (2:24; 3:10-11a, 13; 5:18 [MT 5:17]; 8:15; 9:7). These passages at times contradict what has gone before, even using the same terminology, denoting the "glass-half-full" approach of the Optimist. Whereas Qohelet speaks of the drudgery of toil under the sun (1:3b; 2:17-19; 2:22; 8:17a) and observes "evil" under the sun (4:1, 3; 5:13 [MT 5:12]; 6:1; 10:5), the Optimist sees life "under the sun" as a blessing (5:18 [MT 5:17]; 8:15; 9:9). Qohelet refers to "wisdom under the sun" as "dross" (2:19), while the Optimist sees "wisdom under the sun" providing a "great" illustration of wisdom at work (9:14-15a). Qohelet asks what advantage can be found in toil (3:9), and the Optimist responds that the "task" God gave is "beautiful in its time" (3:10-11a). Qohelet warns of future death (3:20; 9:5), and the Optimist counters by counselling enjoyment of life in the present (3:21; 9:7).

Norman Whybray (1982) went against the grain of scholarship on the scroll of Ecclesiastes when he claimed that Qohelet was a preacher of joy. Whybray's original article claimed that the whole of the scroll is dominated by optimism, but his later commentary is a little more nuanced:

> [Some claim] it is the dark sayings of Qoheleth which express his true attitude. Yet it is equally possible to argue that it is just this series of positive statements, punctuating the book, which expresses Qoheleth's true

conclusions: that it is only the person who has taken full account of the vanities of this world and faced up to them who is free to receive the divine gift of joy in simple things. (1989, 24–25)

I have accepted a text variation in 2:25 attested by Greek and Syriac witnesses that asks, "Who can relish and who can enjoy more than *him*?" (against the MT that reads "me" instead of "him"). In the mouth of the Host, this statement becomes an affirmation for the Optimist's relish for life.

We observe, however, that the Optimist frequently resorts to aphorisms (4:6, 9-12; 6:9a; 7:1a, 9-12; 9:4; 11:1-3) as well as trading pithy sayings with others in 10:1-13. Such sayings, like their counterparts in the books of Proverbs and Job, prove true in the right context but have the potential to sound shallow when misapplied.

The Pietist. Like the Optimist, the Pietist refers regularly to God, but rather than relishing in the good gifts of God, the language that predominates for the Pietist is "fear" of God. Given that the context of the Pietist's contributions is often the judgment of human beings, the verb "fear" (*yrʾ*) is an appropriate one. We should note, however, that this verb can be translated "revere" or "worship," so it is not entirely negative in its meaning. As it happens, exhorting others to be "God-fearers" (7:18; 8:12) puts the Pietist in good company in the Hebrew Bible. This term is used in only two other contexts: of Abraham when he is commended for being willing to sacrifice his son Isaac (Gen 22:12) and of Job as part of his description of being a "blameless and upright" man (Job 1:1, 8; 2:3).

The Pietist, while aware that God will bring all things to judgment, believes that God's judgment will be just (3:17; 7:18; 8:6, 12; 11:9b; 12:14). This perspective contrasts with that of Qohelet who has no faith in the righteous being rewarded and sinners punished (3:16; 7:15; 8:14).

Commentators who argue that the scroll of Qohelet represents a single voice tend to remove moral implications from their translations. Roland Murphy, for example, claims that the terms "good" and "sinner" in 2:26a should be translated "lucky" and "unlucky" on the basis that elsewhere the scroll denies a distinction between good and evil (1992, 26–27). If understood as the perspective of a God-fearing interlocutor, however, we would expect an ethical stance to be stressed. Elsewhere in the scroll the Pietist equates behavior with consequences (8:12-13; 11:9b; 12:14).

The Pietist and the Optimist use imperative verbs more frequently than Qohelet. Both are surer of their positions than he. The Pietist is the surest in that he claims the last word in the scroll, even after the statement "End of words. All has been heard" (12:13). The judgmental attitude of the Pietist is underscored by the fact that his last word is "evil" (12:14). In similar fashion to the use of the scroll of Lamentations, Jewish tradition dictates the repetition of the second last verse at the completion of reciting the scroll to avoid this lasting negative note.

Role Models? Could any of these three panelists be role models for reenactment by contemporary people of faith? The scroll itself does not suggest how the voices relate to each other; it just places them side by side as in a talk show panel. Two of the panelists draw conclusions to their presentations: Qohelet claims "All is dross" (12:8) and the Pietist insists "Fear God and keep his commandments" (12:13). The last words of the Optimist sound suspiciously like the summation of the book of Judges:[90] "Walk in the ways of your heart and in the desires of your eyes" (Eccl 11:9a), and "In those days there was no king in Israel, and everyone did what was right in their own eyes" (Judg 21:25). Yet, just as the time poem exhorts, there is a "right time" for all things: for enjoyment of the good gifts of life; for fear of God; and for honest assessment of the human condition. As we will consider below, there is wisdom for *our* time in each of these voices.

Performative Aspects of the Scroll

The scroll of Ecclesiastes has a rhetorical style that adapts well to performance. The repetition of the key phrases "all is dross," "herding wind," and "under the sun" keeps the listener focused on the combined message of the ephemeral and futile nature (dross, herding wind) of human existence (under the sun). The contrasts offered in the time poem (3:1-8) and Qohelet's lists of people types (9:2a) allow listeners to find their place in what is being described.[91] These implied invitations along with the occasional rhetorical question draw the audience into the performance, as do ready-mades that evoke familiar concepts and then surprise the audience by twisting their expectations.

Ready-mades. References to David (1:1) and kings (1:1, 12; 2:12; 4:13; 5:9 [MT 5:8]; 8:2a, 4; 9:14; 10:16-17, 20) in the context of a book searching for wisdom remind us of Solomon in both positive and negative ways. Chapter 2, where Qohelet describes his achievements in Jerusalem, echoes the successful portrait of Solomon painted in the book of 1 Kings but also the excesses that led to his downfall. The word *šiddāh* (and plural form *šiddôt*, 2:8) that occurs only here in the Hebrew Bible was translated as "cup-bearers" by the LXX but is usually translated "concubine" in modern translations, perhaps influenced by the assumption that the portrait of Solomon lies behind the description. As we saw in the chapter on the scroll of the Song of Songs, *šdh* underlies words for mountains and breasts. The extravagant description of the life of this king along with the assessment that all is "dross and herding wind" agrees with the Deuteronomistic summing up of Solomon's life (1 Kgs 11:1-6). Yet the phrase "the wise heart" (8:5) that comes later in Ecclesiastes is used of Solomon also (1 Kgs 3:12). The combined effect of these contrasting portrayals serves to support the theme of the scroll that wisdom, even if gifted to humans, is full of contradictions.

References to Jerusalem (1:1, 12, 16; 2:7b, 9) and the "house of God" (5:1 [MT 4:17]), "holy place" (8:10), and "sacrifice" (5:1 [MT 4:17]; 9:2a) could have reminded audiences of the centrality of the temple for Israelite life. Yet for the Pietist, fools also enter the house of God (5:1 [MT 4:17]), and in Qohelet's view there is no significant difference between those who sacrifice and those who do not (9:2a). An audience would be left wondering whether there is inherent value in the Jerusalem temple.

Unsurprisingly, since this is part of wisdom literature, there are references to God as creator and specifically to the Genesis account of creation. Frequent references to "Adam" and "sons of Adam" (translated in my script as "human being" and "sons of humanity") would no doubt have meaning for ancient audiences and, indeed, more recent audiences up until postmodern times. My choice of translation was based on sensitivity to inclusive language, which is a more recent concern for audiences of biblical literature.[92] Heavens and earth (5:2 [MT 5:1]), light and darkness (2:13; 11:7-8; 12:2), sun, moon, and stars (12:2), birds (9:12; 10:20; 12:4) and beasts (3:18-19), and the number seven (seven pairs in the poem of 3:2-8; 11:2) are all associated with Genesis 1, the first creation story. Moreover, like God in Genesis 1, the Optimist sees what is good (5:18 [MT 5:17]). Mention of the dust from which we come (3:12; 12:7), the life-breath (3:19a, 21; 11:5; 12:7), naming of human beings (6:10), and the gardens with fruit-bearing trees (2:5) evoke memories of the second creation story of Genesis 2–3. The unusual terms *pardēsîm* (2:5, "paradises," often translated "parks") and *bᵉrēkôt māyim* (2:6, "blessings of waters," often translated "pools") add to a positive vision of the created world where there is no notion of disobedience, yet these positive descriptions give way to the assessment by Qohelet that all that is good in creation is "dross."

Another unusual word that occurs only in the scroll of Ecclesiastes is *ḥešbôn* ("reckoning," 7:25; also 9:10). This word is a homonym for a city in the Transjordan regions of the Amorites and Moabites. The following verse (7:26a) has the word "bitter" (*mar*) and reference to "the woman who snares." Given the proximity of Ecclesiastes to Ruth in the *Megillot*, could this reference in Ecclesiastes be a sly critique of the tale of Ruth? If so, the author of Ecclesiastes is aligning himself with those who see foreign wives as a dangerous element in Israelite life.[93]

There could also be allusions to the scroll of Esther. A "wise heart" is associated with obedience to the word of a king (8:4-5). Later in the scroll (10:17) we hear the word *baštî* (pronunciation: "vashti"). Its translation in this context is "drunken stupor" and therefore invokes the scroll of Esther through both name and emphasis on excessive drinking. If these allusions are deliberate, they could be understood as another negative reference to foreign wives or Israelite women who countenance foreign marriages.

On the other hand, there are key themes in the scroll of Ecclesiastes that are also themes in other scrolls in the *Megillot*, though portrayed differently. "Fate" (*miqreh*) in Ruth 2:3 is a fortuitous "chance" with a happy outcome but for Qohelet is the resignation that all that awaits the human being, whether wise or a fool, is death (2:14; 3:19a; 9:2b). The concept of "remembering" is important in most of the scrolls of the *Megillot*. Its role differs both between and within scrolls. In Ecclesiastes, the Optimist counsels enjoyment of the moment, "for he will not much *remember* the days of his life" (5:20 [MT 5:19]). Qohelet says the opposite: "*Remember* the days of darkness for many there will be" (11:8b). The Pietist exhorts *remembrance* of the Creator while there is capacity to do so (12:1). For all three, the remembering is a human activity. In the scroll of Lamentations, the keeners beg *YHWH* to *remember* the suffering of Jerusalem. The scroll itself is used to ensure that the memory of suffering is kept alive for the Jewish community. In the scroll of the Song of Songs it is the chorus who ensures that *remembering* takes place, allowing the words of the loving couple to continue to inspire new audiences. And remembering is key to the scroll of Esther. The story pivots on the king *remembering* what had been done by Mordecai, changing the fate of all the key players.

Time is a key theme in the scroll of Ecclesiastes. Two words can be translated "time," and the ancient Greek witnesses illustrate the difference between them by translating *zᵉmān* as *chronos* and *ʿēt* as *kairos*. I have translated "season" and "time" respectively. *zᵉmān* is also used in Esther and Nehemiah in reference to appointed dates, but *ʿēt* has the meaning of the "right" or "critical" time.[94] Rather than asserting that there is a "right time" for a particular activity, however, the word is used to claim that *all* activities have equal "rightness" (3:1-8). Moreover, no matter how successful human activity is, whether by human effort or human ingenuity, the "right time" that will come to all is the fate of death (9:11). Neither of the time poems refer to God, but the use of seven paired lines in 3:2-8 suggests that "the number seven [was] pointedly chosen because of its traditional association with the sacred" (Alter 2019b, 685). One can imagine different assessments of God's control over time by the three panelists. For the Optimist it is an opportunity to celebrate God's timely gifts, for the Pietist it is a sign of God's just control over the world, and for Qohelet it reveals God as indifferent and inscrutable.

Wordplay. Wordplay is seen as the word *hevel* is echoed in other similar-sounding words scattered throughout the scroll, and I have tried to replicate these examples in my translation by using words that have similar sounds to that of "dross," my choice of translation for *hevel*. Thus, *tᵉvahēl* is translated "drivel" in 5:1 (MT 5:2); *vᵉhivvēl* is translated "dismiss" in 5:6 (MT 5:5); and *ĕvel* is translated "drooping" in 7:2, 4. Undoubtedly there is also deliberate use of the homonym *ḥevel*, translated "demolished" in 12:6.

The word *rûaḥ* is difficult to translate. The same word is used for the wind that blows over the earth at the end of the flood, the blast of YHWH's nostrils that holds back the waters of the Reed Sea, the breath of life, and the spirit of God hovering over the waters of chaos. The word occurs hundreds of times in multiple contexts. Although I have translated "wind" for most of its occurrences in Ecclesiastes in the phrase "herding wind," on a few occasions *rûaḥ* as "life-breath" is necessary for a contrast with *hevel*, the "expelled breath" that follows inspiration in the breath-cycle.

The perspective of life as an unending cycle is not often promoted in Hebrew Scripture, probably because it is representative of ancient Near Eastern fertility religions that stand in opposition to the historical faith of the Israelites. Nonetheless, the language and imagery of the scroll of Ecclesiastes encourages this cyclical view. The opening speech of Qohelet is full of participle forms that with their continuing movement emphasize the unending rhythm of the circle of life:

> 1:4 A generation goes and a generation comes,
> and the earth forever stands.
> 1:5 And it rises—the sun, and it sets—the sun
> And back to its place it hurries, it is rising there.
> 1:6 It goes to the south, and round to the north
> Around and around it goes—the wind,
> and over and around him comes the wind.
> 1:7 All the rivers are going to the sea, and the sea is not full.

> To the place where the rivers are going, there they
> return to go again.

Depending on one's perspective, this circle of life could be viewed as dependability or relentlessness. Qohelet uses the expression "I turned" on several occasions (2:11a, 12, 20; 7:25) but never in the prophetic sense of "repentance" (see Ezek 14:6), only in the sense of restlessness: "he turns in one direction and then another, but of course all proves to be mere breath and herding the wind" (Alter 2019b, 682). Repetition of sounds stress the idea *mah-šehāyāh hû' šeyyihᵉyeh* ("what is, that is what will be," 1:9), and similar-sounding phrases follow in 3:15, 8:7, and 10:14.

I agree with Wesley Fuerst, who notes that *tov shem mishemem tov* (7:1a) is "an extraordinarily pithy and memorable saying, playing skillfully on words and sounds in Hebrew" (1975, 129), and have therefore retained the Hebrew as spoken by the Optimist in the talk show but have also provided the translation "a good name is better than good oil."

The Hebrew script includes rhyming in several verses. Here I have attempted translations that include rhyme to illustrate the effective use of rhyme in the original:

> *bānîtî lî bātîm / nāṭa'tî lî kᵉrāmîm* (2:4)
> I built for myself dynasties / I planted for myself wineries
> *'ēt livkôt / vᵉ'ēt liśhôq // 'ēt sᵉpôd / vᵉ'ēt rᵉqôd* (3:4)
> A time for grief / and a time to laugh // A time to weep / and a time to leap
> *ṭôvāh ḥokmāh 'im-naḥalāh* (7:11)
> There is merit in credit if inherited
> *sôf dāvār / hakol nišmā'* (12:13a)
> End of words / all has been heard

Although there is no rhyme in the phrase found in 7:6, repetition of the sounds k/q, s, and l and the vowel sound î illustrates paronomasia. This soundplay is picked up in the translation "Like the crackle (*kᵉqôl*) of the nettle (*hassîrîm*) under the kettle (*hassîr*)—this is the laughter (*śᵉḥoq*) of the fool (*hakkᵉsîl*)" (cf. Fox 2004, 45).

The repetition of the phrase *vᵉ'ēn lāhem mᵉnaḥēm*, "not any for them comfort," in 4:1 deserves comment as an effective example of wordplay. Scott Noegel understands this as an example of antanaclasis in which a repeated word or phrase is used in two different senses and thus requires a different translation for the second use. He suggests: "Behold the tears of the oppressed with no one to comfort them; / And the power of their oppressors with no one to avenge them" (2021, 169). Taking the Hebrew at face value, I agree with Alter's interpretation that Qohelet "registers the suffering of the oppressed as a given fact without the slightest indication, as in Psalms or elsewhere, that God will rescue them from their suffering, and without any exhortation, as in the Prophets, that we must act to rescue them" (2019, 687). Simple repetition of the words underscores the hopelessness and pathos of the situation.

Noegel is helpful, however, in pointing out numerical polysemy in 4:8-12 (2021, 209–10). Repetition of the numbers "one" (six times) and "two" (five times) is used idiomatically to represent a lone person in contrast to someone with a companion. It is notable that in verse 8 there are three ways to express the only child: "one," "without a pair," "no son or brother for him." The section ends with reference to a "three-fold thread" (4:12). The repeated numbers underscore the point that it is not good to be alone.

Embodiment. Since ancient times the poem of 12:2-7 has been understood as an allegory for the deterioration of the body. Although not every element of the poem can be easily equated to body parts, the poem is a reflection on the process of aging and impending death and seems apt as the last full speech of Qohelet. It commences with a reference to darkness and clouds returning after rain. Since clouds usually clear away after rain, there is a pessimistic tone set at the beginning of the poem. Continued reference to darkness at the windows is suggestive of the dimming of the sense of sight, and references to the lowering of sound can be understood as loss of acuity in hearing. Sounds become indistinct in noisy places such as the souk (12:4). Legs become unstable and can no longer hold up the "housing" body. The "grinding women" (*haṭṭoḥanôt*) is a feminine plural noun that later is a word used for molars (Alter 2019b, 706) and so probably represents teeth that in old age are few and lose their strength. There are several allusions in 12:5. Almond blossom is white and may denote white hair. A grasshopper that drags is one that has lost the spring in its step, and the "breaking of desire" is the inevitable loss of potency with aging. Parallelism in the penultimate verse stresses the destruction of water sources (well and bore) that are necessary for life, and appropriately the body returns to dust, which is earth that lacks life-giving water and breath. Qohelet's lament that all things are coming to an end, felt within his own body, attests to the personal embodied experience that, as we have noted already, undergirds the wisdom of this scroll.

Prevailing Wisdom

As one hears the words of Ecclesiastes, one becomes conscious that many phrases and ideas from this scroll have entered the vernacular and still have a contemporary ring to them:

- Whatever will be will be (1:9)
- Eat, drink, and be merry (for tomorrow we may die) (2:24; 3:13; 5:18 [MT 5:17]; 8:15; 9:7)
- For everything there is a season (3:1)
- Ashes to ashes, dust to dust (3:20)
- An only child has no end of toil (4:8a)
- It is not good for a man to be alone (4:8-11)
- A threefold cord is not easily broken (4:12)
- Naked we came, naked we shall return (5:15 [MT 5:14])
- Easy come, easy go (5:16a [MT 5:15])
- Man does not live by bread alone (6:7)
- No point arguing with fate (6:10)
- The former days were better than these (7:10)
- It takes one to know one (7:27c)
- Just walk away (8:3a)
- There is wisdom in knowing we can't find wisdom! (8:17a)
- Enjoy life while you are able (9:10)
- Time and chance befall all (9:11)
- Cast your bread on the waters (11:1)
- Take each day as it comes (11:6)

Some of these ideas are picked up elsewhere in the Scriptures, not least in the teachings of Jesus of Nazareth, who in his Sermon on the Mount advocated,

> Do not worry about your life, what you will eat or what you will drink, or about your body, what you will wear. Is not life more than food, and the body more than clothing? . . . Can any of you by worrying add a single hour to your span of life? (Mt 6:25-27, NRSV)

> Do not worry about tomorrow, for tomorrow will bring worries of its own. Today's trouble is enough for today. (Mt 6:34, NRSV)

> Is there any among you who, if your child asks for bread, will give a stone? Or if the child asks for a fish, will give a snake? If you then, who are evil, know how to give good gifts to your children, how much more will your

Father in heaven give good things to those who ask him! (Mt 7:10-11, NRSV)

Others may hear affinities with Buddha's teaching that life is inseparable from suffering and detachment from desire is the spiritual goal of humanity (Ostriker 2005, 7).

While there is no systematic philosophy that can be drawn from the scroll as a guide for living wisely, each of the panelists in our Ecclesiastes talk show has something worthwhile to say about how we might live in our world today.

The Optimist counsels us to embrace life by living in the moment and enjoying good things as gifts from God. For the Optimist, relationships bring fulfilment beyond mere utilitarian value. Time is part of God's gift to humanity, and each experience in life has value.

For the Pietist, human beings have the capacity to experience a conscious relationship with the creator God. We need to recognize, however, that what we do in life will have consequences and so we should live knowing that God will ultimately judge our actions.

Qohelet would tell us that although there is pain in knowledge, there is privilege in being conscious of our existence, in being able to reflect on experience and test our thoughts against learning. Qohelet's observations include the negative along with the positive—there is wisdom in honestly facing up to both. Even if life is summed up as no more than expelled breath, expelled breath follows inspired breath. Breath is "close to nothing, but not quite nothing" (Ostriker 2005, 7). Where there is breath, there is life.

All three panelists are aware that human beings are fallible, and all three recognize the limits of human existence. It is often observed that the scroll of Ecclesiastes sits uncomfortably alongside other books in the Hebrew Bible, even while accepting that it belongs there. Michael Fox, for example, states,

> Koheleth has some unusual things to say, and his views should not be forced to fit presuppositions of what a biblical book *must* say. One need not grant the truth of all his opinions; the other biblical authors would not have. Koheleth's hard and lonely theology is only one man's view of the world and his glimpse of the Infinite. All truths are partial, all thinkers inadequate. Koheleth's teachings are one motif—a poignant and significant discord—in the larger symphony of the biblical canon (2004, ix)

This scroll refers to God with the universal name Elohim. As such, it becomes a conversation that has relevance for all humankind.

Connections with Ecclesiastes

At times I have used the term "pessimist" for Qohelet's persona, contrasting him with the perspectives of an Optimist and a Pietist. We could be justified in going a step further and diagnosing that Qohelet is suffering from depression. As noted above, the scroll emphasizes Qohelet's search for wisdom and meaning as not merely theoretical but as embodied experience. Even as a literary persona, Qohelet puts into words many of the doubts and uncertainties that have plagued humankind since creation. With his universally consistent assessment that everything is *hevel*, he cannot see any meaning in anything he examines. For Qohelet, cycles of nature repeat themselves without ceasing, toil has no profit, righteous living brings no better reward than wickedness, and God is no solution because it is God who has given the evil task to the sons of humanity (1:13b). Qohelet has the same caustic assessment of all matters: there is no value in hard work, wealth, possessions, power, or the quest for knowledge and understanding. Alicia Ostriker notes that he is equally caustic towards himself, "recording the twists and turns of mood, the exasperating ricochet of emotions" (2005, 8). Qohelet's severe case of *ennui* reaches a low point in his assertion that a man who has lived a long life is worse off than one who was miscarried (6:3), and "the day of death is better than the day of one's birth" (7:1b). In short, Qohelet exhibits recognized symptoms of severe depression.

Contemporary descriptions of clinical depression include symptoms of cheerlessness, loss of interest and energy, psychomotor agitation or wandering, concentration difficulties, indecisiveness, feelings of guilt or worthlessness, thoughts of death or suicide, sleeping disorders, decrease in appetite, and weight loss (Kruger 2005, 189). Qohelet reports unhappy feelings that are unable to be alleviated in his repeated refrain "all is dross." Agitation and wandering concentration are seen in the "irregularity and repetition" of his thoughts (Fox 2004, ix). Sleep disturbance is implied in the comments "in the night his heart will not lie down" (2:23) and "no rest for him when he sleeps" (5:12 [MT 5:11]). Although there is no overtly expressed death-wish as we see with the biblical characters Jonah (Jon 4:3), Elijah (1 Kgs 19:4), Jeremiah (Jer 15:10), and Job (Job 3:11), Qohelet is obsessed with the question of death (2:16; 3:19a; 4:2; 6:3; 7:1b; 8:8; 9:2-3; 12:2-7). His poem that describes the aging process includes loss of vitality and energy (12:5). A decrease in appetite is not apparent in the scroll of Ecclesiastes; indeed the listener is exhorted to enjoy food and drink, yet Qohelet observes that strangers will relish such things instead of himself (2:18-19; 6:2).

The World Health Organization estimates that, globally, 5 percent of adults suffer from depression, and a higher percentage is reported for older people.[95] This is not surprising in that older people are more likely to undergo losses of roles and significant others and to experience an increase in physical illness, including dementia. At any age, however, depression may become a serious health condition, affecting the ability to function well in social and work settings and, at its worst, leading to suicide.

Mental health is an important issue and offers an appropriate connection with the scroll of Ecclesiastes. It is not often discussed as a "biblical" issue. Paul Kruger (2005, 188) speculates that this may be for several reasons: emotions have been seen as irrational and subjective and not worthy of serious study; the field of Biblical Studies deals with ancient cultures that can no longer be empirically observed; and mentality and emotions are assumed to be culture-bound rather than universal. Current consensus, however, assumes that there are similarities as well as differences in the expression of emotions across cultures.

A more holistic view of mental health that includes mental, physical, social, and spiritual dimensions will aid in dispelling misconceptions and allowing us to see that mental health falls on a spectrum of normality. Every person can experience periods of anxiety, distress, and the feeling of being disconnected. Moreover, doubt, uncertainty, and disagreement are integral facets of religious discourse (Verbin 2002, 33). Open acknowledgment that such difficulties occur for everyone reduces the stigma and discrimination that can be associated with mental illness. Many of these issues and experiences are temporary and can be effectively managed. For more serious illness there is a range of treatment available including counselling, cognitive behavior therapy, medication, and other therapeutic measures.

It is not clear what causes clinical depression but genetic vulnerability, personality traits, life stressors, substance intake, and medical conditions can all have a contribution. Importantly, while a diagnosis of clinical depression can help guide treatment, it should not dominate the perception of that person in the same way that any illness is never the whole story defining a person's identity. I have found little literature relating depression with Ecclesiastes, but several articles find links between depression and religious practice (Keady 1980; Kruger 2005; Krause and Pargament 2018). Qohelet's depression, if we take his words at face value, is largely driven by his observations that distortion and inequity pervade the world made by a God of justice. And while God is mentioned over forty times in the scroll, there is no direct relationship between God and the speakers in the scroll. Each of the aforementioned characters in the Hebrew Bible who express a desire for death are spoken to directly by God, whether in chastisement or comfort (Wohlgelernter 1981), but there is no such response for Qohelet. As Alter has commented, "Qohelet has enough of a connection with tradition that he never absolutely denies the idea of a personal god, but his *'elohim* often seems to be a stand-in for the cosmic powers-that-be for fate or the overarching dynamic of reality that is beyond human control" (Alter 2019b, 676–77). Verbin asserts that uncertainty about relating to God is a common experience:

> Various forms of spontaneous instinctive doubt underlie the way we talk to, and about God. They have to do with the ambiguity of our experience of the world, with our experience of happiness and pain, of goodness and evil, of hope and despair, of beauty and ugliness. They have to do with wonder, with primitive uncertainty about the meaning of life, and with primitive uncertainty about the future. (2002, 28-29)

Ostriker, reflecting more specifically on the scroll of Ecclesiastes, views Qohelet's vision of God as impersonal, contradictory, and morally unreliable, concluding, "'God' is the name for everything I cannot understand" (2005, 13). Ostriker helpfully reminds us that "what disperses mist [*hevel*] is sunshine, and the sun of enlightenment shines periodically through Qoheleth's mist" (2005, 10). It is the *persona* of the Optimist in Ecclesiastes (8:15) that recognizes the simple healing power of regular doses of sunshine. This is one of the measures of self-care recommended for those suffering from mental disorders since light exposure increases levels of serotonin and melatonin, affecting mood and the circadian rhythm of the body.

The scroll of Ecclesiastes encourages us to recognize the importance of mental health and to be supportive of those in our communities who experience challenges in this area. Conversations are key to being supportive, including asking simple questions about a friend's well-being and the preparedness to listen with an open mind.[96] Although I have envisaged the scroll of Ecclesiastes as a conversation, I have noted how the three panelists allow each other space but do not engage with each other. Considering the scroll in the light of mental health raises this hermeneutical issue and invites us to use the scroll itself as the basis for a conversation about well-being.[97]

We are separated from the community that produced, received, and transmitted the scroll of Ecclesiastes by many degrees. The early Israelite community was pre-scientific, theocratic, and located in a different physical and socioeconomic world. On the other hand, illness and well-being are relevant in all human communities in every generation. Attention to embodiment in the scroll of Ecclesiastes reminds us that the goodness of life was reflected in the bodily state, not in any otherworldly realm. As we read this scroll, we are encouraged to attend to the well-being of each other in our communities.

Attending to the different perspectives in the scroll of Ecclesiastes reminds us that mental well-being is also a spiritual issue. The biblical authors knew that faith is relevant to every aspect of life. For people of faith, the Jewish and Christian Scriptures are frequently a source of comfort and encouragement when we encounter difficulties, whether mental, physical, social, or spiritual. There may be words that offer comfort in a time of need or words that echo our own "instinctive doubt" as we face life's challenges. Either way, it is good to know that the Scriptures do not recoil from engaging with the negative side of existence and hence provide connections for contemporary readers and hearers of these traditions.

The Scroll of Esther

Introduction

This is the second of the scrolls in the *Megillot* named for its heroine. Esther is the Persian name of Hadassah, a Jewish orphan who rose to prominence by being chosen from amongst hundreds of beautiful virgins to be the new queen of King Ahasuerus, ruler of the kingdom of Persia, following the banishment of his first queen Vashti who refused to obey his command. Watched over and encouraged by her close relative Mordecai, Esther was able to use her position as queen to preserve the Jewish population in Persia from a genocidal plan concocted by Haman, the villain of the piece. Full of lavish banquets, eunuchs, satraps, and governors of provinces, the story could have come straight out of *1001 Arabian Nights*. Shimon Levy describes the scroll of Esther as "dramatic, thrilling, and comic" (2000, 104). As such, it is an unusual addition to the canon of sacred Scripture. It has a historical flavor with its many dates, names of places and people, and references to edicts, letters, and annals. Yet "the portrait of King Ahasuerus and the Persian court makes no pretense of serious correspondence to historical reality, as the original audience surely must have known" (Alter 2019b, 713). Elaborate descriptions, repetition and reversal of events, elements of irony and hyperbole, exaggerated caricatures and cleverly woven subplots all point to a tale crafted to be read aloud to entertain an appreciative audience. Its sober subtext of survival of a people group against all odds has meant that the story has continued to be embraced and celebrated by peoples under threat as "a practical, radical, and political theology of hope" (Queen-Sutherland 2016, 204).

The Scroll and the Festival of *Purim*
Of all the *Megillot*, the scroll of Esther is most directly tied to its associated festival. The scroll, especially in the last two chapters, describes the etiology

of the festival in the casting of "Lots" (*purim*) to determine the planned day of Jewish annihilation (3:7; 9:1), authorizes its annual commemoration, and models how it should be celebrated (9:20-22). *Purim* is the only biblical festival that is not authorized in the Torah, and so the book of Esther gives the justification and instruction for the feast that is missing elsewhere.

The festival emulates the events in the story by mandating days of joyful feasting on the days in Adar that the lots fell, which were turned around to become the days that Jews avenged their enemies instead of being annihilated. Distribution of gifts to loved ones and donations to the needy are important aspects of the festival. The scroll is read aloud in the synagogue both on the evening of *Purim* and on the following morning. Traditionally, attendees (children and sometimes adults as well) dress in fancy costumes and masks in order "to highlight the notion that things are not always as they appear" (Brawer 2008, 209). As the scroll is read, there is a pause at every mention of the villainous Haman (54 in all) in order for the congregation to boo, hiss, and rattle noisy "gragers" in an effort to drown out his name. A carnival atmosphere dominates the festival with mock reenactments of Esther that may include cross-dressing or adoption of unrelated costumes and excessive drinking. A famous Talmudic injunction (Talmud *b. Meg.* 7b) encourages participants to get so drunk that they cannot distinguish between "cursed be Haman" and "blessed be Mordecai" (Berlin 2004, 1623). Special foods are used including triangular poppy-seed-filled pastries known as *hamantaschen* ("Haman's pockets") or *oznei Haman* ("Haman's ears").

The month of Adar falls in the spring in the northern hemisphere. The jubilant *Purim* festival thus also serves as a celebration of the end of winter and may have origins in ancient Mesopotamian spring festivals. Adele Berlin notes that the frivolity of the festival is uncharacteristic of Jewish celebrations, and the calendar now in use mandates that *Purim* can never fall on a Sabbath, avoiding conflict between observations (2004, 1625). She also notes that the Qumran community did not observe *Purim* as it would always fall on the Sabbath in their 364-day calendar, and this may explain why Esther is the only biblical book for which no trace has been found amongst the Dead Sea Scrolls.

Purim occurs around the same time of the year as Mardi Gras, the excessive period of feasting and frivolity that precedes the Christian Lenten season with its focus on penitence and fasting. Although there is no religious association between the purposes of *Purim* and Mardi Gras, they share a human enjoyment of temporary suspension of normal societal structures and relationships made possible through costumes and masks.

The Background of the Scroll

The story of Esther has been circulating in more than one version since early in its history. The version in the Hebrew Bible and Christian Old Testament is based on the Masoretic Text (MT). The MT is shorter than its counterparts and is distinctive for what is absent in the text. There are no references to God, Torah, or covenant; no mention of the land of Israel or the temple; no Jewish customs of prayer, Sabbath, or dietary restrictions; no reference to sin or repentance or lament; and no concern about endogamous marriage. The scroll of Esther shares many of these characteristics with the scroll of the Song of Songs, and the two scrolls form bookends for the *Megillot*. There is, however, reference to mourning and fasting in Esther. In addition, Haman's accusation underlying the edict to destroy the Jews of Persia was that the laws of the Jewish people differed from all other people and that they did not keep the king's laws (3:8). In various periods in the history of the Jewish people this comment accurately reflects adherence to the Torah above the laws of the empire or state. In the scroll of Esther the word for "law" is *dāt*, a Persian loan-word, rather than the Hebrew *tôrāh*, so this reference to their laws is implied rather than direct.

The version of Esther in the Greek Septuagint (LXX) includes six additions that serve to rectify these omissions, adding the name of God, prayers, resistance on Esther's part to non-kosher food, and a reference to the king as uncircumcised. St. Jerome, the author of the Latin Vulgate, noticed these additions and moved them to the end of his translation of Esther. In current Catholic Old Testament translations, the additions are included but identified as chapters A–F within the text.

Several copies of another Greek translation of Esther known as the Alpha-Text (AT) suggest that a different underlying Hebrew tradition was circulating at the same time as the one underlying the MT. The major difference is a lack of reference to *Purim* origins and instruction, indicating that the story of Esther and Mordecai existed before it was linked to the practice of *Purim*. In AT, a two-day memorial was instituted that was called Phouria rather than *Purim*. A reference in 2 Maccabees 15:36 to 14 Adar as "the day of Mordecai" suggests that the tradition of AT was more influential at that time. The book of 2 Maccabees describes an additional fast day (Nicanor's Day) that preceded the two-day feast of Mordecai's Day. Nicanor was a Syrian general who threatened Jewish survival and independence by attacking on the Sabbath and was killed by Judas Maccabaeus in 160 BCE (2 Macc 15:1-37). His head was hung from the citadel in Jerusalem as "a clear and conspicuous sign to everyone of the help of the Lord" (2 Macc

15:35, NRSV). This action emulates the display of the bodies of the sons of Haman in the scroll of Esther (9:12-14).

Another version of the story is found in Antiquities of the Jews (c. 93 CE) by Flavius Josephus, a Greek speaking Jewish historian and advisor during the Roman Empire. These volumes gave a Hellenized account of Jewish history from creation to the Jewish wars, using the Septuagint and Jewish midrashim as the primary sources. Josephus identifies the Persian king as Artaxerxes (Cyrus), son of Xerxes who had overseen the rebuilding of Jerusalem's walls and temple. Rather than simply translating an existing version, Josephus paraphrases and adds expository input to the story. For example, when Esther enters the king's court unbidden, she is described as swooning in his fearsome presence:

> He was sitting on his throne, in his royal apparel, which was a garment interwoven with gold and precious stones, which made him seem to her more terrible, especially when he looked at her somewhat severely, and with a countenance on fire with anger, her joints failed her immediately, out of the dread she was in, and she fell down sideways in a swoon: but the king changed his mind, which happened, as I suppose, by the will of God, and he was concerned for his wife, lest her fear should bring some very ill thing upon her, and he leaped from his throne and took her in his arms, and recovered her, and embracing her, and speaking comfortably to her, and exhorting her to be of good cheer. (1997, 299–300)

Josephus's version is worth noting because it has been influential on religious art. There are several examples in classic art of Esther swooning before Ahasuerus, and Michelangelo's Sistine Chapel portrayal of a crucified Haman may be due to Josephus's use of the Greek word *stauros* (cross) rather than the LXX's *khulon* (tree, gallows) for the Hebrew *ēts* (tree).[98]

The question of which of these versions reflects the earliest tradition is debatable. Many argue that the version that has no reference to God (MT) is likely to be earliest, as it is hard to believe that pious Jewish scribes would remove references to God from traditions they had received. On the other hand, Kandy Queen-Sutherland, following David Clines, proposes that the MT tradition deliberately removed such references "in order to emphasize a more subtle theology that God works behind events and circumstances in which no divine participation is apparent" (2016, 192). Suggesting that the scroll was circulating in both Hebrew and Greek versions during the antagonistic Greek period, Queen-Sutherland proposes that both forms were protests against Hellenistic rule:

> The MT . . . may well have been signaling obstinately to the Greeks that even without appeal to Judaism's God, the survival of the Jews and Judaism is a certainty. Once the scroll is translated into Greek, the emphasis shifts to defending the certainty that the God of Judaism will not be compromised, despite Hellenistic attempts to do so. Taken together, the MT story assures certainty of Jewish survival even without God's presence, and the LXX story assures certainty of Jewish survival even under the Hellenistic demands of forced cultural assimilation. (2016, 200)

Josephus and many after him have attributed the scroll of Esther to historical characters and events, but there are many reasons why this assumption is misguided. The opulent and bureaucratic portrayals of the Persian Empire in the scroll are well backed up by Greek writings from the ancient period, but the Persians were meticulous record-keepers and no evidence for the individuals named in the scroll has been found. As Mark Biddle wryly comments, "When one king, two queens, and two prime ministers are missing from the historical records, one must account for the situation" (2013, 75). The king's name in the Hebrew text is Ahasuerus, a name, Yehuda Radday points out (1990a, 295), that sounds comical in Hebrew ("Ahashwerosh") but is similar enough to the known Persian king Artaxerxes for that name to be used in Greek translations. But Persian records do not record names that sound anything like Vashti or Esther for the wives of the historical Artaxerxes, nor are the names of Haman or Mordecai recorded for any high officials. On the other hand, key names in the scroll can be associated with Babylonian and Elamite deities: Mordecai is similar to Marduk and Esther to Ishtar, the principal Babylonian god and goddess; Haman (Humman) and Vashti (Mashti) echo Elamite deities, reflecting the Mesopotamian cultural setting for the scroll and perhaps echoing folk tales from that setting. Susa, the setting for the scroll, was an Elamite city that had been incorporated into the Persian empire. Details such as the six-month-long drinking party for the entire leadership structure of the empire (a great time for invasion!) or a one-year warning that a pogrom is coming (a great time for emigration!) must be understood as farcical rather than realistic. The Persian Empire was known for its tolerance for ethnic minorities, a fact celebrated within the biblical record because it was so unlike other empires that subjugated the land of Israel. Thus an edict for the eradication of a particular people group within the Persian empire is unlikely, backed up by the lack of any such historical records. Indeed, using the setting of the Persian court for the story of Esther may have only been possible because it was a safe target for satire.

The scroll of Esther was written or edited by an unknown author who was acquainted with Persian customs and governance, knew of the practice of *Purim*, and was a good storyteller, using wit and comic timing effectively in his story of Jewish individuals outwitting an empire. On the basis of familiarity with Persian customs and "the abundant borrowings of Persian words," Alter proposes a date of composition within the Persian period (2019b, 713). Kirsten Nielsen wonders why the festival of *Purim* is not mentioned in other Persian-era biblical texts and on that basis proposes a later date (1998, 187). Whether written in the Persian period (fifth to fourth century BCE) or the later, more hostile, Greek era (third to second centuries BCE), the author uses Persia as a "cypher or code for empire" (Biddle 2013, 92) and employs humor as a weapon to inspire and encourage Diaspora Jewish communities. See below in the commentary section for a more detailed discussion of the use of humor by the author of the scroll of Esther.

History of Reception

The scroll of Esther has had a mixed reception in both Jewish and Christian circles. Its canonicity was debated at length, up until the third or fourth century CE in both Jewish and Christian traditions. In one debate over whether it "defiled the hands," the conclusion was drawn that it was composed to be recited and not written (Queen-Sutherland 2016, 187). Yet in some Jewish manuscripts the book is placed immediately after the Torah (Fuerst 1975, 32)! By the Middle Ages it was popular, with Mordecai "the Jew" (2:5; 3:4; 5:13; 6:10; 8:7; 10:3) representing the survival of the Jewish people through history:

> His victory is the victory of the Jewish people. Yearnings, pleasures, and fears of centuries are touched by the story of Esther and Mordecai; the book directly addresses the problems of life and existence for those Jews who were scattered over the world—in the dispersion or Diaspora as it is often described—without a national security. (Fuerst 1975, 41)

Early Jewish readers were troubled by the lack of reference to God and Jewish practice, however, and midrashim "solved the problems" by adding detail that is not present in the MT, claiming that Esther's marriage was unconsummated and her diet was kosher (Berlin 2004, 1624). As will be discussed further below, other rabbinic literature recognized its comedic style and "add[ed] to the fun by their preposterous embellishments of the story and its characters" (1623). In rabbinic tradition Esther has the honor of being regarded as one of the seven prophetesses in Israel (Sarah, Miriam, Deborah, Hannah, Abigail, Huldah, Esther).

Unsurprisingly, early Christian readings included allegorical interpretations relating Esther to the Virgin Mary and Mordecai to Christ with the gallows ("tree") foreshadowing the cross. Others, however, could not find useful Christian connections and were disturbed by the violence meted out against Jewish enemies at the end of the scroll. No Christian commentary was written on Esther for centuries, and it was often not included in lists of books approved as canonical. Martin Luther in the fifteenth century famously derided its value as Scripture, claiming, "I am so great an enemy to the second book of the Maccabees, and to Esther, that I wish they had not come to us at all, for they have too many heathen unnaturalities." Queen-Sutherland points out that Luther's negative views can be explained by his anti-Jewish and pro-Christological perspective on all of Scripture (2016, 189).

For contemporary readers the question of violence in the scroll of Esther is an important one. At one end of the discussion the violence is understood as integral to the humorous narrating of the story and therefore not to be taken seriously, hence Kathleen O'Connor can claim that "the violence of the Jews functions like comic book violence—zap, boom, pow!—the good people defeat insidious, overwhelming evil!" (2003, 55). At the other end, John Collins warns that "Esther cannot be held up as a model for relations between ethnic groups . . . Violence, and even the fantasy of violence, most often begets just more violence" (2004, 543). Whichever end of the spectrum we fall on, the scroll of Esther raises the issue of violence as one that demands attention, and we will return to it in the connections section of this chapter.

The Literary Character of the Scroll
I will consider the creativity of the scroll of Esther in more detail below, focusing particularly on its dramatic qualities, but some comments on its literary style are warranted in this introductory section.

The scroll of Esther is entertaining due to its use of repetition, duplication, hyperbole, irony, and reversals. Characters are paired with each other in various ways, paralleling and contrasting their personalities, motivations, and the consequences of their actions. Thus we see the oppositions of ambitious Haman and humble Mordecai, independent Vashti and compliant Esther, a foolish king and a crafty second-in-command, and disobedient Vashti and disobedient Mordecai, both refusing to flatter the egos of someone of greater status and both setting a train of consequences into action that affected whole populations. Pairing and repetition of events also occurs: contrasting excessive drinking with fasting; the king handing authority to two separate people;

and the sending out of edicts to the whole nation on three occasions. There even seems to be two gatherings of virgins (2:2-3, 19). Exaggeration abounds with some notable examples being the number of provinces in Ahasuerus's kingdom (127),[99] the length of the first drinking party (180 days), the length of beauty treatments for women in the harem (12 months), the amount of silver Haman offers for the Jews (10,000 talents), and the height of the gallows built to hang Mordecai (50 cubits, approximately 75 ft or 25 m). Repeated drinking parties[100] and lush palace descriptions emphasize the excesses of Ahasuerus's kingdom, and the overuse of messengers (eunuchs, attendants, servants and maidservants, scribes, couriers) satirizes the officiousness of the Persian Empire as we see them carrying information and writs back and forth to every province in the kingdom.

In other scrolls in the *Megillot* I have commented on the importance of the information conveyed in the center of the scroll. In the scroll of Esther there are two candidates for this central function.

As the scroll stands, the events of the ten chapters pivot on chapter 6, which begins with the king's sleepless night when he calls for royal records and rediscovers the loyalty of Mordecai in uncovering an assassination plot. This fateful night comes between the two drinking parties planned by Esther, and it proves to set into motion a "deliciously" ironic reversal of fortunes of Haman and Mordecai (see O'Connor 2003, 53–54). Up until this point Haman has been favored by the king and flattered by Esther's invitation to her private drinking party. In the meantime, he had been planning the destruction of the Jewish population and constructing the gallows in the expectation of gaining permission from the king to hang his nemesis Mordecai. When asked by Ahasuerus how a favored man should be honored, Haman assumed he was to receive the honor and described an extravagant ritual of robing, crowning, and being paraded through the streets on the royal steed. Instead, he is commanded to perform the ritual for Mordecai. Within a few verses Haman goes from a state of hubris to acting like a servant, while his enemy Mordecai moves from a nobody at the gate to being honored by the king himself. As the story goes on, the reversal continues in the same trajectory. Haman, depressed and infuriated, is rushed to the second banquet where he is exposed as the potential murderer of Esther herself along with her people, and his desperate plea for his life turns into a death sentence as his action of throwing himself on her mercy is misunderstood as an attempt at molestation when the king returns to the room. Within moments Haman himself is hoisted on his own gallows. His household and belongings are handed over to Mordecai, and the political authority that once was Haman's becomes Mordecai's instead. The duplicated bestowal of the king's signet ring, first to

Haman (3:5) and then to Mordecai (8:2), cements the reversal of power in the story.

I want to suggest, however, a second centerpiece for this scroll. A number of scholars including Sidnie Ann White (1989, 164), following David Clines (1984a), argue that the verses in 9:20–10:3 were an addition to an already complete story. These verses summarize the story (9:24-25) and describe the festival of *Purim*. On this calculation, verse 14 of chapter 4 would fall at the center of the original scroll:

> For if to keep quiet you are quiet in this time, respite and deliverance will stand up for the Jews from another place, and you and the house of your father will be annihilated/ and who knows? If for a time like this you have made your mark on the kingdom. (4:14, my translation)

This is Mordecai's message to Esther following discovery of Haman's plot and it could be understood as the theological center of the scroll. The unusual word *rewaḥ*, usually translated "relief," is from the same root letters as *rûaḥ*, the word for wind, breath, or spirit. My decision to translate the word "respite" is to make that connection obvious and to convey the underlying theological subtlety that it was divine intention that the Jewish people be preserved, and Esther was to choose whether to align herself with the divine spirit even with the human uncertainty of the outcome. While reference to God is not obvious in the scroll of Esther, this high point of challenge at its story center reminds us that "human initiative combines with poetic justice in ways that seem to imply divine providence" (Strawn 2020, 149).

The Purpose of the Scroll

I would suggest that this subtle message of providence contributes to the purpose of the scroll of Esther. It is not merely an etiological explanation for the festival of *Purim*, nor is it merely an entertaining story of Jewish survival. Both descriptions fit the scroll well. By the time this scroll came together, the Jewish community was spread across the Diaspora. A number of stories in the Hebrew Bible and Deuterocanonical collection address the issue of survival of the Jewish people and religion in environments that could be hostile. In the absence of land and temple there was a new emphasis on what *could* be preserved of Jewish culture: laws, stories, and rituals. People with a minority status depended on community solidarity, wise leadership, and good relations with their host nation. Yet each particular situation would demand a different response. In some circumstances segregation was called for, and in others assimilation. Stories of Shadrach, Meshach, Abednago,

Susanna, and Judith encourage Jews to hold up Jewish customs and practice at all costs. The stories of Daniel, Joseph, and Esther show that reaching a high social position in a foreign country without divulging one's Jewish heritage is possible and legitimate, perhaps even necessary for the salvation of the race. As Queen-Sutherland states, "Circumstances may push Jewish self-definition to new limits, calling for innovation, compromise, and even deception, but those actions do not negate the certainty of affirming one's identity as a Jew" (2016, 204).

Along with solidarity and preservation of identity, courage and hope are needed for a people surviving without a homeland. Using humor to laugh at and ultimately overcome hostility allows for courage. The confidence that respite and deliverance will come by one means or another instils hope. A story in which fortunes and power are reversed and a beauty queen faces death to preserve the life of her people is a story to celebrate!

Creativity in Esther—A Pantomime

There is no difficulty in discerning the dramatic quality of Esther. Shimon Levy is representative of many scholars when he says,

> The story of *Esther* is a dramatic plot, replete with theatrical effects from the very beginning . . . *Esther* contains similar materials and motifs to those found in some of the best-known plays in world drama: political scheming, ambition, honor, sex and power; and existential questions about life and death, not only for the individual, but for a whole nation. (2000, 104)

Esther has been the subject of religious plays across history, with a surfeit of plays in the post-medieval period according to Dorothée Sölle (1994, 232). Dramatic features include clearly discernible scenes, multiple dialogues, subplots, caricatures, and complexity in characters with see-sawing emotions, props, and costuming that are integral to the plot.

The way this scroll is used in the Jewish celebration of *Purim* suggests to me that improvising the script for pantomime or melodrama is appropriate. The word "pantomime" in ancient Greek and Roman times denoted masked players in one-man mime performances supported by a chorus telling the story of a mythological subject (Baldrick 2015). The term reemerged in the Renaissance referring to a type of performance rather than a performer. In the Italian *Commedia dell'arte*, key figures were *Arlecchino, Columbina*, and *Pulcinella* who became forerunners for the well-known characters of Harlequin, Columbine, and Punch (from Punch and Judy shows) and inspiration for the hero, heroine, and villain in contemporary pantomime. These historical entertainments were "improvised, rumbustious and earthy, based on a broad storyline that all the players knew" (Taylor 2007, 12). They found their way into English fairs and then theaters with the first recorded pantomime using the Harlequin characters in England in 1721. Over time, new storylines, a greater number of actors, music, dance, and comedic elements were introduced. Pantomime has been adapted for American audiences since the late 1800s (Taylor 2007, 13). Here they are referred to by the term "Panto," which, perhaps correctly, removes the reference to "mime" that is hardly relevant to modern renditions of this art form. A parallel term for this form of family entertainment is melodrama.

Pantomime as a form of entertainment has thrived by maintaining traditional elements within a structured framework while at the same time using improvisation to encompass modern trends and topics. Ellacott and Robbins note that "The fable or fairy tale has to be well told, incorporating the all-important elements of good battling against evil, and emerging triumphant. In this respect, the concept varies little from the medieval morality plays, performed on village greens" (2002). Pantomime and melodrama are forms of entertainment that deliberately break down barriers between performers and audience with the audience being involved vocally, physically, and emotionally (Taylor 2007, 123). Actors directly addressing the audience, participating in cued (and rehearsed) responses, and joining in well-known songs are all ways in which audiences are invited to take part in the performance. Often standard routines such as "it's behind you" and "oh no it isn't" are included, as these ready-mades are expected and enjoyed by audiences.

In the present day, pantomime continues to be family-oriented participatory entertainment that adapts popular traditional quest stories. Costumes, songs, slapstick comedy, cross-dressing, and mild adult innuendo are often incorporated. Pantomime has become associated with the ritual of Christmas activities for many people and is therefore an activity that is closely tied to a particular time of the year. Similarly, the scroll of Esther is routinely "performed" as a *Purim* ritual. In both pantomime and *Purim*, carnival, feasting, merrymaking, and religious festivals are closely related (see Taylor 2007, 18). Costume-wearing is a key aspect of the *Purim* celebration, embraced by both children and adults. Noisy audience participation is encouraged. The story has an obvious hero, heroine, and villain, and the audience is expected to cheer for the stars of the story and heckle the rogue. While the scroll of Esther relies on the subtler humor of irony rather than slapstick, messengers have an important role rushing back and forth between the different levels of court hierarchy and providing "obvious potential for on-stage commotion" (Levy 2000, 107). Heather McKay notes that it is significant that these messengers are eunuchs, as this draws attention to their ambiguous state in gender, class, and ethnicity (n.d., 2). Alongside eunuchs who oversee harems of virgins and concubines, the cast incorporates caricatures with King Ahasuerus as a buffoon and Haman an irrational egotist. Three groups of extras with tongue-twisting names provide additional entertainment in *Purim* performances, with lectors encouraged to read each group of names in one breath. Aspects of the story of Esther are akin to fairy tales, such as the standard trope of a beauty contest to select a new queen. Characterizing the scroll as a pantomime celebrates such features as appropriate to the genre.

In preparing a pantomime script of Esther I have made the following adaptations.

I have left out the final part of the scroll (9:20–10:3), which is often considered a later addition, as discussed above. This allows for the key challenge that Esther faces to be the center of the performance, with Act 1 ending on a cliff-hanger. It also removes unnecessary repetition of detail. I have taken some creative license by inserting the name *Purim* into Mordecai's final speech, even though it does not appear until 9:26 in the longer ending.

Although there are a number of dialogues in the scroll that enhance its dramatic potential, I have placed some of the narrated material into speeches of other characters. Significantly, this gives King Ahasuerus the opportunity to pronounce the three groups of tongue-twisting names, adding humorous potential to his portrayal.

I decided to allow one of the eunuchs, Harbonah, to narrate the tale where narration was unavoidable. As McKay points out, eunuchs had easy accessibility to all characters and all places: ". . . totally free to move about. The city gates and doors to the chambers of the king provide literary and figurative boundaries through which many characters and messages must pass, but none pass so easily as the eunuchs" (n.d., 2). When Harbonah suggests to the king that Haman's gallows are available for his execution (7:9), it implies that he already knows when and why they were built. O'Connor also notes Harbonah's "access to a reliable web of gossip among the eunuchs" (2003, 56). In my script I have referred to this character as "the eyes and ears of the palace."

In "Production Notes" to the script I have emulated pantomime scripts available to community theater groups, but this is not to be taken too seriously as commentary on the scroll.[101] The script includes instruction for audience response, and I envisage these as held up on placards by a stagehand as cues for the audience. As noted already, there is a tradition in *Purim* of drowning out the name of Haman whenever it is heard. The name occurs fifty-four times in the scroll but is only heard eighteen times in my script, hence additional cues are suggested. The line "Look out behind you" is such a well-known routine in pantomime that I have incorporated it in two of the scenes in which Haman appears.

Scenes have been divided with the usual criteria of changes in actors, locations, and time. In addition, the Hebrew diacritics (*setumah* and *petuchah*) are useful in knowing when to divide the scenes. Although not relevant to my script that ends at 9:19, it is worth noting that the scroll does not conclude with a *petuchah* as one might expect, leaving it open-ended. The scroll concludes on a positive statement describing Mordecai as "seeking good for his people and speaking peace to all his seed" (10:3b), expressing a hope that will remain true for all time.

A final comment is warranted regarding my improvised translation. Although I originally translated the scroll of Esther according to principles outlined in the methodology chapter, I have adapted it for a pantomime script to form rhyming couplets for each line as this is a convention in pantomime. I have attempted to maintain some features of my original translation, but word order of the original Hebrew has been largely sacrificed to produce an entertaining rhyming script. Humorous aspects of the scroll that were noted above, such as hyperbole, drinking parties, excessive numbers, and overuse of messengers, have all been incorporated into the script.

CCC Pantomimes Presents
PANTO ESTHER
Adapted from the Scroll of Esther

PRODUCTION NOTES

SCRIPT. Esther is a superb story with superb characters. To read straight through the scroll aloud would take around 45 minutes, but to act it out as a pantomime with added songs and an interval will pad out to a little less than 2 hours, appropriate for a family show. It should be played with energy and comedic flair. Don't let characters talk *to* each other but let them talk to the audience. To use a Broadway expression, the cast should "Grab the audience, not each other" in every scene. Have a stagehand hold up the name of each scene as well as placards (cheers, boos, etc.) to aid the audience in responding appropriately to the heroes and villains at the designated places in the script. Be prepared for additional responses as they begin to warm to their role and wait if necessary to ensure audience noise does not drown out the performance. The villain should always enter from the left and the hero/heroine from the right.

MUSIC. Short, popular songs can be inserted throughout the script if the cast are competent singers and there is access to an orchestra or band. Suggested songs have been added to the script below, inserted at natural breaks in the script marked by the *setumah* or *petuuah*. The songs should be adapted and shortened as appropriate, to last no longer than two minutes. Let the introduction overlap the preceding dialogue so there is no waiting for the song to start, and above all, keep them short.

COSTUMES. Costumes should be colorful and outrageous. The style is Persian—long flowing robes of rich silks and satins, curling beards and high hats for men, jeweled headpieces and veils for women. There is potential for cross-dressing, especially amongst eunuchs, though the majority will have simple sleeveless tunics and chunky jewelry. At least one eunuch should be completely bald. Tattoos are optional. Virgins and/or maids can be dressed as belly-dancers. Changes of clothes are necessary for only two actors. Esther begins as a simple peasant girl but is transformed to beautiful virgin prepared to meet the King and then to regal Queen, with appropriate robes, jewelry and a crown. Mordecai begins with dark plain tunic but changes into torn sackcloth for Scene 10. For Scene 14 he is dressed in robes similar to the King's and in the final scenes he wears purple/blue and white robes with a large crown. Other characters can remain in the same costume throughout, although the King should replace his crown with a nightcap for Scene 14.

FINALLY. Two golden rules: pace and good nature. Never let the show flag even for a second. Ensure that the show is displaying a good mood. The audience will participate as required as long as they are having fun. Leave them wanting more!

CAST

Harbonah	Eunuch attending the King, the eyes and ears of the Palace
Ahasuerus	King of Persia
Vashti	1st Queen of Persia
Memucan	A Prince of Persia
Hegai	Eunuch in charge of the Virgin Harem
Mordecai	a Jew, son of Jair, son of Shim'i, son of Kish, a man of Benjamin
Hadassah/Esther	Abihail's daughter, Mordecai's cousin, a beautiful virgin, 2nd Queen of Persia
Bigthan)	Eunuchs who are scoundrels
Terash)	
Haman	son of Hammedatha, an Agagite
Zeresh	Wife of Haman
Hatak	Eunuch appointed by the King to serve Esther

EXTRAS

Mehuman)
Biztha)
Charbona)
Bigetha)   Eunuchs in attendance of the King
Abagtha)
Zethar)
Carcas)

Carshena)
Shethar)
Admatha)   Nobles and Princes of the Provinces
Tarshish)
Meres)
Marsena)

Shaashgaz, the Eunuch in charge of the Concubine Harem

Firmament)
Workday)

Garden   )
Radiant   )   Seven maidservants for Esther[102]
Quick   )
Lamb   )
Rest   )

Virgin girls, all beautiful
Servants at the gate of the king
Townsfolk
Scribes
Runners
Riders
Jews living in Susa and other provinces

SCENES

ACT 1

Scene 1	Drinking Parties	Full-stage of Throne Room	(1:1-15)
Scene 2	A Welcome Decree [for some]	Full-stage of Throne Room	(1:16-22)
Scene 3	Beauty Pageant Plans	Full-stage of Throne Room	(2:2-4)
Scene 4	Introducing the Heroes	Front of Curtain	(2:5-7)
Scene 5	Beauty Pageant Preparation	Full-stage of Harem	(2:8-15)
Scene 6	Beauty Pageant	Full-stage of Throne Room	(2:16-18)
Scene 7	A Dastardly Plot Thwarted	Front of Curtain	(2:21-23)
Scene 8	Introducing the Villain	Full-stage of Gate of Palace	(3:1-7)
Scene 9	A Dastardly Decree	Full-stage of Throne Room	(3:8-15)
Scene 10	Mordecai's Challenge	Front of Curtain and right-stage Esther's Quarters	(4:1-17)

ACT 2

Scene 11	Esther Risks All	Full-stage of Throne Room	(5:1-5)
Scene 12	Esther's 1st Drinking Party	Right-stage Esther's Quarters	(5:6-8)
Scene 13	Haman's Mixed Feelings	Left-stage Haman's Quarters	(5:9-14)
Scene 14	The King's Sleepless Night	Full-stage of Throne Room	(6:1-10)
Interlude	Mordecai Paraded as a Hero	Front of Curtain	(6:11)
Scene 15	Haman's Fury	Left-stage Haman's Quarters	(6:12-14)
Scene 16	Esther's 2nd Drinking Party	Right-stage Esther's Quarters	(7:1-9)
Interlude	Haman Hangs	Shadow on Closed Curtain	(7:10)
Scene 17	A New Decree	Full-stage of Throne Room	(8:1-14)
Scene 18	Party-time	Front of Curtain opening to Full cast on empty stage	(8:15-9:4)
Scene 19	The Great Turnaround	Half-stage Throne room with shadows on closed half-curtain	(9:5-11)
Finale	The Festival	Curtain opens to full cast on empty stage	(9:12-19)

PANTO ESTHER

ACT 1

(Audience response)

Scene 1   **Drinking Parties**   (Full-stage of Throne Room)

HARBONAH   This happened in the days of the Persian king,
 The one who ruled over 'most everything,
 From far Hoddu to the province of Kush,
 The one they call Ahasuerush.
 He was sitting—the king—on the throne in his place
 The might of the Persians and Medes 'fore his face.
 And for all those nobles and all those princes
 He sent invitations to come for drinkses.
 (Cheers)
 The party went on in his glorious place
 For well-nigh eighty and a hundred days!
 And after that, for the great and the meek
 In the capital Susa were drinks for a week.
 (More cheers)
 His wealth on display in the curtains with tassels,
 Couches of silver and wine in gold vessels.
 Not any restraint, for drinking was law.
 The king had decreed man should do as he saw.
 And Vashti the queen would not be left out
 She made some drinkses for the women about.
 (Women cheer)

   Ensemble: The Drinking Song (The Student Prince)

ב

   When good was the heart of the king with the wine
   He issued an order that seemed to him fine:

AHASUERUS (to eunuchs)	Biztha, Carbona, Bigetha, Mehuman, Carcas, Abagtha, Zethar my man *(takes a big breath)*, Bring to my face crowned Vashti my queen, So her beauty by peoples and princes is seen.
EUNUCHS	She refuses to come at the word of the king! *petuchah*
AHASUERUS (to nobles)	I'm angry, my wrath is burning within. Carshena, Shethar, Meres, Memucan, Admatha, Tarshish, Marsena my man *(takes a big breath)*, Tell me the law when a queen does not come: Vashti refuses—now what should be done?

Vashti: Let it Go (Frozen)

ס

Scene 2   A Welcome Decree [for men]   (Full-stage of Throne Room)

MEMUCAN (to King)	Not over the king alone she did wrong But over all men in the kingdom belong. For it will get out—this deed of your wife— No end of contempt from our women means strife! If it seems good, then let it go out— A law of the king so there isn't a doubt, All women must honor their masters and lords, And Vashti from now will just be ignored. *(Women boo and men cheer)*
HARBONAH	The word was good in the eyes of the king And he did like he said—Memucan's thing. He sent letters afar in everyone's mouth, That men should be princes within their own house.

The King: Master of the House (Lés Miserables)

פ

Scene 3   Beauty Pageant Plans   (Full-stage of Throne Room)

HARBONAH   Not long after these things the king's fire went out
He remembered his Vashti and started to doubt
So the young men attending him started to urge him:

ATTENDANT   Let them seek young girls, beautiful virgins, *(Men cheer)*
(to King)   From all of the provinces both near and far,
Let Hegai the Eunuch put each through the Spa,
And the girl who is good in the eyes of the Rex
Can reign in the place of your troublesome ex.

Virgins: Barbie Girl (Aqua)

כ

Scene 4   Introducing the Heroes   (Front of Curtain)

HARBONAH   There are people in Susa I'd like you to know,
Let me now introduce the stars of our show. *(Cheers)*
Mordecai son of Kish is a Benjaminite,
He came from the homeland when the exiles took flight.
He was father and mother to orphaned Hadassah,
AKA Esther, a beautiful lass, eh?

Scene 5   Beauty Pageant Preparation   (Full-stage of Harem)

HEGAI   Of all the young girls watched over by me,
Esther was best of all I could see.
I hastened her spa times and singled her out,
And found seven maidens to help in her house.
(Cheers)

MAIDS (introduce themselves)	Firmament Workday Garden's my name Radiant Quick Lamb also came I serve on day Seven, and my name is Rest, I'm not sure why, it was Esther's request.
HARBONAH	Now Mordy had told her she mustn't reveal Her people or birthplace for woe or for weal. *(Oooooh!)* But he would walk by every day near the harem To check on her welfare and how she was farin'. *(Cheers)*
HEGAI	A year passed by—six months rubbed with myrrh, And six months with perfumes for this was the law. When the time came to go into the king, The maidens could take with them most anything. In the evening she went, in the morning she came And didn't go back unless called by her name. And the turn finally came for Esther the valid. What happened to her could be sung in a ballad.

Scene 6   Beauty Pageant   (Full-stage of Throne Room)

AHASUERUS (to Esther)	Four years have passed since starting my quest To find from the girls the one I love best. Esther, of all virgins, you found my favor Your beauty and kindness is something to savor *(Cheers)* The crown of the kingdom I set on your hair And now you may reign from Vashti's old chair. I think the occasion calls for a party! Raise your glass one and all, and cheer very hearty *(Cheers)* Princes and servants and out in the sticks

	Take a break from your work and enjoy my great gifts!
HARBONAH	And Esther remembered she mustn't reveal Her people or birthplace for woe or for weal. Esther will do what Mordy commands Even when queen of the vast Persian lands. *(Oooooh!)*

Esther: Dancing Queen (Abba)

ɔ

Scene 7   **A Dastardly Plot Thwarted**   (Front of Curtain)

HARBONAH	One day Mordecai just sitting around Suddenly heard a worrying sound The raging voices of Bigthan and Terash Two of the eunuchs of King Ahasuerush A dastardly plot—he heard them make plans Intending to dispatch the king with their hands! *(Gasps)*
MORDECAI (to Harbonah)	Harbonah! Report now to Esther the Queen The dastardly plot Cousin Mordy has seen.
HARBONAH (to Esther)	Esther, your highness, a message to give To the king—he may have no longer to live If those dastardly eunuchs Terash and Bigthan Are given the chance to send out their hand!
ESTHER (to King)	Mordecai at the gate has discovered a plot You'd better arrange for those men to be shot!
AHASUERUS	Let's hang them instead in the sun's dying rays. *(Cheers)* Now write all this down in the book of the days.

Harbonah & Mordecai: The Story of Tonight (Hamilton)

פ

Scene 8   Introducing the Villain   (Full-stage of Gate of Palace)

HARBONAH	It's time for the villain to enter the gate. *(Boos)* Haman son of Hammedatha was made great, Raised up by the king and set on a throne, An Agagite! Not even one of our own. *(Boos)* The king said that all should be bowing and kneeling, For this is Haman with whom they are dealing. But look! Mordecai was refusing to kneel. The servants were wondering how he could feel Such contempt for the thing that the king did command.
SERVANT (to Mordecai)	Why have you let this get so out of hand?
MORDECAI (to servant)	Look, maybe this bowing is OK for you, But it isn't for me—for I am a Jew.
SERVANT (to Haman)	O Haman, you might think that Mordecai's rude, *(Boos)* He hasn't bowed down—it might be the feud Between his folk and yours that goes back to King Saul! We thought you should know—now it's your call.
HAMAN (to servant)	Well thank you for pointing this out to me now. It fills me with wrath that this man will not bow. But I'm not going to bother with him on his own, Instead I will see the whole Jewish race groan. Bring my *pur*, let me throw for the month and the date When all of his people I will terminate! *(Boos)*

Haman: You'll Be Back (Hamilton)

ס

Scene 9   A Dastardly Decree   (Full-stage of Throne Room)

HAMAN   One people across all your kingdom is scattered
(to King)   Who think that the laws of your land never mattered.
                It won't profit the king to leave them to rest,
                I'll annihilate them if you think that's best,
                Ten thousands of talents of silver I'll weigh
                For the king's treasuries on that fateful day.

AHASUERUS   I'm twisting the signet ring off in my bower
(to Haman)   And handing to you whatever the power
                You need for this deed for the good in your eyes.
                Bring paper and ink and all of my scribes!
                Send the letters afar in everyone's tongue,
                All that Haman decreed shall ever be done.

HARBONAH   And runners took letters from out of the gate,
                To destroy and to kill and to ann-i-hilate
                Every Jew in the land on the thirteenth of Adar,
                In addition that day for their spoil to plunder.
                The runners went out, the law was expounded.
                They sat down to drink; Susa confounded.

Haman: Exterminate (Snap)

פ

Scene 10   Mordecai's Challenge   (Front of Curtain and right-
                                         Stage Esther's Quarters)

HARBONAH   Mordecai tore his clothes and walked in a sack,
                And cried out a cry, his bitter heart wracked.
                And in every province the king's word was reaching,
                Was mourning and fasting, lamenting and weeping.

HATAK/MAIDS   Esther, your highness, we've heard in dispatches,
(to Esther)   That Mordy your cousin is sitting in ashes.

ESTHER   I'm powerfully affected and worried a lot,
(to Hatak)   Take clothing for him and ask him what's what.

MORDECAI (to Hatak)	Tell Esther that Haman is bad to the core. *(Boos)* He's bribing the king to write up a law To annihilate Jews all over the place. She must go for her people and plead to his face!
HATAK (to Esther)	O Esther that Haman is bad to the core. *(Boos)* He's bribing the king to write up a law To annihilate Jews and now Mordy says You must go for your people and plead to his face!
ESTHER (to Hatak)	Go tell my cousin for me these fine words, What he is asking is simply absurd. It is death for the subject as everyone knows Who goes into the king when they haven't been chose, Unless with his scepter he gives them reprieve, And it's now thirty days since the king called for me! *(Gasps)*
HATAK (to Mordecai)	What you are asking just cannot be done, Every one, man and woman, is under his thumb. The law says its death if they come in uncalled, What you are asking has left her appalled.
MORDECAI (to Hatak)	Tell Esther that 'you must not think you are safe In the house of the king o'er the rest of your race. Your silence means death for the house of your father, Respite and deliverance will come from another. Who knows? If this prospect has come to your hand? So YOU make YOUR mark on this Persian land.'
HATAK (to Esther)	What he said.
ESTHER (to Mordecai)	Go, gather in Susa all of the Jews, And fast for me three days and nights if you choose. I and my maids will be also unsated, Then I'll go to the king to be annihilated! *(Gasps)*

HARBONAH   Mordecai did what Esther commanded,
          And she on her part took the fate she'd been handed.

   Esther: Que sera sera (Doris Day)

ა

INTERVAL

ACT 2

Scene 11   Esther Risks All   (Full-stage of Throne Room)

HARBONAH
After three days of fasting she dressed in fine garb,
And stood near the house of the king in the yard.
The king to her beckoned, his scepter extended,
And Esther came in, she hadn't offended. *(Cheers)*

AHASUREUS
(to Esther)
What's up with you Esther, and how do you do?
Ask away—half my kingdom I'm giving to you.

ESTHER
(to King)
Just one thing if good to the king as he thinks,
I'm inviting your kingship and Haman for drinks.
(Boos)

AHASUERUS
(to Haman)
Hurry up Haman, for Esther's invite. *(Boos)*
Let's go to her party that's starting tonight.

Scene 12   Esther's 1st Drinking Party   (Right-stage Esther's Quarters)

AHASUERUS
(to Esther)
Good wine my dear Esther, now what will it be?
Ask away—up to half of my kingdom from me.

ESTHER
(to King)
If favored am I and my wish brings no sorrow,
Let them come, King and Haman, for more drinks tomorrow.

Scene 13   Haman's Mixed Feelings   (Left-stage Haman's Quarters)

HAMAN
I am so favored, there's joy in my belly, *(Boos)*
But wait, isn't Mordecai turning to jelly?
It fills me with wrath that this man will not bow.
But I will control myself, if only for now.

(to family)
Ho, Zeresh my wife, my loved ones, my friends.
The king favors me, and the queen she intends
To invite me again for drinks in her palace.
If only that Jew wasn't feeding my malice.

The Scroll of Esther

ZERESH (to Haman)	Dear Haman, now listen, I have an idea. *(Boos)* Make a gallow, a high one, right outside here. Go in the morning and speak to the king, Then come back and hang Mordecai on that thing. *(Boos)*
HARBONAH	It seemed very good, to take this advice.
ZERESH	'Make it eighty feet high',
HARBONAH	Suggested his wife.

Zeresh: Stand by Your Man (Tammy Wynette)

פ

Scene 14   The King's Sleepless Night   (Full-stage of Throne Room)

AHASUERUS	It's night but my sleep, it wanders away. Bring for me now the book of the days. Bigthana and Teresh, ah, yes I remember That Mordecai told me they planned to dismember My royal person—now what has been done To honor this loyalty under the sun?
ATTENDANT (to King)	Not anything, sir, we're ashamed to report.
AHASUERUS (to attendant)	What is that noise? Who's out in the court?
ATTENDANT (to King)	*Look out behind you!* Behold, it's Haman! *(Boos)*
AHASUERUS (to Haman)	Well let him come in, as quick as you can. What should be done for a man I admire?

HAMAN (aside)	It must be MY greatness that set him on fire!
(to King)	Bring royal robes and a right royal crown,
	One royal horse that you've ridden around,
	Clothe him and mount him and lead him outside
	By the hand of one of your nobles with pride,
	Let him then call out to those in the crowd,
	'This is a man who has made the king proud.'
AHASUERUS	Hurry! Bring clothes and a right royal crown,
	One royal horse that I've ridden around,
(to Haman)	Do all you have said, as quick as you can,
	Go and find Mordecai—he is the man! *(Cheers)*
HARBONAH	So he took royal robes and a horse and a crown,
	Clothed and mounted the Jew, and took him downtown,
	And led him and called out amongst all the crowd,
	'This is a man who has made the king proud.'

Interlude   Mordecai Paraded as a Hero   (Front of Curtain)

Scene 15   Haman's Fury   (Left-stage Haman's Quarters)

HARBONAH	Haman left Mordecai at the gate of the king,
	And stumbled off home, head bowed and mourning. *(Boos)*
HAMAN	Oh, Zeresh my wife, my loved ones, my lads,
(to family)	You wouldn't believe the day that I've had.
	The king made me honor that despicable Jew,
	What shame has fallen on me and on you.
ZERESH	If Mordecai comes from some Jewish seed,
(to Haman)	You'll fall at his face, you'll never succeed.
HARBONAH	We are the king's eunuchs, we don't like to pester,
(to Haman)	But you are now late for the drinkies with Esther.

Scene 16 Esther's 2nd Drinking Party (Right-stage Esther's
                                        Quarters)
                                        (Boos at Haman)

AHASUERUS   More good wine Esther, now what will it be?
(to Esther)   Ask away—up to half of my kingdom from me.

ESTHER   If favored am I and my wish brings no strife,
(to King)   Let be given to me and my people, my life!
                    For we have been sold, my people are hated,
                    To be killed and destroyed and annihilated,
                    If only as servants and maids to be sold,
                    I wouldn't be letting my troubles be told.

                                    ᴑ

AHASUERUS   Who?! He?! This?! Where?! This?! He?!
(to Esther)   What blackened heart wants to do this to thee?

ESTHER   A man who is enemy, a man who is foe,
(to King)   It is Haman the Bad, this one that we know! *(Boos)*

HARBONAH   O'erwhelmed with wine was the king and with wrath.
                    He stepped into the garden to calm down his breath.
                    Meanwhile in the chamber a panicking scene,
                    Look out behind you! Haman reached for the queen.
                    He stumbled and fell on the bed and on Esther,

                                    ᴑ

                           The king came back in . . .

AHASUERUS   What? Now a molester?
(to Haman)

HARBONAH   As the word went out from the mouth of the king,
                    Bad Haman saw it was finished for him.
(to the king)   Behold, there's a gallows which Haman has built,
                    A high one, eighty feet, just ready for guilt,

>   Though he made it for hanging Mordecai the
>   brave . . .

AHASUERUS   Hang Haman upon it—that villainous knave! *(Cheers)*
(to Harbonah)

Interlude   Haman Hangs   (Shadow on Closed Curtain)

> *Harbonah: Hit the Road Jack (Ray Charles)*

פ

Scene 17   A New Decree   (Full-stage of Throne Room)

HARBONAH   In that day the king gave to Esther the news
               That she had the house of the foe of the Jews,
               And Mordecai came to the face of the king,
               For Esther had told him that they were close kin.

AHASUERUS   I've twisted the signet ring off once again,
(to Mordecai) And given it this time to you, my good man.
               Esther can give you whatever she likes,
               Maybe the house of Haman Agagite! *(Applause)*

HARBONAH   Esther came in again to plead with the king,
               For the law was still standing for annihilating *(Gasps)*
               All the Jews in the kingdom. His scepter of gold
               Was stretched out to touch her, and she became
               bold.

ESTHER   If favored am I and it brings the king joy,
(to King)   Let a new law be written that doesn't destroy
               All the Jews who are living all over this place,
               For Aghhhh! must I see the death of my race?

AHASUERUS   Write to the Jews what is good in your eyes,
(to Esther)   And seal with my ring to stop any replies.
               For that which is writ in the name of the king
               Cannot be turned back by, heck, anything!

(to attendant)	Bring paper and ink and scribes let them come! Send letters afar in everyone's tongue, Send out to each province from Hoddu to Kush One-twenty-seven from Ahasuerush.
HARBONAH	And letters were written and sealed as seemed right, And riders this time were sent out in the night, To give to the Jews, by one certain date, The right to destroy and to kill, annihilate Each non-Jew around who was set to PURSUE them, Who had proven themselves an enemy *to* them. *(Applause)*

Ensemble: Another One Bites the Dust (Queen)

ס

Scene 18   Party-Time   (Front of Curtain)

HARBONAH	As the riders on horses went out with great speed. In the capital Susa was party indeed, For Mordy was honored in robes and a crown, And gladness and joy lit up the whole town. *(Cheers)*
MORDECAI	In province by province, in each neighborhood, The word of the king made a day of great good, Gladness and joy at the wonderful news, That day many Persian folk called themselves Jews! And in the twelfth month through all of the lands, The power was taken from enemy hands. Where once Haman's law with a hatred had burned, The slaughter intended was now overturned! *(Cheers)*
HARBONAH	All the princes and satraps and governors too Were fearing and raising these jubilant Jews. In the house of the king there came a new name: The great Mordecai could now bask in his fame. *(Cheers)*

Mordecai: This is Me (The Greatest Showman)

פ

Scene 19 The Great Turn-around   (Half-stage Throne room with shadows on closed half-curtain)

AHASUERUS The people have killed your enemy's sons.
(to Esther) Is there anything more you'd like to be done?

ESTHER Just one thing, if good to the king, let me see
(to King) The sons of my enemy hung on a tree.

AHASUERUS Parshandatha and Dalphon, Aspatha and Aridai
              (Boos)
(to servants) Poratha, Adalia, Vaizatha and Arisai
              Parmashta, Aridatha *(takes a big breath)* string them up high
              As a warning to any who cross Mordecai.

Finale   The Festival   (Curtain opens to full cast on empty stage)

MORDECAI From now every year on the fourteenth of Adar,
          Come together with gladness and gifts for your neighbor.
          Raise a glass for a toast, for this day I deem
          Forever from now is the Feast of *Purim*. *(Cheers)*

Ensemble: The Purim Song (The Maccabeats)

פ

THE END

All Bow   Ecstatic Applause

Commentary on Esther

My commentary will step back from the fun of a pantomime script to take a more serious look at the *cast* of characters and how they are portrayed in the scroll. Although there is potential to kill humor by analyzing it, the scroll of Esther warrants a discussion of the way it has functioned as *comedy* with a subversive slant. Finally, I will use the theatrical concept of *chiaroscuro* to explore how this comedy has both light and dark sides to it.

Cast

My script has revealed a large cast of characters in the scroll of Esther. There are several speaking parts, with the action revolving around five major actors: Esther, Mordecai, King Ahasuerus, Queen Vashti, and Haman. As we have seen, however, characters with only minor speaking roles such as Zeresh and the eunuchs can have a profound effect on the course of events.

Ahasuerus. The scroll opens with a description of the king of a vast empire reigning from Susa, the winter capital of the kingdom. In Jewish legend Ahasuerus was the richest of all kings, informed by this lavish portrayal of luxury, leisure, and generosity. He hosts drinking parties, first a six-month event for *all* his princes and his servants (1:3) and then a seven-day party for *all* the people of Susa, from the greatest to the smallest, hosted in his own garden-court (1:5). The unlikely length of these occasions along with comment that "drinking was like law, without any restraint" (1:8) suggests that Ahasuerus is being ridiculed by the storyteller rather than admired, shown to be irresponsible and debauched. Reference to Vashti's own drinking party for women (1:9) and a chance remark in Nehemiah 2:6 that reports a Persian queen sitting beside the king on a public occasion indicate that the drinking parties hosted by Ahasuerus were for men alone. This assumption is underscored when Ahasuerus sends seven eunuchs to bring Vashti "to show the peoples and the princes her beauty" (1:11). The story makes clear that this desire was motivated by an excess of alcohol (1:10), and it is likely the rabbinic tradition was correct to infer that he was expecting her to appear naked before his audience (*Midr. Esth. R.* 3). This would also explain her refusal, which is not otherwise made clear in the scroll (1:12, and see below). Ahasuerus swiftly turns from appearing expansive and generous to "exceedingly angry, burning with wrath" (1:12). Shimon Levy describes the king as dependent, emotionally excitable, arbitrary, and rash (2000, 106). When others speak to him, they defer to him by using third-person speech ("let the king . . ."), which both enables gratuitous repetition of his title and persuades him to think the ideas are his own. Even Esther, his queen, must use flattering and manipulative language:

> To survive within a system of domination requires calculation, manipulation and trickery. These are highly developed skills of people with no other way to affect the course of events. They are the diplomatic strategies of any people with no power and one of the strategies at which women have excelled for centuries. They are not to be scorned. The sorrow is that anyone ever has to use such demeaning tactics to get around immovable power. In this book, Esther's manipulative speech, exaggerated and excessively fawning, points not to her flaws of character but to the king's. She is cunning and skilled in manoeuvring around her husband for the sake of her people. (O'Connor 2003, 60)

Ahasuerus typically turns to others for advice and readily agrees to what he hears. In fact, as O'Connor notes, "the king himself is incapable of thinking or making any decisions whatsoever. Every royal decision in the book of Esther is first prompted by another character" (2003, 57). Many of the decisions, moreover, seem prompted by self-indulgence or apathy. He agrees to a law mandating mastery of the house, to the idea of auditioning countless young women for the queen's replacement, to Haman's plan for eradicating the Jewish population, to Esther's mysterious invitations to her own drinking parties, and to her request that new orders be sent out allowing Jews themselves to respond to their enemies with violence. He acts without thought and jumps to conclusions. Settling down to drink after signing a death warrant for thousands (3:15) is typical of his self-absorption, as is his misreading of the situation when, coming back from the garden, he finds Haman at Esther's bed (7:8). Two symbols of his royal power are important props in the story for defining his erratic use of power. His golden scepter symbolically separates him from all others, since the law insists that unless he holds it out, a death sentence awaits the approaching subject, including his own queen. Yet the signet ring, with which unbreakable laws could be ratified, is handed over with ease first to Haman and then to Mordecai.

Ahasuerus is portrayed as a toothless tiger in the scroll of Esther. Purportedly rich, famous, and powerful, he nonetheless is swayed by advisors, manipulated by Esther, and happy to abdicate authority to others. He is a comic book character who may well have influenced the portrayal of the hapless Sultan in Disney's 1992 animated version of Aladdin. Just as in that tale, the "unchangeable" law of the king is easily adjusted when necessary to enable the story to end happily for its Jewish readers.

Vashti. For a character who has no speaking lines and may not even appear on stage, a lot of attention has been given to Vashti within scholarship dealing with this scroll! She is a rare biblical woman who has a mind of her own and is held up by feminist scholars as a role model (Niditch 1995, 33). As such Vashti is, at times, even preferred to the compliant Esther who follows Mordecai's commands (2:10, 20), allows Hegai to guide her (2:15), and is willing to submit herself to preparations for a night with the king. Perhaps it is deliberate wordplay that the name Vashti, though Elamite, has similar sounds to the Hebrew word for drinking parties, *mišteh*.[103]

A story told by Herodotus forms a helpful background to the incident. A Lydian king Candaules was so proud of his wife's beauty that he insisted his bodyguard Gyges should see her naked. Due to the unwillingness of Gyges to cooperate, the king arranged for a clandestine viewing. The queen discovered the plan and gave Gyges a choice between murdering Candaules or being slain himself (Her 1:8-12). Herodotus explains, "for among the Lydians, and indeed among the barbarians generally, it is reckoned a deep disgrace, even to a man, to be seen naked" (Her 1:10). Written in 430 BCE, the Histories of Herodotus may have been known to the author of the scroll of Esther. His recounting of the story of Candaules suggests it was a known tradition and that the moral stance of the queen in the story was likely common across the ancient world.

Nonetheless, whether she was expected to appear naked or not, the king's summons was an insult to Vashti. His motivation for demanding her presence was self-indulgent, as it would expose her to the gaze of men so that they would, in turn, envy the king. By refusing, "Vashti deflates the king's hubris, together with the surrounding pomp, with her laconic, unexplained yet clearly understandable refusal" (Levy 2000, 106).

The response to her refusal is part of the scroll's hyperbole. Ahasuerus asks what should be done with the queen, according to the law. Rather than simply answering the king's question, Memucan, the king's advisor on this occasion, claims that Vashti's wrongful action was directed not only at the king but "over all the princes and all the people who are in all the provinces of the king" (1:16), resulting in "no end of contempt and fury" (1:18). He recommends a law be written up that would apply to all households in the land, great and small, that women must give honor to their masters (1:20). A minor action on the part of Vashti, therefore, had far-reaching consequences. In this respect, Vashti could be likened to Mordecai, whose minor action of refusing to bow to Haman (also a command of the king) resulted in an edict that threatened the well-being of every Jew in the kingdom.

Vashti is mentioned once more in the scroll, as Ahasuerus calms down and remembers her, "and what she had done and what had been decided about her" (2:1). His law had decreed that Vashti should never again come into his presence (1:19), and it is clear that those advising the king were keen for him to forget her and exploit the opportunity to gather new women to the court. This has left a gap in the story that others have filled, such as the assumption by the rabbis that she was executed, although this could be motivated by a desire that Esther not be implicated by the taint of adultery.

Susan Niditch suggests that for the writer of Esther, "Vashti's foolishness is the foil for Esther's wisdom, her dismissal justified and, indeed, from a narrative point of view, the spark that commences the story" (1995, 33–34). Her removal clearly makes way for the heroine Esther to appear, and for that Vashti's role in the scroll is significant.

Mordecai. Mordecai is introduced as a Jew from the tribe of Benjamin with a known patronage going back to Kish (2:5). His Jewish race is mentioned first as the heritage of Mordecai and is fundamental to the story. Although his forebears had Jewish names, his own was derived from Marduk, the Babylonian deity, "a reflection of the degree to which the Judahites exiled to Babylonia had adapted themselves to the new culture" (Alter 2019b, 721). Reference to him being amongst the exiles with Nebuchadnezzar (2:6) is one of the factors considered to undermine suggestions that the story is historical since the Persian setting places events much later than would allow Mordecai to be one of the exiled group. This reference, however, gives the impression that his family were among Judean nobility. The names Kish and Shim'i may have been ready-mades for the original audience as both names are associated with King Saul (1 Sam 9:1; 2 Sam 16:5). Rabbinic tradition assumes that the resistance Mordecai showed to Haman the Agagite was due to Mordecai's connection to Saul for whom Agag, king of the Amalekites, was a bitter enemy (1 Sam 15). Such intertextual references may also be intended to contrast Mordecai's success with Saul's failures (Thambyrajah 2021, 28).

Mordecai is the reason that Esther, the heroine of the scroll, is present in Susa at this critical moment. The tender verb *'mn* is used to describe the relationship between Mordecai and Esther, describing the close relationship between a child and an adult who is not her parent (2:7). Elsewhere it is translated nurse (Num 11:12; 2 Sam 4:4; Isa 60:4; Ruth 4:16), guardian (2 Kgs 10:1, 5), or foster father (Isa 49:23). I have translated it this way: "He was the one *mothering* Hadassah, who was Esther, daughter of his uncle." As we noted in the chapter on the scroll of the Song of Songs, *dod* ("uncle") is another affectionate term, here implying a close family relationship. One might wonder if allowing her to be taken into the harem indicated true care of her, but the script removes his agency by noting "she was taken" (2:8) and underscores his concern for her welfare by describing his daily vigilance at the court of the women "to know the welfare (*shalom*) of Esther and what was being done with her" (2:11).

Mordecai's character is hard to pin down. His presence "at the gate of the king" (2:19, 21; 3:2-3; 4:2, 6; 5:9, 13; 6:10, 12) may be a technical term for a royal courtier (White 1989, 165), and his action of reporting an assassination plot against Ahasuerus proves his loyalty to the king (2:21-23). Yet he is normally on the fringes of the action, not able to pass the boundary of the gate and needing to rely on messengers to communicate with Esther. His refusal to bow down to Haman is unexplained other than his response, when asked, that he is a Jew (3:4). As the stories of Joseph (Gen 42:6) and David (1 Sam 24:8 [MT 9]) show, respectful bowing to people of authority was not forbidden to Jews, only bowing to idols. Hence the rabbinic explanation of the multi-generational family feud.[104] White considers Mordecai's refusal as foolish and his reaction to Haman's edict as excessive:

> We see the victim of shock in Mordecai, who goes into a panic, putting on mourning and wailing through the city streets (4:1). These actions are, of course, acceptable means of expressing grief in the Ancient Near East, but they do not help avert the crisis. Mordecai's one idea seems to be to bring the crisis to the attention of Esther. (1998, 169)

As Esther becomes aware of the situation and is challenged by Mordecai to use her position to influence change, their roles reverse. Where once Esther had been willing to do all that Mordecai commanded (2:10, 20; 4:8), the tables turn when she decides to act, and the scroll tells us that "Mordecai did all that Esther commanded him" (4:17).

Even though Mordecai's loyalty to the king is remembered and rewarded by the public parade honoring him (6:10-11), his status does not change as a result of the incident. Instead he is returned to the gate (6:12), still on the outside.

By the end of the scroll Mordecai is upheld as the hero. The king's signet ring has been handed to him and his words are carried across the empire with the king's authority. The final short chapter in the scroll speaks only of Mordecai, his authority, his strength, his greatness, and his legacy (10:1-3). Yet the more detailed earlier chapters 8 and 9 indicated that he still relied on Esther's interactions with Ahasuerus to counter the plans of Haman by re-issuing an edict permitting Jews to defend themselves and to shame the house of Haman by displaying the bodies of his sons. There may have been different versions of this story circulating, one focused entirely on Mordecai. If so, the final editors of the scroll have countered the emphasis on Mordecai by naming the scroll after the heroine Esther.

Esther. When the heroine of the story is introduced, the only details that are given are her name, her orphaned status, and her beauty. Her Jewish name Hadassah, meaning "myrtle," is only mentioned once (2:7), but on two other occasions (2:15; 9:29) she is referred to as "daughter of Abihail" (*ʾabîḥayil*), a name that translates "father of valor," hence my reference to her as "Esther the valid" (Scene 5). The Persian name "Esther," like Mordecai, seems derivative of the Babylonian deity Ishtar but could also be deliberate wordplay as it sounds like the Hebrew word *hastēr* that means "concealment" (Radday 1990a, 300). Although no reason is given for Mordecai's instruction to Esther to keep her Jewish identity hidden, it serves as an important plot device. Since Haman is unaware of her Jewish identity, he does not know that the edict the king had sanctioned would have an impact on the queen.

Esther's character develops through the scroll from orphaned child to object of pleasure to frightened queen to courageous, intelligent, independent woman (Levy 2000, 114). We are told that, unlike the usual expression to "find favor," Esther actively "wins" the favor of those around her: first Hegai the eunuch (2:9), then "in the eyes of all who saw her" (2:15), and finally the king (2:17; 5:2). Until the turning point of the story, Esther allows herself to be instructed and prepared by others. Her lack of access to those beyond the palace gate is shown in the use of messengers between Mordecai and herself. Her longest speech in the scroll is given in response to Mordecai's "command" to go to the king and implore favor for her people:

> All the servants of the king and the people of the provinces of the king are knowing that every man and woman who go into the king to the court of the inner court who has not been called—his one law—are put to death, unless the king extends to him the scepter of gold will they live / And I have not been called to come into the king this thirty days. (4:11)

The dividing *athnach* comes close to the end of the verse, implying that her desperate plea could be spoken in one breath. Mordecai's response, as noted above, is the centerpiece of the scroll, challenging Esther to align herself with divine providence (4:14). Recalling that her father's name means "father of valor," Mordecai's reference to "the house of your father" was a clever piece of rhetoric on his part and may have swayed her decision. Once

Esther accepts the challenge of Mordecai, she takes charge of her situation. *She* commands *him* to follow her orders, to gather all the Jews in Susa and fast along with her and her maids for three days. The courage needed for this decision is seen in the fatalistic statement "And then I will go to the king which is not like the law, and if I am annihilated, I am annihilated" (4:16b).

Shimon Levy also sees this part of the scroll as signaling a turning point in Esther. He writes that as she clothes herself in royal garments in preparation to go before the king (5:1), her costume is "an external, theatrical sign of [her] inner conversion . . . for the first time she has become really resolved to behave like a queen" (2000, 108).

The path that Esther takes by requesting the presence of the king and Haman at a private drinking party rather than directly requesting favor for the Jews as she had been commanded not only contributes to the drama but also reveals her intelligence, wit, and wisdom. She removes the issue from the public eye (thus not making the same mistake as Vashti), raises the curiosity of the king, and lulls Haman into a false sense of security. The invitation to a second party could only increase those responses. When Esther finally reveals her request (7:3), the Hebrew diacritics again indicate how dramatic tension is used in the scene. Esther begins as she has on the two earlier occasions, "if it is good for the king" (5:4, 8), but the *athnach* indicates a dramatic pause before her surprising revelation. She rushes on, saying, "for we have been sold—I and my people—to be destroyed and to be killed and to be annihilated," and another pause is indicated by the *athnach* before an astute reference to how these circumstances affect the king himself. The *setumah* that follows this revelation indicates that it is taking time for the information to sink in, and the king's almost incoherent response, literally "who, he, this, and where this, he" conveys him spluttering with rage and precipitating Esther's final revelation: "A man who is enemy and foe, Haman the bad, this one!" (7:6). After this there is no need for Esther to speak again—Haman, even if accidentally, engineers his own downfall and death sentence.

It is also possible to fill these pauses with a different interpretive vision. As Stan Goldman suggests,

> One could infer from the gaps of silence in the text that the beautiful Esther has manipulated both men by arranging herself in a seductive manner on the couch. Thus when the king enters the room, the combination of Haman's fall and Esther's beauty compels the sentence of death. Since Esther does not hesitate to seek vengeance later in the tale, the portrayal of a shrewd theatrical female manipulator is very plausible and appealing. (1990, 19)

With her increased confidence, Esther's role becomes more commanding in the latter part of the scroll. She is given the property of Haman and admits to the king her relationship to Mordecai, after which he is raised to the position that Haman once held (8:1-2). While she must still depend on the extension of the scepter to allow her to make requests of the king (8:3-5), he consults her more readily (9:12). Her need for skillful manipulation of the king with the repetitive "if it is good for the king" (8:5; 9:13) indicates that while her character developed, that of the king remained unchanged.

Haman. As the villain of this performance, Haman is as much a caricature as Ahasuerus, presenting as wily, manipulative, and erratic as an advisor. We are not told why this foreigner (an Agagite), albeit with Persian-sounding name and patronym, was promoted over "all the princes" (3:1) but, as Clines notes, "the unaccountable promotion contrasts nicely with the inexplicable overlooking of Mordecai in the previous scene" (1984, 293). The link between Saul and Agag the Amalekite as mentioned above along with an oracle of Balaam that named Agag as an enemy of Israel (Num 24:7) meant that his designated role as "enemy of the Jews" (3:10; 8:1; 9:10, 24) was unsurprising.

Like Esther, Haman uses the phrase "if it is good for the king" to get his own desires filled (3:9). In other respects he mirrors the king. He, too, takes advice from others and acts on it without consideration (5:14). He, too, is self-absorbed, assuming he is the subject that the king desires to honor (6:6), not questioning why he was singled out to drink with Esther and the king (5:12), and seemingly unaware of the way his pleading for his life to Esther on her bed would appear to others (7:8). He is moody, swinging from hubris to fury to depression. His casting of lots (3:7) indicates a superstitious bent. Yet his easy access to the king (3:8) and the king's decree that others should bow to him (3:2) suggests that he was powerful and influential, free of the restraints that others faced.

The villainous nature of Haman is undisputed. His arrogance is excessive and his hypersensitive pride irrational. When Mordecai refused to bow to him, the scroll tells us Haman "disdained" to deal with him (3:6) but instead devised a plan to wipe out all Jews. Later, however, when humiliated by the ironic reversal of positions as Mordecai was honored, Haman readily agrees to the suggestion that he build gallows to hang Mordecai. The plan that would go ahead even when Mordecai was removed was instigated with bribes and excessive use of bureaucracy, a plan "to destroy, to kill, to annihilate" and, on top of that, "to plunder" the Jews (3:13).

The downfall of this villain, as befits a comedic script, is based on a misunderstanding. After Esther's revelation and in the absence of the king,

Haman turns to Esther to plead for his life (7:7). In doing so he falls "on" or "beside" Esther's bed while she is reclining on it, no doubt in the eastern manner of dining and partying, and is thus caught in an apparently compromising position when the king returns (7:8). The accusation the king makes uses the verb *cbš*, a verb that in most circumstances could be translated as "rape." As the word leaves the king's mouth, "the face of Haman fell"—he can see there is no escape for him.

Ultimately Haman's fate is tied directly to the perception of Ahasuerus. Haman rose to power swiftly, and he fell from power just as fast, both at the whim of the easily manipulated king.

Zeresh. A brief comment should be made about the character Zeresh, the wife of Haman. Like the eunuchs in this story, she has a significant role despite her few lines. On the one hand, she represents a softer side to the villain, as she is mentioned along with "loved ones" (5:10, 14; 6:13) and is clearly the mother of the ten sons of Haman that are hanged following his downfall (9:7-10). On the other hand, her words reveal her as equally capable of callous villainy. Zeresh is named first in suggesting that Haman build exaggerated gallows to rid himself of the annoying Mordecai (5:14). Later, she joins Haman's "wise ones" in uttering a prophetic word about Haman's own inability to withstand Mordecai (6:13). Even the loyal wife of the enemy of the Jews must recognize that they are invincible!

Comedy

Esther has been said to be "the only book in the Bible . . . that can be classified, start to finish, as a comedy" (Biddle 2013, 73). Its humorous bent is conveyed predominantly through irony, a type of reversal where a character or audience member may expect one thing but the opposite is true instead. In the scroll of Esther this theme is summed up in a nutshell: "In the days when the enemies of the Jews had hoped to master over them, overturned it was so that the Jews mastered over the ones hating them!" (9:1).

The verb *hpk*, which I have translated "overturned," is used elsewhere in the Hebrew Bible with a similarly ironic meaning, such as in Deut 23:5 where it is recalled that Balaam's curse was overturned to a blessing or in Jonah 3:4 where the prophet's famously short prophecy "yet forty days and Nineveh is overturned" is fulfilled in an unexpected way by the city's complete and fulsome repentance. It is used again in the scroll of Esther in 9:22 where sorrow is overturned to gladness for the Jews. The scroll begins with excessive partying by the Persians and ends with a two-day party for the Jews alone.

Countless details in the scroll are marked by this sense of ironic reversal. Ahasuerus is introduced as a man of power and influence but is manipulated by all around him. In the opening scene the king is said to decree that every man should do as he desires (1:8), yet the first person who follows their own wish is Vashti the queen. Vashti's punishment for refusing to come to the king is to be banned from coming to the king! Ironically, she gets exactly what she wants. This queen is banished but Esther, her replacement, is also shown following her own desires, willing to risk her life by breaking the law of the king, this time entering his presence *un*invited.

The most extreme levels of irony are reserved for the characters of Haman and Mordecai, emphasized by references to rising and falling. Haman rises to prominence rapidly—the king "raised him up and set his throne over all the princes with him" (3:1). All are commanded to kneel before him, but Mordecai remains upright. Haman's fury extends beyond the individual Mordecai with a plan to eliminate all Jews—with an exaggerated threefold description "to destroy, to kill, to annihilate" (3:13). Mordecai's response is to dress in sackcloth, bringing himself so low in appearance that Esther sends garments to clothe him (4:4). In their subsequent exchange (conveyed by the eunuch Hatak) Mordecai challenges Esther to use her position of high rank to the advantage of her people. Yet when she gains the ear of the king she merely invites him and Haman to a drinking party (5:8). After this Haman boasts to his family and friends how he has been raised above all others, and yet he feels belittled by Mordecai's lack of respect. He readily agrees to the suggestion of a high gallows on which to hang Mordecai, knowing he must first get the king's permission. With ironic timing, it is just as he comes to court to seek permission that the king has rediscovered the good deed of Mordecai and wants to reward him. Haman's fortuitous appearance means it is he who advises the king. Assuming the man to be honored is himself, Haman suggests an elaborate plan of raising the man on the king's horse dressed in the king's garments and paraded by one of his subjects. Another reversal ensues as it is Mordecai raised on the horse and Haman below calling attention to him: "Thus is done for the man whom the king delights to honor him" (6:11). Now it is Mordecai who sits high above all others.

No wonder Haman returns home feeling low (6:12). The words of his loved ones drive home the reversal—"you have begun to fall before the face of Mordecai" (6:13). The storyteller seems to delight in hastening this downfall of Haman: "Yet while they were speaking with him, the eunuchs of the king arrived and were in a terrible hurry to bring Haman to Esther's drinking party which she had made" (6:14). Shimon Levy describes this verse as "a short but viciously funny interlude" (2000, 111). It is at this second drinking party that Esther reveals that Haman's plan would mean her own destruction—an irony in itself given the pains she has taken to conceal her identity. As Haman falls at Esther's feet and the king returns, Haman is condemned to death for assault of Esther—ironically a crime he did not commit! Being raised on his own extraordinarily high gallows is the last twist in Haman's tale—his final elevation is his final downfall. In the meantime, Mordecai's relationship to Esther is revealed to the king, and by virtue of their kinship he is raised to the level of power and authority that had formerly been Haman's.

I have referred above to the use of hyperbole and exaggeration in this scroll, especially the number of provinces said to be under Ahasuerus's control, the length of the drinking parties and beauty treatments, the amount of silver in Haman's bribe, and the height of the gallows. Goldman refers to this feature as "irony of language," suggesting that "such numbers are historically unbelievable but ironically believable, for the strategy of exaggeration heightens the absurdity and incongruity of the tale—the very heart of irony" (1990, 21).

The scroll of Esther celebrates the survival of the Jewish race amongst the diaspora. As O'Connor suggests, "Esther's humour is a work of political satire, a survival tactic, and an act of hope . . . Humour at the expense of the Persians functions in Esther as a survival tactic of the Jewish community as they face exclusion and genocide in the post-exilic Diaspora" (2003, 53). The humor did not stop with the words themselves in the Masoretic Text. A tradition of its transmission prescribes that the names of Haman's sons be written in a particular way: seven letters smaller and one larger to convey their minor status (Radday 1990b, 72). Moreover, the names are often written directly under each other with the rest of the page left empty as if they are "hanging" on the scroll. This may aid in the custom of reading the names in a single breath. Rabbinic expansions add other elements of humor. A Talmudic elaboration on the scene of Haman leading Mordecai through the streets on the king's horse claims that Haman's daughter was watching the proceedings from the roof and assumed the man on the horse was Haman and the man leading the horse was Mordecai. She empties a chamber pot on the one she thinks is Mordecai but instead targets her father (B. *Meg.* 16a)!

It is, in fact, ironic that the Persians should be chosen as the target of this satirical portrayal, since it was this empire that was most benign towards the Jews, allowing them to return to their homeland and rebuild their temple. As well as laughing at the enemy, therefore, the writers of this humorous tale may also have been laughing at themselves (see Goldman 1990, 25). We have already noted the lack of typical Israelite focus on cultic concerns. The author seems to be at pains to tell a Jewish story but write as a non-Jew. If this scroll was indeed directed at a diaspora audience, it may have been suggesting that accommodation to the non-Jewish environment was necessary for survival. To live amongst foreigners, it is necessary to act like foreigners. Mordecai and Esther both adopted Persian names and were integrated into the palace hierarchy. They also seem to adopt the methods of their enemies. As matters are overturned following the death of Haman, the same action that had been planned against the Jews is carried out by the Jews themselves at the behest of Esther and Mordecai. An edict goes out allowing the Jews to "to destroy, to kill, and to annihilate, and to plunder" (8:11). Two details prevent wholesale assimilation, however. The scroll takes pains to claim that the Jews did *not* plunder their enemy (9:10, 15, 16) and there is reference to "many peoples of the land calling themselves Jews" (8:17). Motivated by fear, there was nonetheless willingness on the part of foreigners to embrace Jewish identity, just as these diasporic Jews seemed willing to fit into their new context.

Chiaroscuro

Chiaroscuro, literally "light and shadow," is a theatrical concept that uses the contrast between dark and light to affect interpretation of a composition. As Levy comments, "sometimes one well-aimed spotlight can do the job of many words" (2000, 113). As we look back at the scroll of Esther we can see that some issues are in the spotlight, and others remain on the dark edges. Even the heroic characters have shadow sides, and the reputation of the entire scroll threatens to fall under a shadow.

One of the strengths of the story of Esther is its compelling characters. We want to like Esther and Mordecai, hate Haman, and laugh at Ahasuerus. To an extent, we admire Vashti and Zeresh, women who hold influence over men in a time and place where that is unusual. The ironic unfolding of events elicits satisfaction, seeing the downfall of the bad guy and the triumph of the good guys.

What the scroll itself spotlights, however, leads to wry smiles rather than admiration. Many verses are used to describe drinking parties (seven in all) and edicts sent out across the empire, first by the king (four) and then by Mordecai (one). Almost a chapter is devoted to the description of preparations for a beauty contest to select a new queen. And there is much interest in appearing before others in demonstrations of status.

Mordecai is introduced in parentheses early in the second chapter. While the audience expects him to be the starring hero, he has few lines and most of the time is at the edge of the action, outside at the gate while parties are going on inside the palace. Opinions of his role vary, from wise courtier who is in charge of all that happens to a foolish, panicky victim of shock (see

White 1989). We are not given enough information to make judgments of his reasons for challenging Haman, but his action without doubt endangered his compatriots and his own cousin's well-being. At the end of the scroll (perhaps an addition from a Mordecai source?) he is spoken of in glowing terms, second to King Ahasuerus, seeking good for his people and peace for his seed, yet the ambiguous phrase "acceptable to many of his brothers" (10:3) indicates he was not universally acclaimed.

Esther also has had mixed reception, indicating that she is a flawed heroine. She has been critiqued both for her submissiveness to and compliance with the men around her (Niditch 1995, 33) and for her aggressive and manipulative action (Goldman 1990, 20). Though she fits into the fairy-tale model of the ideal beautiful heroine, contemporary readers struggle to find inspiration from a woman who must use outward beauty and manipulation to achieve success. Both of the heroic protagonists of this scroll, therefore, have their shadow sides.

For many interpreters, the character of Haman represents irrational anti-Semitism, the "black hatred of the Jews" on the basis of their "otherness." Haman's edict is motivated by the claim that "their laws differ from all people" (3:8). Sölle speaks of the irony that the name of God is never spoken in the scroll, "yet it is this holding on to a different God that made this people different, separate, and the target of irrational hatred" (1994, 225). Following the demise of Haman, however, the retaliation of Esther, Mordecai, and all the Jews of the land is equivalent to what he was planning. It plays out like black comedy with an emphasis on exaggerated violence with a countable death toll, leaving the audience both darkly amused and deeply unsettled. I minimized this shadow side in the script of "Panto Esther" out of respect for its "family entertainment" focus, but it is important to turn now and face it.

Connections with Esther

As we discovered when finding connections with the scroll of the Song of Songs, it is possible to appreciate and enjoy the artistry of the scrolls of the *Megillot* and at the same time allow them to conscientize us about important issues.

Violence and genocide are real issues in the scroll of Esther. Haman's decision to engender an edict for the wholesale slaughter of the Jewish race may have had its roots in a blood feud reaching back generations. If so, it reminds us that violence breeds violence and can spiral out of control if unchecked. On the other hand, if it were merely his pride that was offended and he considered himself "too lofty to lay hands on one man alone"

(Queen-Sutherland 2016, 278), Haman's decision to persecute the entire Jewish race would suggest the irrational and dangerous megalomania of someone who has access to power.

The festival of *Purim* is an annual reminder that the Jews have been threatened over and over throughout history and yet have survived to this day. Persecution with both political and religious motivation saw millions of Jews marginalized, attacked, expelled, and scapegoated, culminating in the horror of the Holocaust instigated by Nazi Germany where six million Jews were killed in just four years (1941–1945).

The systematic slaughter of a face or group of people in the name of a god or ideology is not limited to Jewish experience. Other genocides within recent decades include the Killing Fields of Cambodia, ethnic cleansing in Bosnia, the black Africans of Dafur, the Tutsis and Hutus of Rwanda, the Armenians of Turkey, the Rohingyas in Myanmar, the Uyghurs in China, and many more. Indigenous populations from colonized countries continue to draw attention to "Frontier Wars" that aimed to remove local populations to make way for invaders. For such populations, colonization has ongoing impacts on self-determination, culture, language preservation, and land rights.

Unfortunately, as we return to the scroll of Esther, we see that the Jewish heroes of the story did not facilitate an end to violence but instead responded in like manner to the violence that had been planned against them. Although the scroll notes three times (9:10, 15, 16) that the Jews did not take spoil from their enemies, which would be normal practice in warfare, in the counter-decree of Mordecai (8:11) and the further requests of Esther to kill enemies in Susa and hang the bodies of Haman's ten sons (9:13), the scroll makes it clear that Mordecai and Esther were not merely defending their people: "like Lamech's seventy-sevenfold vengeance in Genesis, the Jewish attack [of Esther 9] is a tragically ironic *expansion* of violence" (Goldman 1990, 23, my emphasis).

The fact that the scroll does not use the name of God is of some comfort, as it places violence in the hands of human initiative rather than divine. It may be that the MT edited religious aspects out of the Hebrew version precisely to signal that what happens in the scroll is not exemplary (Strawn 2020 150). As Biddle has noted, "The book of Esther does not ratify violence—either Persian or Jewish. It does not endorse revenge. It ridicules imperial decrees, whether drafted by Haman or Mordecai. It ridicules puppet kings and power-drunk Persian ministers of state" (2013, 91). Yet the scroll is still part of Scripture and therefore God's word to faithful communities. How, then, should we respond to the violence within it? Even satirical or comic-book violence has dark undertones that should be addressed. Thom Stark reminds us that since such offensive texts exist as part of Scripture, it allows us to confront issues within them honestly rather than pretend they do not exist or have nothing to do with faith. It is worth quoting Stark at length on this issue:

> Just as history's madmen have justified their genocides in utilitarian, ideological, and moralistic fashion, we have been trained to justify the genocides of our spiritual ancestors in the name of Israel's physical preservation, Israel's "right" to land, and in the name of the moral depravity of Israel's enemies. Our scriptures have trained us to reason like war criminals, and whether we like it or not, that capacity abides in us. To ignore these texts is to push that reality out of our sight, where we are powerless to chasten it. We must keep these texts in our liturgies, so that God can speak through them, urging us not to be yet another people willing to kill in the name of some land, some ideology, or some god. [We must allow] God to speak through them, calling upon us to see our pathological selves within them, calling upon us to hold ourselves in judgment long before we even begin to approach our enemies. (2011, 223–24)

I was living in Cape Town, South Africa, at the time when Nelson Mandela was released from prison and the ruling National Party under the leadership of F. W. de Klerk dismantled South Africa's apartheid system and introduced universal suffrage to the country. In the leadup to these events the media often conveyed widespread fear that black South Africans would retaliate with violence and hatred on the basis of the long history of human rights abuses and violence perpetrated against them by the white-minority government. Instead, Mandela became President of South Africa in a peaceful election process in 1994 overseen by de Klerk, and de Klerk was appointed Deputy President of Mandela's coalition Government of National Unity. The two men were jointly awarded the Nobel Peace Prize in 1993.

The new South African government chose to deal with the violence of the past by establishing a Truth and Reconciliation Commission (TRC) focused on restorative justice. The TRC began hearings in 1996, chaired by Archbishop Desmond Tutu, Anglican Archbishop of Cape Town. Victims of human rights violations gave statements about their experiences and perpetrators of violence were also invited to give testimony and apply for amnesty from prosecution. The commission kept a record of submissions and made recommendations on the granting of amnesty to perpetrators and reparation to victims. In addition, a register of reconciliation enabled ordinary South Africans to express regret and remorse for past failures.

Although no human-instigated system will ever be perfect, the TRC was an admirable and creative response to breaking the cycle of violence. Like Stark's attitude to violence in Scripture, the people of South Africa were prepared to face and examine the dark side, to practise forgiveness, and to use the experiences to envisage a different way of dealing with each other in the future. Since South Africa's TRC, the model has been used in many other places, including Congo, Sierra Leone, Chile, Nepal, and Germany on human rights violations in the former East Germany. In addition, commissions focusing on the mistreatment of indigenous peoples in colonized countries have been activated in Canada and Australia.

One of the most challenging issues facing people of the Judeo-Christian faith is the Israeli-Palestinian conflict. Jews and Arabs had lived together peacefully in Palestine across history as the region had been subject to the rule of different regimes. Following the Second World War and in the wake of Holocaust revelations, the United Nations adopted a Partition Plan for Palestine to enable an independent Jewish state. Surrounding Arab leaders rejected the plan and the Jewish Agency unilaterally declared the independence of Israel in 1948. In the subsequent Arab-Israeli War of 1948 and ongoing conflict, Israel has taken sovereignty over most of the mandated territories including parts of the West Bank, Golan Heights, and Gaza Strip. New Israeli settlements continue to encroach on Palestinian land. Despite multiple discussions in the Israeli-Palestine peace process, sporadic violent conflict continues between the Israeli government and the Palestinian Liberation Organization.

People of good will on both sides are working for peace in Israel-Palestine. Colum McCann's novel *Apeirogon* (2020), named for a shape with a countably infinite number of sides, ruminates on the many facets of the conflict and the many attempts at peacemaking. It tells the stories of Palestinian Bassam Aramin and Israeli Rami Elhanan who both lost daughters due to violence in their homeland. They met through the organization Combatants for Peace and now tour the world together to speak about their experiences, telling how they share the same pain and are committed to sharing their land instead of just sharing graveyards. They advocate for a peaceful end to the conflict in Israel-Palestine, recognizing that concession is needed on both sides. Might we envisage one of those concessions as a type of Truth and Reconciliation Commission to allow for the healing power of honesty and forgiveness?

Stories of redemption have long been found in Jewish tradition. Journalist Shaul Magid in an article titled "The Dark Side of *Purim*" (2014) recounts a Hasidic tale of a rabbi leading his people to "blot out Amalek" during a *Purim* feast. As they enter an inn where Polish peasants are engaged in revelry, the place falls silent. The rabbi walks to the center of the dance floor and holds out a hand. One of the peasants steps forward and takes it, and they begin dancing together. In a matter of minutes, the group of Hasidic Jews and the Polish peasants are all dancing joyfully.[105] In his article, Magid suggests that to blot out Amalek today, Jews need to enter a mosque and offer a hand to start dancing. Reaching out a hand to the enemy would enable a transformation of *Purim* from a story of redemptive violence to a story of redemptive peace (Queen-Sutherland 2016, 487).

As I was writing this chapter I heard of the death of Holocaust survivor Eddie Jaku OAM at 101 years of age. Eddie came to live in Australia after surviving the Second World War including interment at Buchenwald, a French prisoner-of-war camp, and finally Auschwitz, described by him as "hell on earth." His book, titled *The Happiest Man on Earth* (2020), was published as he turned 100. In a Ted Talk in 2019, speaking with a pin lapel that spelled out the Hebrew letters *zakhor* ("remember"), Eddie said, "I do not hate anyone. Hate is a disease which may destroy your enemy but will also destroy you in the process."[106] He claimed his long and healthy life came from a commitment to being positive, happy, and prepared to help others.

The stories of Mandela and de Klerk, Aramin and Elhanan, the Hasidic parable, and Eddie Jaku inspire us to believe that violence need not always be met with violence. The scroll of Esther encourages us to believe that reversal is possible, but the sad history of conflict in our world invites us to see that the reversal that is needed is the turn *away* from violence, a reversal that will be of benefit for all people.

The *Megillot*—Concluding Comments

Reading the *Megillot* as a Collection

In the introduction chapter of this volume, I proposed that human experience is the theme that draws this disparate collection of scrolls together. There is no question that these scrolls are part of the Scriptures of the Hebrew Bible and Old Testament, yet the presence of God within them is elusive: God is not directly mentioned in the bookending scrolls of the Song of Songs and Esther and is silent in the remaining three. The key to interpreting this portion of Scripture, therefore, is life itself.

The content of the five scrolls covers the major events of life—the milestones that are observed in most human cultures: birth and youth, betrothal and marriage, work and retirement, anniversaries and memorials, ageing and death. Along with these events come associated emotions and experiences. Love and sexual intimacy, loyalty, conversion to another's faith, the choice to shirk or take on responsibility, feelings of despondency and *ennui*, grief and physical pain, longing for the presence of another, yearning for meaning, faithful attention to the welfare of relatives, fear of the enemy, making hard decisions, acting with courage, celebrating success, and taking pleasure in ordinary things. We have also seen a range of social and global issues to which these scrolls speak: loss and death, family relationships, mental health, domestic abuse, violence and war, threats to home, country, and planet.

The poem on "time" found in Ecclesiastes 3:1-8 is a succinct summary of the range of events, experiences, and emotions covered in the five scrolls. Kandy Queen-Sutherland has described the words of this poem as "poster words" that "read well [and] are easily agreed to" but have come together "without much thought" (2007, 220). The poem covers the majority of life's experiences in paradoxical pairs, claiming that each has value in its time. According to Queen-Sutherland, it represents a view of history that moves in circles without purpose or goal, putting it in contradiction to much of Old

Testament theology. By contrast, after spending some time reflecting on the faith implicit within the *Megillot*, I view the poem as deeply truthful. Life *does* include many experiences that are the opposite of each other: birthing and dying, planting and uprooting, killing and healing, grieving and laughing, weeping and leaping, loving and loathing, keeping and releasing, silence and speech. This poem is well situated in the wisdom tradition of the Israelites because there is profound wisdom in accepting the ebb and flow of life's experiences and recognizing the way in which they resonate with each other. After experiencing war, we better comprehend the value of peace. The joy of new birth can be healing for a family after the loss of a cherished family member. Living through a global pandemic teaches the wisdom of refraining from embracing and the joy of embracing again!

The breadth of human experience reflected in the *Megillot* collection is not the only unifying characteristic. Each scroll deals with potentially explosive content with admirable discretion. The Song of Songs expresses sensuality without any hint of pornography. In Ruth, women's plans are hatched and fulfilled under the cover of darkness, with a powerful and influential man protecting the reputation and dignity of the women within the surrounding community. Lamentations accuses YHWH of desertion and cruelty yet tempers this indictment with admission of human failure. Furthermore, the exquisite crafting of the poetry in the scroll of Lamentations allows us to see beauty even in the midst of suffering. Ecclesiastes presents debate with balance and respect rather than heated censure. Esther offers a heroine who is brave without boasting and calm and gracious in the face of threatened disaster. The scroll of Esther also uses humor as a defiant weapon against those who would try to destroy.

As we have noted, another common characteristic is that the center of each of the five scrolls has significance.

For the lovers in the Song of Songs, the verbal exchange emulates their lovemaking with a climax as the Man comes to his "garden" and eats and drinks until full (4:16–5:1). Although this is a superbly private consummation, there is an immediate appeal to us as audience to embrace the celebration of love that is being offered for our delight.

In the scroll of Ruth, the tide of fortune turns for the two widows from Moab in the middle of the scroll and in the middle of the night. It is on the threshing floor that Boaz recognizes the value of Ruth as a valiant woman and acknowledges his own kinship responsibility to care for her (3:10-13). He begins to make plans that will reverse her status as a foreign, childless widow so that by the end of the scroll she is married, a mother, and incorporated into the Israelite family.

In the middle of the third of the five poems of Lamentations, the first words of hope amongst the poems appear (3:21-23). These words, expressing faith in the kindness and compassion of YHWH, set a new tone for the scroll. Although overt confidence in the saving power of the deity falls away again, the final two poems express the possibility of a new future, and the petitioning community's face and words turn towards YHWH at the end of the scroll in contrast to the downcast and distant description of an observer at the beginning.

The author of Ecclesiastes has so carefully structured the composition that it begins, ends, and is divided into two equal halves by the expression "All is dross"—the pessimistic catch cry of the scroll (1:2; 6:9; 12:8). By uncritically interweaving other perspectives into the debate, however, the author invites the audience to consider also that life is a gift that comes from God (the Optimist) and will be best lived in obedience and worship (the Pietist).

Finally, the scroll of Esther also has a turning point at the center of the plot. Mordecai's challenge to Esther (4:14) is to recognize her position as the Persian queen as a divine appointment enabling salvation for her people. A number of commentaries suggest that the words "respite and deliverance" in the verse encapsulate the divine presence that is otherwise unacknowledged in Esther, giving it another claim to be the climactic moment of the scroll.

Another benefit of reading the *Megillot* in the order set for the Jewish festivals is that it provides a metaphor for the lifelong relationship between God and a person of faith. At Passover, the Song of Songs is read with its focus on the love between a betrothed couple representing the beginning of the relationship between God and the beloved. The scroll of Ruth highlights Ruth's commitment to Naomi, her people, and her faith. It is fittingly read at *Shavuot*, which remembers the foundational covenant between God and the chosen people that took place at Sinai. All relationships go through trials and painful episodes, making Lamentations a meaningful reflection on failing within a relationship yet refusing to let it go. Mourning with others and in the presence of God, albeit a distant deity, can be valuable in a process of healing. The scroll of Ecclesiastes with its mixture of skepticism and optimism encourages us to see that life includes challenges and questions, and these should be faced while at the same time opportunities for enjoyment must be seized. The use of this scroll during *Sukkot* with its memory of the wilderness wanderings is a reminder that relationships can survive and be enjoyed even in precarious times. The scroll of Esther commemorates surprising reversal of fortune and survival against all odds. Relationships that survive the vicissitudes of life and stand up against forces that threaten to destroy them ought to be celebrated with partying and largesse, just as is the practice for the feast of *Purim*.

Reenacting the *Megillot*

Faithful readers of the scripts of the *Megillot*, while appreciating the varied artistry and issues inherent within them, will nonetheless view them as the word of God. Scripture has remained authoritative and relevant down through the ages because it has been continually performed, reenacted, and improvised in the light of new communities of faith, new settings, and new audiences. This book has suggested some ways in which we might reenact these scripts in our time, and I hope it will inspire new and different reinterpretations and reenactments as they are read in other places and circumstances.

The Song of Songs celebrates human love as a gift of God. The original author(s) and circumstances of the poetry are unknown, but audiences down through the centuries have made the words their own and applied them to their own relationships. Some have found that application most palatable when viewed as the love between God and the individual, or God and the church. Others have embraced the poetry as expressive of the focused, committed, passionate relationship between human lovers. Some, like myself, have incorporated words from the scroll into their own marriage vows and into memorial services for loved ones:

> Place me like the seal over your heart,
> Like the seal over your arm.
> For strong like death is love,
> Fierce like Sheol is passion,
> Its sparks are sparks of fire—
> A flame of Yah! (8:6)

The scroll of Ruth presents such lively characters that we will not find it difficult to identify with them, especially if we honestly recognize our own perspective and accept the challenge offered through that standpoint. For the outsider, the refugee, or the needy, the scroll is an invitation to trust in the good provision of God through people of kindness and valor. For the insider, the landowner, and the wealthy, this story is an invitation to provide for those in need and use all means available, including legal solutions, when they are prevented from full participation in the community due to unjust systems. Contemplation of the bitterness of Naomi, the unwillingness of the *P'loni Almoni* to fulfil obligations, the faithful kindness of Ruth, and the committed resolve of Boaz raises challenges for us to consider in our relationship with God and each other.

The scroll of Lamentations inspires us with its beautifully crafted but forthright words of hurt and anger in both individual and communal voices. It encourages us to incorporate such lament language into our own prayer and into our times of gathered worship. Even if, at times, my own suffering is minimal, I can pray in solidarity with those with whom I fellowship who experience loss, anxiety, and personal calamity.

The scroll of Ecclesiastes includes more than one perspective on life's challenges, thus offering food for thought that will apply at different levels of relevance depending on the season of one's own life. At times we will identify with the doubtful cynic, at other times with the cheerful optimist. Our faith traditions may undergird and strengthen us or may be brought into question. Wherever we are in life's journey, we are invited to recognize that life is a good gift of our Creator despite its times of struggle and despair. Ecclesiastes encourages us to be in conversation with others, listening with an open mind and a willingness to encounter different worldviews. It reminds us that faith does not recoil from the difficulties of life.

The scroll of Esther offers reflection on how we might use the power of our position and circumstances to bring about change in our world. Our predominantly democratic contexts are different from the monarchies and theocracies of the ancient world, and yet we will no doubt have opportunities to "make our mark" (4:14), even if only in small ways. Voting in elections, writing to members of the government, participating in petitions or protest action are all opportunities to exercise power in our time. Esther's story and the festival of *Purim* have a further moral impact, recognizing that there is potential for violence in all of us. Escaping violence directed towards us should not automatically mean turning that violence against our enemy. We can appreciate the entertaining nature of the scroll of Esther while simultaneously letting it question the dark side that may lurk beneath the surface in our own relationships. Perhaps it will inspire commitment to a nonviolent lifestyle.

The *Megillot* have been preserved in the Hebrew Bible tradition as a collection for use in festival time. These scrolls are therefore intended not only to challenge us to continue embodying faithful practice as we connect with their themes in our own time and place but also to aid us in ongoing faithful performances of commemoration and celebration.

Works Cited

Alter, Robert. 1985. *The Art of Biblical Poetry*. New York: Basic Books.

———. 2019a. *The Art of Bible Translation*. Princeton: Princeton University Press.

———. 2019b. *The Hebrew Bible: A Translation and Commentary. Volume 3: The Writings Ketuvim*. New York: W.W. Norton & Co.

The Arabian Nights. 2008. Trans. Malcolm C. Lyons and Ursula Lyons. London: Penguin Classics.

Assis, Elie. 2007. "The Alphabetic Acrostic in the Book of Lamentations." *The Catholic Biblical Quarterly* 69, no. 4: 710–24.

Baker, Warren, and Eugene Carpenter. 2003. *The Complete Word Study Dictionary: Old Testament*. Chattanooga, TN: AMG Publishers.

Baldrick, Chris, ed. 2015. *The Oxford Dictionary of Literary Terms*. Oxford: Oxford University Press. www.oxfordreference.com

Bandstra, Barry L. 1995. *Reading the Old Testament: An Introduction to the Hebrew Bible*. Belmont, CA: Wadsworth.

Bellis, Alice Ogden. 2021. "I am Burnt but Beautiful: Translating Song 1:5a." *Journal of Biblical Literature* 140, no. 1: 91–111.

Berlin, Adele. 2004. "Esther." In *The Jewish Study Bible*, ed. Adele Berlin and Marc Zvi Brettler, 1623–39. Oxford: Oxford University Press.

Bertman, Stephen. 1965. "Symmetrical Design in the Book of Ruth." *Journal of Biblical Literature* 84, no. 2: 165–68.

Bial, Henry. 2004. *The Performance Studies Reader*. London: Routledge.

Biddle, Mark E. 2013. *A Time to Laugh: Humor in the Bible*. Macon, GA: Smyth & Helwys.

Bier, Miriam J., and Tim Bulkeley, eds. 2013. *Spiritual Complaint: The Theology and Practice of Lament*. Eugene, OR: Pickwick Publications.

Boase, Elizabeth. 2006. *The Fulfilment of Doom? The Dialogic Interaction between the Book of Lamentations and the Pre-exilic/Early Exilic Prophetic Literature*. London: T. & T. Clark.

Brady, Christian M. M. 2005. "Lamentations." In *Theological Interpretation of the Old Testament: A Book-by-Book Survey*, ed. Kevin J. Vanhoozer, 179–82. Grand Rapids, MI: Baker Academic.

Brawer, Naftali. 2008. *Judaism: Theology, History and Practice*. London: Robinson.

Brenner, Athalya. 1993. "Naomi and Ruth." In *A Feminist Companion to Ruth*, ed. A. Brenner, 70–84. Sheffield: Sheffield Academic Press.

Brettler, Marc Zvi. 2005. *How to Read the Jewish Bible*. Oxford: Oxford University Press.

Brown, William P. 2017. *A Handbook to Old Testament Exegesis*. Louisville, KY: Westminster John Knox Press.

Brueggemann, Walter. 2002. *Reverberations of Faith: A Theological Handbook of Old Testament Themes*. Louisville, KY: Westminster John Knox Press.

Carvalho, Corrine L. 2018. "The Ethics of Survival in the Book of Lamentations." In *Scripture and Social Justice: Catholic and Ecumenical Essays*, ed. G. Sterling and A. Portier-Young, 65–85. Lanham, MD: Lexington Books.

Christianson, Eric S. 2012. *Ecclesiastes Through the Centuries*. Blackwell Bible Commentaries. Chichester: Wiley Blackwell.

Clines, David J. A. 1984a. *The Esther Scroll: The Story of the Story*. Sheffield: JSOT Press.

———. 1984b. *Ezra, Nehemiah, Esther*. The New Century Bible Commentary. Grand Rapids, MI: Eerdmans.

———. 2009. *Interested Parties: The Ideology of Writers and Readers of the Hebrew Bible*. Sheffield: Sheffield Phoenix Press.

Collins, John J. 2004. *Introduction to the Hebrew Bible*. Minneapolis: Fortress Press.

Conquergood, Dwight. 2002. "Performance Studies: Interventions and Radical Research." *The Drama Review* 46: 145–56.

Dell, Katharine J. 2014. "'A Time to Dance': Music, the Bible and the Book of Ecclesiastes." *The Expository Times* 126, no. 3: 114–21.

Dobbs-Allsopp, F. W. 1993. *Weep, O Daughter Zion: A Study of the City-Lament Genre in the Hebrew Bible*. Rome: Pontifical Biblical Institute Press.

Downer, Alan S. 1955. *The Art of the Play: An Anthology of Nine Plays*. New York: Holt, Rinehart & Winston.

Ellacott, Nigel, and Peter Robbins. 2002. "History." *The Magic of Pantomime*. http://www.its-behind-you.com.

Eskenazi, Tamara Cohn, and Tivka Frymer-Kensky. 2011. *Ruth*. The JPS Bible Commentary. Philadelphia: The Jewish Publication Society.

Euripides. 1963. *Medea and Other Plays*. Translated and with an introduction by Philip Vellacott. London: Penguin Books.

Exum, J. Cheryl. 2012. *Plotted, Shot, and Painted: Cultural Representations of Biblical Women*. Sheffield: Sheffield Academic Press.

Fewell, Danna Nolan. 1987. "Feminist Reading of the Hebrew Bible: Affirmation, Resistance and Transformation." *Journal for the Study of the Old Testament* 39: 77–87.

Fox, Michael V. 2004. *Ecclesiastes*. The JPS Bible Commentary. Philadelphia: The Jewish Publication Society.

Fuerst, Wesley J. 1975. *The Books of Ruth, Esther, Ecclesiastes, The Song of Songs, Lamentations. The Five Scrolls*. Cambridge Bible Commentary. Cambridge: Cambridge University Press.

Gerstenberger, Erhard S. 2013. "Elusive Lamentations: What Are They About?" *Interpretation* 67, no. 2: 121–32.

Goldman, Stan. 1990. "Narrative and Ethical Ironies in Esther." *Journal for the Study of the Old Testament* 47: 15–31.

Gordis, Robert. 1986. "Personal Names in Ruth—A Note on Biblical Etymologies." *Judaism* 35, no. 3: 298–99.

Gottwald, Norman. 1954. *Studies in the Book of Lamentations*. London: SCM Press.

Grossberg, Daniel. 2004. "Lamentations." In *The Jewish Study Bible*, ed. Adele Berlin and Marc Zvi Brettler, 1587–602. Oxford: Oxford University Press.

Grossman, Jonathan. 2007. "'Gleaning among the Ears'—'Gathering among the Sheaves': Characterizing the Image of the Supervising Boy (Ruth 2)." *Journal of Biblical Literature* 126, no. 4: 703–16.

Havea, Jione. 2015. "Stirring Naomi: Another Gleaning at the Edges of Ruth 1." In *Reading Ruth in Asia*, ed. J. Havea and P. H. W. Lau, 111–24. Atlanta: SBL Press.

Herodotus. 2013. *The Histories*. Trans. George Rawlinson. Moscow, ID: Roman Roads Media, LLC. https://files.romanroadsstatic.com/materials/herodotus.pdf.

Higgins, Scott J. 2017. *Boundless Plains to Share?: Australia, Jesus, and Refugees*. Sydney: A Just Cause.

Hillers, Delbert R. 1972. *Lamentations: A New Translation with Introduction and Commentary*. New York: Doubleday.

Hopkins, Gerald Manley. 1953. *Poems and Prose*. London: Penguin Books.

Jacobson, Karl. 2009. "Through the Pistol Smoke Dimly: Psalm 23 in Contemporary Film and Song." *Society of Biblical Literature: SBL Forum*. https://www.sbl-site.org/publications/article.aspx?ArticleId=796.

Jaku, Edward. 2020. *The Happiest Man on Earth: The Beautiful Life of an Auschwitz Survivor*. London: Pan Macmillan.

Kaminsky, Joel S., and Joel N. Lohr. 2015. *The Hebrew Bible for Beginners: A Jewish and Christian Introduction*. Nashville: Abingdon Press.

Kaplan, E. Ann. 2005. *Trauma Culture: The Politics of Terror and Loss in Media and Literature*. New Brunswick, NJ: Rutgers University Press.

Keady, Richard E. 1980. "Depression, Psychophysiology and Concepts of God." *Encounter* 41, no. 3: 263–77.

Klein, Isaac. 1979. *A Guide to Jewish Religious Practice*. New York: Jewish Theological Seminary.

Krause, Neal, and Kenneth I. Pargament. 2018. "Biblical Inerrancy and Depressive Symptoms." *Pastoral Psychol* 67: 291–304.

Kruger, Paul A. 2005. "Depression in the Hebrew Bible: An Update." *Journal of Near Eastern Studies* 64, no. 3: 187–92.

Kynes, Will. 2018. "The 'Wisdom Literature' Category: An Obituary." *The Journal of Theological Studies* 69, no. 1: 1–24.

LaCocque, André. 2004. *Ruth*. Minneapolis: Fortress Press.

Lee, Nancy C. 2002. *The Singers of Lamentations: Cities under Siege, from Ur to Jerusalem to Sarajevo*. Leiden: Brill.

———. 2008. "The Singers of Lamentations: (A)Scribing (De)Claiming Poets and Prophets." In *Lamentations in Ancient and Contemporary Cultural Contexts*, ed. Nancy C. Lee and Carleen Mandolfo, 33–46. Atlanta: SBL Press.

———, and Carleen Mandolfo, eds. 2008. *Lamentations in Ancient and Contemporary Cultural Contexts*. Atlanta: SBL Press.

Levy, Shimon. 2000. *The Bible as Theatre*. Brighton: Sussex Academic Press.

Lieber, Andrea. 2012. *The Essential Guide to Jewish Prayer and Practices*. New York: Alpha Books.

Linafelt, Tod. 2016. *The Hebrew Bible as Literature: A Very Short Introduction*. Oxford: Oxford University Press.

Machinist, Peter. 2004. "Ecclesiastes." In *The Jewish Study Bible*, ed. Adele Berlin and Marc Zvi Brettler, 1603–22. Oxford: Oxford University Press.

Magid, Shaul. 10 March 2014. "The Dark Side of *Purim*." *Forward*. https://forward.com/opinion/194161/the-dark-side-of-purim/.

Mandolfo, Carleen R. 2007. *Daughter Zion Talks Back to the Prophets: A Dialogic Theology of the Book of Lamentations*. Atlanta: SBL Press.

Marin, Louis. 1996. "The Frame of Representation and Some of Its Figures." In *The Rhetoric of the Frame: Essays on the Boundaries of the Artwork*, ed. Paul Duro, 79–95. Cambridge: Cambridge University Press.

Mathews, Jeanette. 2012. *Performing Habakkuk: Faithful Re-enactment in the Midst of Crisis*. Eugene, OR: Pickwick Publications.

———. 2019. "Led Through Grief—Old Testament Responses to Crisis." *Stellenbosch Theological Journal* 5, no. 3: 621–42.

———. 2020. *Prophets as Performers: Biblical Performance Criticism and Israel's Prophets*. Eugene, OR: Cascade.

McCann, Colum. 2020. *Apeirogon, a Novel*. London: Bloomsbury.

McKay, Heather A. n.d. "The Book of Esther and the Festival of *Purim*: A Megillah Provides an Avenue for Social Change." Unpublished paper. Available with a login at https://www.academia.edu.

Meek, Russell L. 2016. "Twentieth- and Twenty-first-century Readings of Hebel (הֶבֶל) in Ecclesiastes." *Currents in Biblical Research* 14, no. 3: 279–97.

Melgar, César. 2015. "Ruth and the Unaccompanied Minors from Central America: Ethical Perspectives on a Socio-economic Problem." *Review and Expositor* 112, no. 2: 269–79.

Murphy, Roland E. 1990. *The Tree of Life: An Exploration of Biblical Wisdom Literature*. New York: Doubleday.

———. 1992. *Ecclesiastes*. Word Biblical Commentary. Dallas: Word Books.

Niditch, Susan. 1995. "Esther: Folklore, Wisdom, Feminism and Authority." In *A Feminist Companion to Esther, Judith, and Susanna*, ed. Athalya Brenner, 26–46. Sheffield: Sheffield Academic Press, 1995.

Nielsen, Kirsten. 1998. "Other Writings (Ruth, Song of Songs, Esther, Daniel)." In *The Hebrew Bible Today: An Introduction to Critical Issues*, ed. Steven L. McKenzie and M. Patrick Graham, 173–200. Louisville, KY: Westminster John Knox Press.

Noegel, Scott B. 2021. *"Wordplay" in Ancient Near Eastern Texts*. Atlanta: SBL Press.

O'Connor, Kathleen M. 2002. *Lamentations and The Tears of the World*. Maryknoll. NY: Orbis Books.

———. 2003. "Humour, Turnabouts, and Survival in the Book of Esther." In *Are We Amused? Humour about Women in the Biblical Worlds*, ed. Athalya Brenner, 52–64. London: T. & T. Clark.

———. 2008. "Voices Arguing about Meaning." In *Lamentations in Ancient and Contemporary Cultural Contexts*, ed. Nancy C. Lee and Carleen Mandolfo, 27–31. Atlanta: SBL Press.

Ostriker, Alicia. 2005. "Ecclesiastes as Witness: A Personal Essay." *The American Poetry Review* 24, no. 1: 7–13.

Pardes, Ilana. 2019. *The Song of Songs: A Biography.* Lives of Great Religious Books. Princeton: Princeton University Press.

Penchansky, David. 2012. *Understanding Wisdom Literature: Conflict and Dissonance in the Hebrew Text.* Grand Rapids, MI: Eerdmans.

Perry, Peter S. 2016. *Insights from Performance Criticism.* Minneapolis: Fortress Press.

Peters, John P. 1919. "Some Uses of Numbers." *Journal of Biblical Literature* 38, no. 1,2: 15–23.

Peterson, Eugene H. 2002. *The Message.* Colorado Springs: Navpress.

Pope, Marvin H. 1977. *Song of Songs: A New Translation with Introduction and Commentary.* The Anchor Bible. New York: Doubleday.

Queen-Sutherland, Kandy M. M. 2007. "A Party Called Faith." In *The Pastor's Bible Study Volume Four*, ed. D. A. Farmer, 193–229. Nashville: Abingdon Press.

———. 2013. "Teaching/Preaching the Theology of Lamentations." *Interpretation* 67, no. 2: 184–93.

———. 2016. *Ruth and Esther.* Smyth & Helwys Bible Commentary. Macon, GA: Smyth & Helwys.

Radday, Yehuda T. 1990a. "Esther with Humour." In *On Humour and the Comic in the Hebrew Bible*, ed. Yehuda T. Radday and Athalya Brenner, 295–313. Sheffield: Almond Press.

———. 1990b. "Humour in Names." In *On Humour and the Comic in the Hebrew Bible*, ed. Yehuda T. Radday and Athalya Brenner, 59–97. Sheffield: Almond Press.

Rees, Anthony. 2015. "The Boaz Solution: Reading Ruth in Light of Australian Asylum Seeker Discourse." In *Reading Ruth in Asia*, ed. J. Havea and P. H. W. Lau, 99–110. Atlanta: SBL Press.

Rhoads, David. 2006. "Performance Criticism: An Emerging Methodology in Second Testament Studies—Part I." *Biblical Theology Bulletin* 36, no. 3: 118–33.

Rossing, Barbara. 2010. "God Laments with Us: Climate Change, Apocalypse, and the Urgent *Kairos* Moment." *The Ecumenical Review* 62, no. 2: 119–30.

Ruiz, Jean-Pierre. 2018. "Ruth: A Woman Crossing Boundaries." *The Bible Today* 56, no. 1: 15–20.

Rulmu, Callia. 2012. "Stumbling Words for a Determined Young Lady: Notes on Ruth 2:7b." *Biblical Theology Bulletin* 42, no. 3: 115–17.

Scolnic, Benjamin Edidin. 1996. "Why Do We Sing the Song of Songs on Passover?" *Conservative Judaism* 48, no. 4: 53–72.

Scott, R. B. Y. 1965. *Proverbs, Ecclesiastes*. The Anchor Bible. New York: Doubleday.

Shusterman, Richard. 2001. "Art as Dramatization." *The Journal of Aesthetics and Art Criticism* 59, no. 4: 363–72.

Smith-Christopher, Daniel L. 2015. "Blues Music." In *The Oxford Encyclopedia of The Bible and the Arts*, vol. 1, ed. Timothy Beal, 99–111. Oxford: Oxford University Press.

Sölle, Dorothée, ed. 1994. *Great Women of the Bible in Art and Literature*. Grand Rapids, MI: Eerdmans.

Spinoza, Baruch. 1670/1991. *Tractatus Theologico-Politicus*. Trans. Samuel Shirley. Leiden: Brill.

Stark, Thom. 2011. *The Human Faces of God: What Scripture Reveals When It Gets God Wrong*. Eugene, OR: Wipf & Stock.

Stern, Elsie. 2004. "The Song of Songs." In *The Jewish Study Bible*, ed. Adele Berlin and Marc Zvi Brettler, 1564–77. Oxford: Oxford University Press.

Stone, Timothy J. 2013. *The Compilational History of the Megilloth: Canon, Contoured Intertextuality and Meaning in the Writings*. Tübingen: Mohr Siebeck.

Strawn, Brent A. 2020. *The Old Testament: A Concise Introduction*. New York: Routledge.

Taylor, Millie. 2007. *British Pantomime Performance*. Bristol: Intellect. Proquest Ebook Central.

Thambyrajah, Jonathan. 2021. "Jews in Susa—The Significance of Setting in the Book of Esther." *Australian Biblical Review* 69: 23–36.

Trible, Phyllis. 1978. *God and the Rhetoric of Sexuality*. Philadelphia: Fortress Press.

Van Heerden, Willie. 2001. "Ecclesiastes 3:16-22: An Ecojustice Reading, with Parallels from African Wisdom." In *The Earth Story in Wisdom Traditions*, ed. Norman C. Habel and Shirley Wurst, 155–67. Sheffield: Sheffield Academic Press.

van Wolde, Ellen. 1997. "Texts in Dialogue with Texts: Intertextuality in the Ruth and Tamar Narratives." *Biblical Interpretation* 5, no. 1: 1–28.

———. 2008. "Sentiments as Culturally Constructed Emotions: Anger and Love in the Hebrew Bible." *Biblical Interpretation* 16, no. 1: 1–24.

Verbin, N. K. 2002. "Uncertainty and Religious Belief." *International Journal for Philosophy of Religion* 51, no. 1: 1–37.

Watling, E. F. 1947. "Introduction." In *The Theban Plays*, Sophocles, trans. E. F. Watling, 7–22. London: Penguin Books.

Webb, Barry G. 2000. *Five Festal Garments: Christian Reflections on The Song of Songs, Ruth, Lamentations, Ecclesiastes and Esther*. Downers Grove, IL: Intervarsity Press.

Weeks, Stuart. 2010. *An Introduction to the Study of Wisdom Literature*. London: T. & T. Clark.

Westermann, Claus. 1981. *Praise and Lament in the Psalms*. Edinburgh: T. & T. Clark.

White, Sidnie Ann. 1989. "Esther: A Feminine Model for Jewish Diaspora." In *Gender and Difference in Ancient Israel*, ed. Peggy L. Day, 161–77. Minneapolis: Fortress Press.

Whybray, R. N. 1982. "Qoheleth, Preacher of Joy." *Journal for the Study of the Old Testament* 23: 87–98.

———. 1989. *Ecclesiastes*. The New Century Bible Commentary. Grand Rapids, MI: Eerdmans.

Wilson, Kelly M. 2012. "Daughter Zion Speaks in Auschwitz: A Post-Holocaust Reading of Lamentations." *Journal for the Study of the Old Testament* 37, no. 1: 93–108.

Wohlgelernter, Devora K. 1981. "Death Wish in the Bible." *Tradition: A Journal of Orthodox Thought* 19, no. 2: 131–40.

Wolfe, Lisa Michele. 2020. *Qoheleth (Ecclesiastes)*. Wisdom Commentary. Collegeville, MN: Liturgical Press.

The Works of Flavius Josephus. 1997. Trans. William Whiston. London: Ward, Lock, & Co.

Zetterholm, Karin Hedner. 2012. *Jewish Interpretation of the Bible: Ancient and Contemporary*. Minneapolis: Fortress Press.

Zevit, Ziony. 2005. "Dating Ruth: Legal, Linguistic and Historical Observations." *Zeitschrift für die alttestamentliche Wissenschaft* 117, no. 4: 574–600.

Notes

1. See sefaria.org/Tanna_debei_Eliyahu_Zuta. This rabbinic parable has similarities to the parable of the talents/minas told by Jesus (Matt 25:14-30; Luke 19:12-27). Although transformation is a key to those New Testament parables, it is hard to know if the subject matter was intended to be interpretation of Scripture traditions as is the case with the Jewish parable.

2. William Brown's *A Handbook to Old Testament Exegesis* (2017) is an excellent recent publication covering interpretive approaches to the Old Testament.

3. The term "critical" is not used in the sense of fault-finding but to convey a method of careful, systematic, open-minded examination of biblical texts.

4. See Shimon Levy's (2000) *The Bible as Theatre*, 5. Levy's work has been inspirational for my own exploration of performance in the Hebrew Bible.

5. The King James Version (1611, 1769) aimed for a literal word-for-word translation and has included such words in italics to convey the fact that these words are implied by being included in the single Hebrew word.

6. The translation principles I have just outlined have guided my initial translations that formed the basis for each of the five scripts, but the character of each individual script has called for an occasional compromise. For example, I have translated *hinnēh* as "look" in the Ecclesiastes script as it seemed more appropriate for the contemporary feel of a television talk show.

7. The man refers to the woman as "bride" several times, but it is not clear that the couple are yet married since they seem to live in separate dwellings.

8. In English translations the name is usually spelled with a single "m," but I have transliterated from the Hebrew text with its double "m."

9. See Pope 1977, 56, for a translation of this *wasf* relating to Sarai.

10. See also Pope 1977, 54–89, for a detailed discussion of parallels for the Song of Songs in ancient Near Eastern love poetry.

11. For examples of critique, see Fewell 1987, 80, and Clines 2009, 94–121.

12. See Levy 2000, 132; Trible 1978, 154; Nielsen 1998, 181; Pardes 2019, 1.

13. My own translation of 8:6 emphasizes the "s" sound prominent in the verse and translates the last word "flame of Yah."

14. Even if readers are not in a position to study biblical Hebrew, there are many podcasts available to hear the Song of Songs chanted in Hebrew, such as https://listen.talkingbibles.org/en/language/heb/22_songofsolomon.

15. Information about Greek plays is partly taken from the E. F. Watling's "Introduction" essay in Sophocles, *The Theban Plays* (1947).

16. See David Clines, who argues strongly for an all-male competition as the implied social context of the Song of Songs (2009, 99–100).

17. On this translation, see "Playfulness" section in the discussion on pg. 55.

18. Note that in the Hebrew Bible Chapter 7 begins at this verse and is made up of 14 verses. The Hebrew Bible and English translations are the same in chapter 8.

19. In Greek plays the chorus "may be as large or small as convenience indicates; fifteen was the regular number in Sophocles's day, but as few as five will serve. Large or small, it is essential that their words should be intelligible; the choral odes should be spoken in unison" (Watling 1947, 21).

20. As discussed above, Jewish writers Ibn Ezra and Shlomo Löwisohn are early proponents of this "three-character scheme" that others have also adopted. See Pope 1977, 35, for other names.

21. Somewhat confusingly, the Arab village where Tel Shunam is located is now called Sulam, although it was known in ancient times as Shunem and was mentioned in the Armarna Letters from the fourteenth century BCE as well as being found in a list of conquered cities in the tenth century BCE by Egyptian Pharaoh Shoshenq I.

22. See a discussion of this verse in Bellis 2021. Arguing that the passage is not about race or ethnicity and noting that all Jewish translators retain the translation "but," Bellis advocates for the translation in the title of her article, pointing out its pleasing alliterative repetition of b's and t's.

23. The phrase is also used in 3:10 in the description of King Solomon's palanquin that was "fitted with love by the daughters of Jerusalem" (3:10). The following verse refers to "daughters of Zion" (3:11), probably for poetic parallelism.

24. "Let us make remembered" is a cohortative plural verb in the *hifil* stem, a causative form of the verbal concept.

25. While translating this verse I was reminded of my years of mothering young children who regularly woke during the night. Though I was sleeping soundly, I would wake at the first peep from one of the children, while their father usually slept on!

26. See also Mathews 2012, 32, and Mathews 2020, 84.

Notes

27. When in 1:13 the Woman uses the actual word for breasts, *šāday*, we are reminded that an ancient name for God, Shaddai, is a word related to a mountain god who enables fertility and abundance. See Baker and Carpenter 2003, #7706.

28. In our own day tourism uses all means of promotion to entice visitors. When I watched the beautifully shot movie *Vicky Christina Barcelona* recently, I was intrigued to discover that the Barcelona Tourist Board had approached Woody Allen, suggesting that he use that city as background for one of his movie productions!

29. "Violence against Women," 9 March 2021, *World Health Organization*, who.int/news-room/fact-sheets/detail/violence-against-women.

30. It is disappointing to me that two of my most admired biblical scholars are guilty in this respect. Phyllis Trible, who has been quoted above, notes the verbal correspondences and differences between the two encounters with the watchmen, stating that on the second time they "not only fail to help but actually assault her," but then she makes no further comment about the incident (1978, 148). Robert Alter *does* comment on the verse in his translation, with the dispassionate "We now realize how dangerous it is for a woman to go out in the streets at night . . . the watchmen decide to punish her for her brazenness by beating her and humiliating her through the stripping away of her veil" (2019b, 603). The implication is that violence occurs because the woman has asked for it by placing herself in a risky situation and therefore deserves punishment! No blame is attached to a man's choice to act violently. In 2021 an Australian documentary series titled *See What You Made Me Do* (directed by Tosca Looby) explored this dichotomy.

31. Teaching Respect for All (UNESCO), the Expect Respect Education Toolkit (UK); Respect Matters Program (Dept Education, Australia); and Teaching Respect for All (South Africa) are a few examples of school education campaigns instigated in recent years.

32. Grace Tame's address to the Canberra Press Club can be found on YouTube (March 2, 2021): youtube.com/watch?v=LJmwOTfjn9U

33. Clines accepts that in this fantasy the lovers are equal, and he also passes over the verse in which the Woman is abused with little comment.

34. See collectiveshout.org, an online grassroots campaign movement launched in 2010 to draw attention to the increasing pornification of culture and the way its messages have become entrenched in mainstream society, presenting distorted ideas about women and girls.

35. Not surprisingly, the Christian celebration of Easter and Pentecost holds very similar symbolism to that of Passover and Shavuot, with the death and resurrection of Jesus Christ at Easter securing freedom from death for the believer and the coming of the Holy Spirit at Pentecost marking the birth of the Christian church.

36. Aron haKodesh and Teivah are modern Hebrew terms. The underlying

biblical Hebrew words *'aron* and *tevah* are both translated into English by the word 'ark'. The latter word is used of the boat built by Noah (Gen 6-9) and the basket Moses was placed in for safety as a baby (Exod 2:3). Although the box housing the tablets is only ever called *'aron* in the Hebrew Bible, the varying names in Jewish tradition suggest an overlap in Hebrew as well as English, an observation underscored by the use of the word *'aron* for the coffin (box) of Joseph (Gen 50:26). Clearly both words indicate a receptacle for safe keeping.

37. See Lieber 2012, 235–49, for a detailed description of the Torah service.

38. Yael Rosenberg, "Reading Ruth: Rhyme and Reason," *Jewish Holidays*, http://www.mazornet.com/holidays/Shavuot/readingruth.htm. The final point is added in a similar list of explanations offered by Eskenazi and Frymer-Kensky (2011, xxvi).

39. See the ten *Toledoth* ("generations") found in Gen 2:4; 5:1; 6:9; 10:1; 11:10; 11:27; 25:12; 25:19; 36:1; 37:2.

40. Examples include the marriage verbs: *nś'* ("took up a wife") is used only in Ruth 1:4 and Ezra 9:12 and *qnh* ("acquire Ruth") in Ruth 4:5, 10, the latter of which becomes a common idiom in later times. See Zevit 2005, 574–600.

41. The chiastic arrangement Bertman suggests is as follows:

    A 1:1-7 Threat to family, death in Moab

        B 1:8-22 Kinship ties are challenged; Naomi afflicted by YHWH; women of Bethlehem speak to Naomi

            C 2:1-23 Ruth and Boaz in the field; Ruth worthy of blessing; food for widows

            C' 3:1-18 Ruth and Boaz on threshing floor; Ruth worthy of blessing; food for widows

        B' 4:1-17 Kinship ties resolved; Naomi blessed by YHWH; women of Bethlehem name Naomi's son

    A' 4:18-22 Family restored; life for the future

42. Idioms retained in my translation: "fell on her face" (Ruth 2:10) "uncover the feet" (3:4; 3:7); "spread your wing" (3:9); "before a man could recognize his neighbor" (3:14); "redeem/uncover your ear" (4:4); "he went into her" (4:13).

43. See Robert Alter (2019a, 22-23, 31-32), who speaks of the difference between "domesticating" and "foreignizing" translations, arguing that the latter is preferable when translating the Hebrew Bible.

44. It should be noted that Alter translates *lalekhet* as "to go."

45. 1 Sam 21:2 (MT v. 3) and 2 Kgs 6:8. In both cases the phrase could be translated "in such and such a place."

46. The meaning of v. 7 in episode 2 is unclear in the Hebrew. Alter states,

"The Hebrew text, which reads literally, 'This is her staying in the house a bit,' seems garbled, and so the translation is no more than a guess" (2019b, 629). Another way of viewing this verse is Hurvitz's suggestion of "words stumbling over words" as a deliberate choice by the author to convey the embarrassment of the overseer (quoted in Rulmu 2012, 117).

47. From the meaning of the name Elimelek and his opportunity to migrate when Bethlehem was in famine, Jione Havea (2015, 113) infers that he was a man of privilege but also countenances the possibility that the choice to move was predominantly Naomi's.

48. Robert Alter claims this is ". . . the most significant literary allusion in the book" (2019b, 630).

49. Proverbs 12:4. In most instances *ḥayil* is translated "army," "mighty [man]," or "wealth."

50. The Catholic and Orthodox Bibles include two apocryphal books that are named for women: Judith and Susanna.

51. Van Wolde also points out that *'arēmāh* ("grainheap") sounds very similar to *'arom* ("naked").

52. As van Wolde (1997, 18) points out, Tamar was in the same situation and also reinterpreted the levirate law to her advantage by seducing the father of her deceased husbands.

53. See Hag 2 and 1 Chr 3 for the genealogy leading from David to Zerubbabel.

54. André LaCocque has a more positive view of Ruth's integration into Israel, describing it as "subversive" due to the prohibitions against Moabites and foreign marriages as noted above (2004, 26).

55. Anthony Rees gives a succinct overview of the recent treatment of refugees in Australian politics in his article "The Boaz Solution: Reading Ruth in Light of Australian Asylum Seeker Discourse" (2015). César Melgar outlines similar responses to refugees from Central America in the United States context: "Ruth and the Unaccompanied Minors from Central America: Ethical Perspectives on a Socio-economic Problem" (2015).

56. "Australia 2021," *Amnesty International*, amnesty.org/en/countries/asia-and-the-pacific/australia/report-australia/. See also Scott J. Higgins, Boundless Plains to Share?: Australia, Jesus and Refugees (2017).

57. "Women," *UNHCR USA*, unhcr.org/en-us/women.html.

58. Hebrew words used to describe such people include *nekar* (one noticed), *ger* or *gur* (sojourner, alien, or foreigner), and *zar* (stranger).

59. See "Human Rights Case Summaries," *Human Rights Law Centre*, hrlc.org.au/human-rights-case-summaries/tag/Refugee+%26+Asylum+Seeker+Rights.

60. See "What is the current situation?" *Justice + Peace Office*, http://justiceandpeace.org.au/people-seeking-asylum-and-refugees/.

61. Indigenous groups could also be addressed in this discussion as they are often denied rights and dignity due to their status. In Australia, government policy demanded integration of mixed-race indigenous children who were forcibly removed from their own communities. The 1996 "Bringing them Home Report" published by the Australian Human Rights Commission exposed Australia to the shameful policies and put individual human faces and stories to the issue, conscientizing individuals and organizations, including churches, and resulting in widespread changes in attitude. See https://humanrights.gov.au/our-work/bringing-them-home-report-1997.

62. O'Connor poses this view and cites several other scholars on this point.

63. "The use of all the letters of the alphabet may imply fullness of expression —everything from A to Z—thereby symbolizing the completeness of the devastation being described" (Grossberg 2004, 1588).

64. Carvalho acknowledges the work of Carleen Mandolfo (2007) and Elizabeth Boase (2006), who have observed the performative nature of this dialogic speech.

65. See Wilson 2012 for a post-Holocaust reading of Lamentations; Lee 2002 on the Balkan crisis; Carvalho 2018 and Queen-Sutherland 2013 on Lamentations and 9-11.

66. See also O'Connor 2002, 14, where she acknowledges that she is following Nancy Lee with this interpretation.

67. Although some performance poetry is spontaneous or improvised, most often it involves performances of prewritten poetry.

68. See Mathews 2020, 159–60, for a description of analogies between performance art and biblical prophets.

69. Sarah Kay and Phil Kaye regularly perform poems together, such as "When Love Arrives." See a performance posted 9 June 2012 at youtube.com/watch?v=mdJ6aUB2K4g.

70. See 2018 interview with Solli Raphael, Australian performance poet and author, at youtube.com/watch?v=g2iwBwXtJak.

71. Yoda, a major character in the Star Wars franchise, speaks English but with a characteristic object-subject-verb pattern ("an unusual way of speaking Yoda has").

72. This translation claims to be the only translation in which each unique Hebrew word is matched and mated with a unique English word. Surprisingly, then, the sample verses Lam 3:7-9 used below to compare translations have two different English words for the same underlying Hebrew word. See biblegateway.com/versions/Jubilee-Bible-2000-JUB/.

73. David Lee, "Lamentations: introducing this version," *ServiceMusic*, http://servicemusic.org.uk/scripture/lamentations/index.php

74. Nancy Lee offers a theological reflection on the purpose of these reversed letters. In her analysis, acrostic poetry is used elsewhere in the Hebrew Bible to convey the theology of retributive justice (*tzaddiq*). The inversion of the two letters that precede the letter *tz* in the Hebrew alphabet signals a rebellion against such a simplistic view of justice (2008, 43–44).

75. Lee, "Lamentations," http://servicemusic.org.uk/scripture/lamentations/.

76. Harry Baker, "A love poem for lonely prime numbers," *TED*, ted.com/talks/harry_baker_a_love_poem_for_lonely_prime_numbers?language=en.

77. Obadiah in the Scroll of the Twelve Prophets is an oracle of judgment against Edom, a neighbouring nation with traditional kinship ties to Israel/Judah through the stories of Jacob and Esau, but evidently no loyalty in times of difficulty.

78. Alison Flood, "Darfur poet triumphs in international poetry slam," *The Guardian*, 4 November 2015, theguardian.com/books/2015/nov/04/darfur-poet-triumphs-in-international-poetry-slam.

79. But see Lee (2008) for a defence of Jeremiah as a speaker.

80. The Hebrew word *daveh* can be translated "faint" or "sick" but is used in Leviticus 15:33 and 20:18 as a euphemism for menstruation. I have hence taken the liberty of transforming "days of my sickness" (1:13) to "all my bloody days" in the performance poem. This not only improves the meter for recitation but also enhances the element of shock that is present in Poem 1 with its description of Daughter Zion exposed and shamed before her enemies.

81. See their website as ipcc.ch/.

82. "Chair's Vision Paper," *Intergovernmental Panel on Climate Change*, AR6 Scoping Meeting, Addis Ababa, Ethiopia, 1–5 May 2017, ipcc.ch/site/assets/uploads/2018/11/AR6-Chair-Vision-Paper.pdf.

83. "Climate change and health," *World Health Organization*, 30 October 2021, who.int/news-room/fact-sheets/detail/climate-change-and-health.

84. See graph at "#ShowYourStripes," *University of Reading*, showyourstripes.info/. For example, for some countries, where records exist, the timespan covered is longer than a century.

85. "Knit for Climate Action," *Common Grace*, commongrace.org.au/knit_for_climate_action.

86. Recent work by Will Kynes (2018) is challenging the appropriateness of the term "wisdom literature" for the so-called wisdom texts of the Hebrew Bible. Historically, grouping of the literature has been diverse. The Babylonian Talmud used the order Job, Proverbs, and Ecclesiastes, but the Septuagint placed Psalms

between Job and Proverbs (followed in most Christian Bibles) while later Jewish tradition grouped Ecclesiastes with the other festival scrolls.

87. The Australian group The Seekers with lead vocals by Judith Durham covered The Byrds' song in the 1960s. See youtube.com/watch?v=VRg9NkIdjVs.

88. While the verb *yld* can be translated "beget" or "sire" (as in 5:14 [MT 5:13]; 6:3), it usually refers to a woman giving birth to a child. Note that Tamar, discussed in the chapter on Ruth, gave birth to twins and named one Perez because he "broke through" (*perets*) ahead of his brother.

89. I have removed the definite article in my own translation because it is not seen in the Hebrew.

90. The Talmud (Tractate Sabbath 306) considered this advice dangerous and for this reason prevaricated as to the suitability of the scroll of Ecclesiastes as canonical (Ostriker 2005, 12).

91. A spiritual director once invited me to use the poem of Ecclesiastes 3:1-9 to discern my spiritual state of mind at that moment in my life.

92. "Sons of Adam" was once a familiar epitaph for the human race. My father taught me a poem by Leigh Hunt (1784–1859) of the Romantic movement that commences "Abou Ben Adhem (may his tribe increase!)," but I am not sure that my own sons would understand the witticism of the parenthesized phrase. Like all literature in the Hebrew Bible, the scroll of Ecclesiastes was undoubtedly written from a male perspective for predominantly male audiences, but see above where I discuss the time poem as potentially written with a female perspective in view.

93. Another creative reading of this difficult verse is suggested by the intrusion of the third-person reference to Qohelet—the only place this occurs in the scroll other than the framing introduction and conclusion. In the MT, the verb "to say" is in feminine singular form, preceding the name Qohelet as we would expect to see the verb preceding the subject, but, as noted above, Qohelet is a noun with a feminine *plural* ending. Could there be a female voice interrupting at this point (perhaps even someone in the studio audience!) such that it would read this way: "See this I have found," she said, "Qohelet! One by one to find a reckoning [it takes one to know one]"? It is worth noting that most scholars understand a scribal error here and explain the *he* at the end of the verb as the definite article preceding the name Qohelet as it occurs in many other places in the scroll.

94. A reference used in the Lamentations chapter in this volume speaks of climate change as an "urgent Kairos moment" for our time, and an influential document engaging South African churches in the anti-apartheid movement of the late 1980s was titled "The Kairos Document."

95. "Depression," *World Health Organization*, 13 September 2021, who.int/news-room/fact-sheets/detail/depression

96. R U OK? is an Australian nonprofit suicide prevention organization that

was established in 2009 to encourage people to have conversations with each other about their mental health and to promote community cohesiveness. See www.ruok.org.au.

97. The scroll of Ecclesiastes has inspired a wide range of literature including novels and poetry, music, and films. These may also be used to initiate conversations about well-being. The following list includes just some of its influence. Novels: *The House of Mirth* (Wharton, 1905); *The Sun Also Rises* (Hemingway, 1926); *Remembrance of Things Past* (Proust, 1922–1931). Poetry: "Vanitas Vanitatum" (William Thackeray, 1885); "Koheleth" (Louis Untermeyer, 1928). Music: Carissimi's "Vanitas Vanitatum" (1620–1677); Brahms's "Four Serious Songs" (1896); Granville Bantock's "Vanity of Vanities" (1913); Pete Seeger's "Turn, Turn, Turn" (1959); Norman Dello Joio's "Meditations on Ecclesiastes" (1956); Stevie Wonder's "Ecclesiastes" (1979); Dave Matthews Band's "Tripping Billies" (1993); John Rutter's "To Everything There Is a Season" (2008); Bono/Johnny Cash's "The Wanderer" (1993). Film: *Platoon* (dir. Oliver Stone, 1986) and *Gattaca* (dir. Andrew Niccol, 1997), both of which open with quotes from Ecclesiastes; *Groundhog Day* (dir. Harold Ramis, 1993); *The Giver* (short film dir. Jamey Foxton and Ryan Simpson).

98. See, for example, Jacopo Tintoretto, *Esther before Ahasuerus* (1547–1548), https://en.wikipedia.org/wiki/Esther_before_Ahasuerus#/media/File:Esther_before_Ahasuerus_(1547-48); Antoine Coypel, *The Swooning of Esther* (c. 1704), https://commons.wikimedia.org/wiki/File:Coypel_Esther.jpg; and Michelangelo, *The Punishment of Haman* (1511), michelangelo-gallery.com/the-punishment-of-haman.aspx.

99. Although the Persian Empire was larger than the preceding Assyrian and Babylonian empires, the Behistun Inscription of Darius lists only 23 provinces in total.

100. The Hebrew word *mišteh* is often translated "banquet," but it is from the verb *šth* (to drink), so "drinking party" is a better translation of its use in Esther (1:3, 5, 9; 2:18; 5:4, 5, 6, 8, 12, 14; 6:14; 7:2, 7, 8; 8:17; 9:17, 18, 19, 22).

101. Sample scripts can be found at www.noda.org.uk.

102. Names given in Jewish tradition that enabled Esther to know which day was the Sabbath (Rest) because she ordered her seven maids to serve her in the same order each week. See Sölle (1994), 230.

103. Although Vashti is generally viewed favorably by modern authors, she was less sympathetically viewed by many ancient Jewish and Christian readers. A ninth century commentary on Esther by Rabanus Maurus, for example, viewed Vashti as allegorical of the Jewish people whose refusal and stubbornness led to the death of Jesus! Note, however, that Josephus portrayed Vashti as refusing out of respect for the law (Thambyrajah 2021, 63, n15).

104. In one Jewish tradition the feud is between Haman and Mordecai them-

selves who had met earlier while serving in the army. Mordecai had done a kindness to Haman that was later forgotten, and the shame of being reminded by his refusal to bow to him prompted the desire to have him killed (Sölle 1994, 230).

105. A similar scene takes place in the musical *Fiddler on the Roof*, except it is a Russian Cossack who first offers the hand of friendship, accepted by the Jewish Tevye who then dances with him.

106. Eddie Jaku, "A Holocaust survivor's blueprint for happiness," *TED*, 2019, ted.com/talks/eddie_jaku_a_holocaust_survivor_s_blueprint_for_happiness/transcript?language=en.